BOEING B-52
STRATOFORTRESS

BOEING B-52 STRATOFORTRESS
WARRIOR QUEEN OF THE USAF

JEANNETTE REMAK

FONTHILL

Fonthill Media Language Policy

Fonthill Media publishes in the international English language market. One language edition is published worldwide. As there are minor differences in spelling and presentation, especially with regard to American English and British English, a policy is necessary to define which form of English to use. The Fonthill Policy is to use the form of English native to the author. Jeannette Remak was born and educated in the USA and now lives in Sunnyside, New York City—therefore American English has been adopted in this publication.

Fonthill Media Limited
Fonthill Media LLC
www.fonthillmedia.com
office@fonthillmedia.com

First published in the United Kingdom and the United States of America 2016

British Library Cataloguing in Publication Data:
A catalogue record for this book is available from the British Library

Copyright © Jeannette Remak 2016

ISBN 978-1-78155-467-8

The right of Jeannette Remak to be identified as the author of this work has been asserted by her in accordance with the Copyright, Designs and Patents Act 1988.

All rights reserved. No part of this publication may be reproduced, stored in a retrieval system or transmitted in any form or by any means, electronic, mechanical, photocopying, recording or otherwise, without prior permission in writing from Fonthill Media Limited

Typeset in 10.5pt on 13pt Sabon
Printed and bound in England by CPI Group (UK) Ltd, Croydon, CR0 4YY

Contents

Acknowledgments   8
Foreword   9

1   The End of the Second World War, Into the Cold War   11
2   Jet Bombers: The New Air Force   32
3   Building a Warrior Queen   59
4   LeMay's Greatest Wish   85
5   From 'A' to 'H': The B-52 Comes to Life   95
6   Vietnam and the B-52   137
7   The Life of a Crew Dog and Coming Home   171
8   Warrior Queen   179
9   Still Defending the Skies   190

Epilogue: The Ghost Rider Soars Again   199
Bibliography   202
Index   205

This book is dedicated to the B-52 crews who flew this aircraft through many wars and missions and continue to fly this magnificent bird today and into the future.

Acknowledgments

The author would like to thank the following for their help and support in the undertaking of this book: the Boeing Corporation and Kevin Kelly for the use of their magnificent photographs; Mike Lombardi, Archivist for Boeing Corporation, for his help and patience in getting information that was not easy to recover; Jay Slater at Fonthill Media and staff for their patience and leadership in producing this book; S/Sgt (Ret.) Ron Alexander for his photographs and memories of McCoy Air Force Base; T/Sgt (Ret.) Dan Freeman for his memories and his photographs of Fairchild Air Force Base and the B-52; Robert F. Dorr, the consummate Second World War author and historian, for his help and photographs; Joseph Ventolo Jr., partner in Phoenix Aviation Research, for his help and support; Mary Anne Ruggiero, Phoenix Aviation Research; the National Museum of the United States Air Force for their photo archives and history; Wesley B. Henry Chief, Research Division, National Museum of the United States Air Force; the Department of Defense for their photographs and their historical archives; *Aviation Week and Space Technology* magazine, for their photographic archive and articles; and the United States Air Force for their history and photographic images. If I have missed anyone, I apologize and thank you sincerely. Last, but by no means least, my little wingman, my Pekingese pup Shanghai, for his valuable support in keeping me sane while writing this book.

Foreword

The B-52 bomber is truly one of the most magnificent aircraft ever to greet the skies. The Boeing Company had already created the B-17 and B-29 bombers for the Second World War and converted the B-29 into the B-50, a more advanced version of the B-29. These bombers helped to win the war. They continued to work in the service of the US Air Force for many years. However, there is only one aircraft in the US inventory that has been in daily service for sixty years. That aircraft is the superlative B-52 Stratofortress. She has served in working status for sixty years and will continue in service until the year 2040. That is unheard of in the life of any military aircraft. She has served in many variations, in many wars with many, many crews; hers is an unparalleled lifespan. In this book, I hope to bring you her glorious history, along with her exploits in war, and those of some of their crews, and her various other services. I hope that this book will help you to appreciate what a tremendous aircraft the B- 52 is and what a brilliant company Boeing is to have created it. There has never been anything like the B-52, and long may she fly in service to the United States.

Jeanette Remak
October 2015

1

The End of the Second World War, Into the Cold War

The Second World War was over, finally. After six hellish years, millions of deaths and the loss of homes and cities, Europe would have years of work ahead to restore some of what was lost. The European war had ended with the Germans surrendering to the Allies after Hitler did the world a favor by blowing his brains out in an underground bunker in Berlin on 30 April 1945. On 7 May, Germany signed an unconditional surrender at Allied Headquarters in Rheims, France, which would take effect the next day. The final battles of the Pacific had concluded dramatically after the United States made the ultimate decision to drop the atomic bomb on Hiroshima on 6 August 1945. With the Japanese still not willing to give up, the second bomb was dropped on Nagasaki on 15 August. The Empire of Japan finally surrendered later that same day, and the peace was formally signed on 2 September 1945. Many thousands of Allied lives were saved from the brutality of a ground invasion of the country. While soldiers were returning home, the US military was still occupied in making the tools of war, and especially the aircraft used for bombing. That was something the mighty US Army Air Corp—soon to become the US Air Force—could not do without. The Cold War would soon begin, and the US needed to be ready for action.

The Soviets started their campaign to establish communist rule across the world by blockading Berlin on 12 May 1949. This blockade became one of the major international crises of the Cold War. Berlin became a hellhole for the unfortunate Germans caught in it, as they tried to pick up the pieces of what was left of their country after the Second World War—and there was not much left. German families, torn asunder by the war and Soviet rule, were virtually helpless, trying to live on rations that could barely have kept a mouse alive, let alone a child. The US military oversaw the massive Operation Vittles in 1947 and 1948, airlifting supplies across the blockade to aid the civilians. Meanwhile, the Russians used the opportunity to push their communist agenda onto a people on their knees; they cut off rail lines and truck depots to further inhibit vital foods and medical supplies from reaching the desperate inhabitants of Berlin. Meanwhile, the threats made by the Soviets were soon carried out as they took over Hungary, Poland, and other countries, forming their 'Iron Curtain', the phrase coined by Winston Churchill in his famous speech of 1946. And worse was to come: Berlin was just the start.

The B-36 Peacemaker—A Helluva' Big Bird

Of all the aircraft made, the B-36 Peacemaker was an awesome sight to behold. She was the largest mass-produced piston aircraft ever made, and with a wingspan of 230 feet, she was the largest aircraft that the USAAF (US Army Air Force) ever produced. The Consolidated Vultee (later known as Convair) Aircraft Corporation built this strategic bomber to be capable of delivering a nuclear weapon from inside her four bomb bays. The Consolidated B-36 was also the first manned bomber with an unrefueled intercontinental range of 9,900 miles, carrying her weight of 73,000 lbs as a maximum payload. The B-36 dates back as far as 1941, just before the United States entered the Second World War. Even before the USAAF sent aircrew and machines to Britain to join the RAF in bombing Germany, it was realised that more advanced aircraft would be needed in the future.

The Consolidated B-36A—an enormous bird. Her size can be judged by the flight crew standing in front of her. (*National Museum of the USAF*)

Research had been conducted into aerial refueling since the First World War, but a system that worked had not yet been designed. The USAAF therefore needed bigger bombers with a greater fuel capacity to achieve their ambition of intercontinental flight without having to land in foreign nations to refuel. The USAAF initiated a design competition for a long-range bomber on 11 April 1941. The USAAF kept this new requirement under wraps and wanted it secret as possible. The requirement asked for a top speed of 450 mph, a 275 mph cruise speed, a service ceiling of 45,000 feet, and a maximum range of 12,000 miles at 25,000 feet. The technology at the time was just not up to these specifications. On 19 August 1941, the USAAF decided to come down to earth and reduce some of the requirements; a maximum range of 10,000 miles was requested, a cruise speed of 240 to 300 mph, a service ceiling of 40,000 feet, and an effective combat radius of 4,000 miles carrying a 10,000-lb bomb load. This would be just high enough to keep the bomber out of the range of Nazi flak.

The request for preliminary design studies was released to Boeing and Consolidated on 11 April 1941, with a fixed cost of $435,263 for the competition. The winner was to be awarded an additional $135,445 and a smaller award went to the loser—the rationale was that the winner got the larger development and production contract and recoup their expenses to make a profit, while the loser was reimbursed for their costs and given a small fee for competing.

Consolidated had been working on their Model 35 idea since September 1940, financed by the company; they used this design as the basis for their entry into the new competition. The high wing aircraft had a 128-feet-long circular fuselage, used two vertical stabilizers, almost like the B-24 Liberator, and four engines on two nacelles. On 27 May 1941, Jack Northrop of Northrop Aircraft was asked by Consolidated for more information on his 'flying wing', an amazing design concept. Glenn L. Martin of Martin Aircraft was also asked for help by Consolidated, but he was working on the XB-33 design and had a Navy contract to uphold and so was unavailable. Other companies like Douglas, who had a contract for the Allison V-3420 air-cooled engine, were asked to be part of the competition. This was to be the engine for the new bomber.

The results were not good, as all the companies were having problems in working out how they could best meet all the requirements.

Consolidated was the more forceful of the competitors from the start as they had two different designs: the Model 35, which was revised from the first design on May 1941, and a second design called the Model 36. This was an unusual design for such an aircraft as it had six engines to a wing and was driven by propellers instead of being pulled in the usual tractor fashion. This was ironic, because USAAF designers at Wright Field, an engineering and design facility run by the USAAF, had been working on an engine pusher design on their own, away from the competition. Consolidated's detailed proposal was submitted on 6 October 1941, and they asked for $15 million plus a fixed fee of $800,000 for development, mock-up, and tooling for two long-range bombers. Consolidated also put their foot down about the 'red tape' issue, saying they wanted none of it and that changes being made to the requirements every ten minutes, every time someone got a new idea, would not be tolerated. In the event, it did not matter what Consolidated wanted; this program ended up in more red tape and confusion than any other project at the time.

The Consolidated proposal was managed by Isaac M. 'Mac' Laddon, the executive vice president who was to be connected with the B-36 for many years to come. By 15 November 1941, contract W535-AC-225352 was signed. On 22 November 1941, the Wright Field engineers felt that the original Model 36, six-engine design was the best, and it was selected instead of the four-engine Model 35.

Consolidated started to build a full-size wooden mock-up in San Diego to check equipment, armament, and crew compartment configurations. The company felt it was going to run straight into a wall with problems based on the aircraft's huge size and high ceiling requirement. The Model 36 had a wing span of 230 feet, powered by six 28-cylinder Pratt and Whitney 'XWASP' air-cooled radial engines. Each of them drove a 19-foot diameter, three-blade Curtis-Wright propeller in a pusher configuration. This was one giant bird and one giant headache.

The original designation was to be Model B-35, but the name changed to B-36 to avoid any confusion with its competitor for a production contract, the Northrop YB-35, which was also being developed.

The early development of the B-36 was beset by delays and political wrangling. One huge factor had to do the US just entering the Second World War after the attack on Pearl Harbor on 7 December 1941 by Japan. The B-36 was pushed to the side so that the B-24 Liberator, which was sorely needed in the European/Pacific theater, could see increased production. After six months of fine tuning to meet the requirements of the USAAF, the first mock-up for the B-36 was inspected by the 'Mock-Up Committee' on 20 July 1942. A month after the mock-up inspection, the B-36 was moved from San Diego, California, to the Fort Worth, Texas, plant, which put production back several months.

The tricycle landing gear system and the initial main landing gear design had enormous single wheels which were found to cause significant ground pressure issues. This would have limited B-36 operations to only three airbases that could handle the aircraft's size; because of this problem, the Air Force mandated that Consolidated come up with a four-wheel design, with a bogey-type wheel

The huge tire of the B-36. The maintenance of this bird was no easy task. (*National Museum of the USAF*)

system for the main gear. A bogie system was comprised of a 'leg' that could carry the wheels of a large aircraft requiring four or more wheels for landing support. This distributed the pressure more evenly and reduced the weight by some 1,500 lbs. The Air Force also ordered a new antenna system to be to be incorporated into the design to accommodate the new radio and radar systems. Pratt and Whitney engines were also redesigned, which added yet another 1,000 lbs—the B-36 was just getting bigger.

A Tough Birth

Consolidated struggled to solve the B-36's problems. The first wind tunnel tests were rough, but after a test with a 1/26 scale model, the company decided on some changes. NACA (National Advisory Committee for Aeronautics) was known for getting the United States through the toughest times during the war by creating solutions for aerodynamic issues, and it helped once again. Consolidated made the change to the NACA 63 airfoil to help the laminar air flow across the wing, although it would take a year before a wind tunnel was available to try it, and another six months before the design was tested at the San Diego plant. The full-scale wooden mock-up was complete.

Fuselage, wing and the vertical stabilizers mounted on horizontal stabilizers were ready to be incorporated into the design.

There were concerns that the vertical stabilizers could shear off during a hard landing or severe flight conditions, and the design continued to be evaluated. This led to the twin tail change in favor of a single 47-foot-high vertical stabilizer. This change reduced the weight by 3,800 lbs, gave directional stability, and lowered the base drag; it followed the trend in aircraft building at the time. The mock-up was very useful in working out the many problems associated with the sheer size of the aircraft.

On 20 July 1942, the B-36 mock-up was inspected. Weight was the main issue; with the aircraft in its current state, the 10,000-mile requirement was going to be tough to hang on to. To counter the weight problem, members of the 'Mock-Up Committee' suggested reducing the defensive armament and the number of crewmembers for the aircraft. Other team members thought those changes would ruin the aircraft and make it too much like the 'X-19 Flying Laboratory.' However, if they could not reach a compromise, the program would be in jeopardy, so the 'Mock-Up Committee' agreed to take out the 'less necessary' equipment—the crew's little galley and some survival equipment—which allowed for significant weight reduction although added to the crew's discomfort. The program went ahead and the Air Force approved the mock-up inspection in September 1942, at which point the entire mock-up was disassembled and packed into railroad cars. Along with 200 engineers, the parts were moved to Fort Worth, Texas, only to find that the plant there was too small to house the complete B-36. A hangar building, completed in 1944, was built near the plant to accommodate the aircraft. The move to Fort Worth was quick, but the B-36 program was set back again because of the urgent need for B-24s and B-32s in the European theater.

Consolidated wanted a commitment from the government to make an order for the completed bomber before both prototypes (experimental bombers designated XB-36) were finished. They felt that another two years would be saved if one complete aircraft could be constructed along with the two prototypes. Consolidated also did their best to explain that they had to line up their sub-contractors, who were busy with war contracts. Supplies were at a premium too.

In the summer of 1942, things started to look up for Consolidated. The USAAF agreed to accept a cargo version of the B-36, called the XC-99, provided one of the two experimental bombers was built three months before the cargo version. However, the cargo version would be ready to fly sooner than the two XB-36s because it would need no crew compartment, armament, or EWO equipment. Consolidated wanted use the cargo version to test engines and landing gear, and to find out more about the flight realm and characteristics of the XB-36.

The production line of the Consolidated B-32 Dominator, which was used in the Second World War. (*National Museum of the USAF*)

Consolidated accepted the government offer and a $4.6 million contract was signed by both the USAAF and Consolidated at the end of 1942. On 17 March 1943, Consolidated merged with Vultee Aircraft and became Consolidated Vultee Aircraft Company, known as Convair. The name was not official until 29 April 1954, when Consolidated Vultee became the Convair division of the General Dynamics Corporation.

In 1943, while the newly named Convair was dealing with all the problems of the B-36, China was near to a complete collapse as a nation and nothing the USAAF had in its inventory could pull the range needed to help them; the B-17, B-24, and the B-29, which were in the early stages of production and designed to achieve this range, were suffering delays. The Consolidated B-32 Dominator was also being built, but it was nothing more than a back-up plan for the USAAF, just in case the B-29 was delayed any longer. However, neither of these aircraft could reach Japan from the US mainland; the Mariana Islands became a bloodbath before they could be used as bases for B-29 and the B-32 operations. Meanwhile, prioritizing the B-36 could give the USAAF a way to hit Japan straight on. Following the 'Trident' Conference headed by President Roosevelt and Winston Churchill in May 1943, Secretary of War Henry Stimson gave the USAAF authority to order the B-36 into production before the two prototypes were finished.

By 23 July 1943, thanks to the input of General 'Hap' Arnold, the USAAF and Department of War ordered a hundred B-36s. The Letter of Intent was signed and the price for each B-36 was agreed at $1,750,000. The B-36 was now a higher priority than it had been, but still not equal to the B-29. A delivery date of August 1945 was set initially, but this was pushed back to 1946 by Convair, and the first XB-36 would not be ready for the USAAF until September 1944. A Letter of Contract (W33-038-AC-7) for the production aircraft was signed on 23 August 1943, replacing the Letter of Intent of a month before. Even with the elevated status, the B-36 was still stuck in the mud. Convair was still worried over the weight of the 'XWASP' engine, and the new Pratt and Whitney engine was slow to materialize. Looking further into the issue, the liquid-cooled Lycoming BX-engine (lower fuel consumption) was discontinued for lack of manpower, materials and the facilities to produce the engine—all of which were focused on war production. The two XB-36 experimental aircraft were delivered in May and November 1944. The first (42-13570) met the light of day at the Fort Worth plant on 8 September 1945. Her first maiden flight was 8 August 1946. The second prototype was now designated YB-36 (42-13571); it was to be the production aircraft that was rolled out on 25 April 1945. It carried a different canopy due to poor visibility in the first aircraft. The YB-36 also still had the single wheel undercarriage for landing. This prototype's maiden flight took place on 4 December 1947. The YB-36 (42-13570) was turned over to the USAAF as of June 1948 and the second prototype (42-13571) was turned to the USAAF on 31 May 1949.

The Airframe

In the meantime, the gigantic B-36 airframe was undergoing all sorts of stability testing; she was two-thirds longer than the B-29, which was already a super bomber. The wing space and the tail height of the B-36 even beat the largest of the Soviet aircraft, the Antonov AN-22, called in Russian the 'Antei' or 'Antaeus.' The AN-22 was a massive freight carrier and the largest mass-produced prop-driven aircraft; her name, 'Antaeus', was derived from that of the giant son of the Greek gods Poseidon and Gaia. Her specifications were span 211 feet 3½ inches, 189 feet 1½ inches in length, 41½ feet in height, with an empty weight of 251,325 lbs, a max speed of 460 mph with a cruise speed of 368–398 mph, and a maximum range of 6,800 miles loaded. It put her in the class of what the USAAF was looking for. Not until years later, when the Boeing 747 came into being, did the US possess an aircraft large enough to compete with the AN-22.

The B-36 carried a crew of fifteen, and as in the B-29, the flight canal and crew compartment were accessed via a pressurized tunnel through the bomb bay. It was 25 feet in diameter and 85 feet long. In the B-36, crewmembers rode through the tunnel on a wheeled trolley by pulling themselves on a rope. The rear compartment featured six bunks and a dining galley—which was soon removed to reduce weight—and led to the tail turret.

One of the remarkable things that came out of the development of the B-36 was the demand to make the skin of the aircraft smooth. The use of pop rivets causes drag because of the rivet heads protruding above the skin. By early 1942, with the help of research engineer Dr Glen Havens, Consolidated had developed a metal adhesive tough enough to support primary aircraft loads. This was a breakthrough not only in the reduction of drag, but also in the speed of manufacturing as it was no longer necessary to use thousands of pop rivets during airframe construction. Consolidated spent almost $3 million to produce the high-strength glue in liquid and tape forms. They called 'MetlBond', then licensed the product to Narmco Corp. and Pacific Laminates, who called it 'Silabond.' By the early 1950s, 30 percent of the exterior skin of the B-36 was built using this new product. It was available in tape and liquid form and greatly reduced drag. It became a staple of the aviation industry.

Hydraulics and the electrical systems were also subjected to weight reduction. With the help of the Wright Field engineers, Consolidated started development on a 3,000-psi hydraulic system pump. Valves and activators were created from scratch and no parts were taken off the shelves.

The wings of the B-36 were colossal. They allowed the aircraft to carry enough fuel to handle super-long missions without any aerial refueling. The widest point around the chord of the wing was 7.5 feet thick. It held a crawlspace that gave the crew some access to the engine. The wing area permitted a cruising altitude above the operating ceiling of any of the 1940s piston-turbine fighters. There would be many variants of the B-36 by the time she left service, but all versions would be able to cruise at 40,000 feet. The mission logs for the B-36 contain details of mock attacks against US cities while flying at 49,000 feet—that was truly a record.

Later in 1954, as the program had progressed, turrets and other non-essential equipment were removed from the aircraft, much like the 'SILVERPLATE' program of the B-29, which caused the aircraft to go to 'featherweight' configuration. This resulted in a 423 mph speed with a ceiling of 50,000 feet, and a dash ceiling of over 55,000 feet or higher. The super large wings of the B-36 allowed for a good sized spread between the actual stall speed and the maximum speed of the aircraft. This made the B-36 more maneuverable at high altitudes than many of the USAF jet interceptors of the day. This was amazing for such a huge aircraft. The fact that the jet interceptors of the period could not attain anything higher than 40,000 feet and would stall out if they attempted it demonstrates the advances that had been made in bomber design.

Landing Gear

The XB-36 featured a single-wheel main landing gear with the largest tires ever produced up to that time. The tires were 9 feet 2 inches tall, 3 feet wide, and weighed 1,320 lbs each. They contained enough rubber for sixty regular car tires. The tires put so much weight per unit on the runways that the XB-36 was restricted to the Fort Worth airfield, just next to the Consolidated plant. Only two other USAAF bases after that were able to handle this stress load. At one point a 'tank like' tread landing gear was attempted, but it was very heavy and noisy and was quickly dropped.

Engines

The propulsion system for the B-36 made her more than just a huge aircraft. The six 28-cylinder Pratt and Whitney R-4360 WASP MAJOR radial engines were unique. The prototype R-4360s delivered a total of 18,000 rpms. The early B-36s required a long take-off run before lift-off, and this problem was solved later on with another version that delivered a significantly increased power output of 22,800 hp. Each engine drove a set of three bladed propellers, 19 foot in diameter, pushing the aircraft. This was the second largest diameter propeller ever built for a piston engine.

Because of the configuration, propeller turbulence from interfacing the airflow over the wing led to insufficient airflow around the engines. This in turn led to overheated engines and in-flight engine fires. The props were so large and slow turning, that when they interacted with the high-pressure airflow behind the wing, a very low frequency pulse at ground level was produced, which gave away any approaching flights. Later, with the arrival of jet propulsion—first incorporated into the B-36D version—a pair of General Electric J-47-19 jet engines were suspended near the end of each enormous wing. These engines were placed on all B-36Bs. The B-36 was configured for ten engines: six radial propeller engines and four jet engines, leading to the popular B-36 catchphrase, 'Six turning, four burning.' The B-36 had more engines than any other mass-produced aircraft ever made.

The engines were accessible for maintenance in flight through the wing. The 10,000-mile range was still the biggest challenge facing the B-36, and to achieve it, Consolidated had to minimize the base drag of the aircraft. They were persistently reminded that it took two pounds of fuel for every pound of extra weight to complete the 10,000-mile range.

The jet pods helped improve take-off performance and dash speed over the targets. To reduce drag and to prevent any foreign object damage, the jet

The 19-foot propellers of the B-36 were the largest ever made. (*National Museum of the USAF*)

The Consolidated B-36B in her colors of orange and bare metal (magnesium). This is the reason why they called her the '*Aluminum Overcast*'. (*National Museum of the USAF*)

engine louvers were manipulated by the flight crew from the cockpit. This action could be performed airborne or on the ground. The two pods combined with the four turbojet and six piston engines gave the B-36 a total of 40,000 hp for short periods of time.

First Flights and New Configurations

The first prototype XB-36 was ready to fly on 8 August 1946. The speed and range of the prototype failed to meet the standards set out by the USAAF way back in 1941. The Pratt and Whitney R-4360s engines were not ready yet, and there was a lack of qualified workers and materials to install them properly. The second prototype, the YB-36, flew on 4 December 1947. It had a redesigned, high-visibility bubble canopy, which was later adapted for production, and the engines used were more powerful and efficient than the earlier prototype. The YB-36 was closer to the real production aircraft.

The first twenty-one B-36As were completed and delivered in 1948. They were the interim airframes intended for crew training and later conversions. There was no defensive armament fitted, since none of the planned weapons were ready. The aircraft that were available, the B36As, were converted to RB-36Es, the reconnaissance version. The first of the B-36 variants meant for normal operations was the B-36B.

The B-36B was delivered in the beginning of November 1948. This aircraft met all the 1941 requirements, but still had some serious issues with engine reliability and maintenance (little issues like changing the 336 spark plugs, dreaded by all the maintenance crews). There was also the matter of the availability of armament and parts. Later versions of the R-3460 engines were improved, along with radar and redesigned crew compartments. The additional four jet engines were put on the outer edges of the enormous wings. This also added to fuel consumption problems and reduced range. The advent of the air-to-air missile also rendered the conventional gun turrets obsolete. By February 1954, the Air Force gave Convair a contract for a new 'Featherweight' program, which helped to reduce the weight and crew size. There were four configurations for 'Featherweight':

Featherweight I:	Defensive hardware eliminated for weight consideration;
Featherweight II:	Took out rear compartment crew galley and bunks and other crew features to allow for hardware needed to carry the McDonnell XF-85 Goblin parasite fighter;
Featherweight III:	Included the six-gun turrets taken out of the Featherweight I feature and reduced the aircraft crew to nine instead of fifteen crew members;

Featherweight IV: Allowed the B-36 to have a higher operating ceiling of at least 47,000 feet, especially critical for reconnaissance missions.

The B-36J-III (the last fourteen that were made) had a single radar-aimed tail turret. The B-36J-III had extra fuel tanks in the outer wings, and landing gear that forced the maximum gross weight to run up to 410,000 lbs. Due to on-going problems in its early stages of testing, development, and later in service, some of the critics of the program referred to the B-36 as 'the billion dollar blunder'.

The B-36 in Real Life

By 1947, the USAAF had become the USAF, a separate service, which it had fought tooth and nail to become. The Air Force used the B-36 for reconnaissance during the Cold War, but not as a bomber. She never fired an angry shot in combat.

The fact that the B-36 needed to be stationed as close as possible to enemy targets meant that she was often based in extreme weather locations, usually in Alaska and Greenland, close to Soviet territory. The aircraft was too large to fit in most standard hangars, so most of the maintenance had to be done outside. In the far north it sometimes reached −60°F. in winter, and in the summer, at some B-36 stations—during the Korean War, for instance—could reach temperatures of 100°F. in the shade, with humidity to boot. It was a tough job for ground crews. Special shelters were provided for the crews of both locations. In the winter, crews also ran the risk of slipping on icy wings over 18 feet off the ground, or getting caught in the prop wash, which ran in reverse.

By 1950, Convair developed a streamlined pod, which looked like an oversized drop tank, mated on each side of the B-36 fuselage. This pod would carry spare engines between bases. Each pod could airlift two engines. When the pods were empty, they were removed and stored in the B-36's bomb bays.

There was the occasional fire with the B-36's radial engines. The phrase, popular with crews, 'Six turning, four burning' has already been mentioned, and then there was, 'two turning, two burning, two smoking, two choking, and two more unaccounted for.' They were not kidding. The problem was worsened by the prop-pusher configuration, which increased carburetor icing. The R-4360 engine was designed to be mounted in the conventional pull or tractor configuration, but on the B-36 it was mounted backwards in the pusher configuration. The carburetor was now in front of the engine, and could not benefit from engine heat. This made more traditional, short-term carburetor heat systems unsuitable. When intake air was cold and humid, ice could gradually obstruct the carburetor intake, which increased the richness of the air/fuel mixture, until the unburned fuel in the exhaust caught fire. There were three engine fires of this nature that were responsible for the loss of US nuclear weapons.

Armament

The B-36 had four bomb bays that could carry 86,000 lbs of conventional armament, which meant iron bombs. That weight was some ten times the load that a B-17 could carry. While the B-36 was not designed to carry nuclear devices, that would change. The period in which the B-36 was designed ran parallel to the top secret 'Manhattan Project', the work of Robert Oppenheimer and the team at Los Alamos, New Mexico, that created the atomic bomb. It would not take long until the B-36 walked right into the role of carrying nuclear devices.

When the B-36 became operational in August 1948 it had everything the Air Force had wanted, except speed. Yet, she was still fast enough to match her Soviet counterpart, the Tupolev TU-95. Production was started on the TU-95 in 1956, and the aircraft was still active in 2014. It seems the Russians had the same idea about this aircraft as the USAF had about the B-52, except that the TU-95 is a propeller aircraft.

The B-36 also carried the T-12 Cloudmaker, a gravity bomb that weighed in at 43,600 lbs. At that size, it was capable of making a huge impact and producing an earthquake effect. This weapon was tested by releasing two of the bombs at different altitudes on a single mission. One bomb released at 30,000 feet and the other at 40,000 feet for a total bomb load of 87,200 lbs.

Nuclear Weapons

By May 1946, the newly formed United States Air Force began the Nuclear Energy for Propulsion Program for Aircraft (NEPA), which was followed in 1951 by the Aircraft Nuclear Propulsion Program (ANP). The ANP used a modified B-36 to study the shielding requirement for the airborne reactor and determine whether a nuclear-powered aircraft was even feasible. Convair modified one aircraft to a B-36H-C-20A (#51-5712) that was damaged in a tornado at Carswell Air Force Base in September 1952. This aircraft was later designated XB-36H, and after that, NB-36H, which was modified to carry a 1 MW air-cooled nuclear reactor in the aft bomb bay. There was a 4-ton lead shield disc installed in the middle of the aircraft, between the reactor and the cockpit, to ensure that the pilots would not be harmed by the radioactivity. In addition, the highly modified cockpit section was cased in lead and rubber with a lead glass windshield a foot thick. Large air intake and exhaust holes were installed in the sides and bottom of the aircraft and rear fuselage to cool the reactor in flight. The reactor was operational, but did not give any of its power to the aircraft proper. Its only purpose was to explore the effects of radiation on the aircraft and its systems. A crane removed this reactor, which weighed in at 35,000 lbs, from the aircraft after testing. Between the years 1955 and 1957, NB-36H completed some forty-seven flights and 215 hours of flight time were recorded in the flight logs. Eighty-nine of these hours had the reactor at critical. It was like flying with a mini-Chernobyl on your back.

Parasites

The 'parasite' experiment was another experiment high on the list for the B-36. The B-36 was modified to carry a parasite fighter that could be launched from the mother ship and later be retrieved by the same aircraft after flying its mission. The parasite fighter was carried either totally or partially in the bomb bay of the B-36. The FICON (flight conveyor) project, as it was called, involved the modification of a B-36D into the GRB-36D 'mother ship', with a RF-84K, a fighter modified for reconnaissance, connected to the bomb bay. The GRB-36D would ferry the RF-84K to the target area, where the RF-84K

Modified for reconnaissance, the GRB-36D would ferry the RF-84K to the target area, where the RF-84K would disconnect and begin its mission. (*National Museum of the USAF*)

would disconnect and begin the mission for reconnaissance. Ten B-36s were adapted to GRB-36Ds and twenty-five RF-84Ks were built, but they saw only limited service.

The 1950s 'Tom-Tom' project comprised the RF-84F and the GRB-36D from the FICON project to test if the B-36 could carry the RF-84K Thunderflash as a parasite bomber. The test went on for a couple of months but it was canceled due to the vortice turbulence which became uncontrollable on the B-36 wingtips. Like the 'Tom-Tom' project, the 'Tip-Tow' project was another parasite program involving the docking of an F-84 Thunderflash to the wing tips of either the B-29 or B-36 to see if the USAF could promote an extended range in flight. It was canceled when the EF-84D and a modified EB-29A crashed, killing all on board.

As the last word on the B-36, there were 360 aircraft produced for Strategic Air Command (SAC) and the last one rolled out of the giant assembly building at Fort Worth, Texas, just clearing the hangar with its 47-foot tail. The delivery of the last production model to the USAF was on 14 August 1947. In truth, she was one 'helluva' big bird, and one of the finest.

Strategic Reconnaissance

Reconnaissance was the greatest offering of the B-36 program, and this was particularly crucial in this period of the Cold War. The USAF lacked a superior reconnaissance system and was forced to recycle Second World War aircraft to do the work while they came up with a solution. By 1952, during the Korean War, six RB-36Ds from the 5th Strategic Reconnaissance Wing were sent to the 9th Strategic Reconnaissance wing in Yokota, Japan. This was the first deployment of the RB-36 into the Korean theater. While not used for any combat missions over North Korea, RB-36Ds conducted high altitude aerial reconnaissance over Chinese Manchuria and Soviet East Asia while serving with the 91st Strategic Reconnaissance Group (SRG). One of SAC's initial missions was to plan strategic aerial reconnaissance on a global scale. First efforts in aerial photo reconnaissance were tough for the small group of ELINT professionals, also known as 'Ferrets', who were spying on the transmissions of enemy nations via electronic intelligence. Weather reconnaissance was also part of the system, looking for anything, especially atomic testing, that would leave radioactive residue in the air.

There was also the issue of the USSR's air defense systems, which in the 1950s were effective only up to 40,000 feet. Any aircraft above that level was virtually undetectable. The first aircraft to put this theory to the test was a specially fitted RB-36D, carrying a crew of twenty-two instead of the usual fifteen. The additional members were there to operate and maintain the reconnaissance equipment. The forward bomb bay, which was pressurized in this aircraft, carried fourteen cameras. The compartment also held its own little darkroom, where a photo technician could develop film. The second bomb bay held eighty T-86 photo flash bombs, and the third bay carried an extra 3,000 gallons of fuel in a disposable tank. The fourth bomb bay carried all the electronic countermeasure equipment. All defensive armament, which consisted of sixteen M-24A 20-mm cannons, was held in the fourth bomb bay. The extra tanks increased the flight range to up to fifty hours, and with an operational ceiling of 50,000 feet, the Soviets would not be able to see her. A lightweight version of the RB-36III could even reach as high as 58,000 feet.

RB-36s were distinguished by the bright aluminum finish of the camera compartments which contrasted with the dull magnesium of the rest of the fuselage. There was also a series of radar domes under the aft fuselage, varying in both number and placement. Only US aircraft had enough range to fly over the Eurasian land mass from bases in the United States with the capacity to carry the very heavy and bulky high-resolution cameras of the day.

The standard RB-36D held up to twenty-three cameras, mostly of the K-17C, K-22, K-38, and K-40 varieties. There was a very special 240-inch focal length camera known as the 'Boston' camera in honor of the university that designed it. It was tested on aircraft #44-92088, which was also re-designated ERB-36D. The first RB-36D (#44-92088) made its first flight on 19 December 1949, six months after the first B-36D flew. The 28th Strategic Reconnaissance Wing based at Ellsworth Air Force Base in South Dakota got its first RB-36D on 3 June 1950. Due to severe materiel shortages, the new aircraft did not become operational until May 1951.

Twenty-four RB-36Ds were built; some were modified to be 'featherweight' configuration, discussed earlier in this chapter. These aircraft were re-designated the RB-36III. Modifications were carried out by Convair, starting from February 1954 to November 1954. The RB-36Ds were able to explore the borders of the USSR's arctic region in 1951. Although onboard equipment showed that the Soviets could detect the aircraft, there was not much they could do given the high altitude of the RB-36D.

The RB-36B, stationed at RAF Sculthorpe in England, made a number of flights over Soviet arctic bases, especially a new nuclear weapons test site at Novaya Zemla. The RB-36s performed a number of reconnaissance missions and were believed to have frequently overflown Chinese and Soviet airspace under the directions of SAC chief General Curtis LeMay.

In 1950, Convair converted the B-36As to a reconnaissance role. Included in the conversion was the YB-36 (#42-13571). All these converted aircraft were re-designated RB-36E. They were equipped with the four YJ-47 jet engines that were fitted to the RB-36Ds. The normal crew was twenty-two, but five additional gunners were added to man the new 16M-24A-1 20-mm cannons. The last conversion was finished in July 1951. More than a third of the B-36s were now reconnaissance models.

Advances in Soviet Air Defense systems limited the RB-36 to flying outside the borders of the USSR and Eastern Europe. In the mid-1950s, the jet-powered Boeing RB-47E was able to push its way into Soviet airspace and produce a number of overflights of the USSR. Some flights went very deep into the heart of the USSR, grabbing as much photographic and radar information that they could to provide targets for SAC bombers should they need them. These flights were highly dangerous, which is why crews were known as 'silent warriors.' When these airmen went on these missions, they did not talk about it with wives, family, or friends—their loved ones would only learn about their activities if something tragic happened, and even then they would not always be told. These flights into mainland USSR were called SENSIT (Sensitive Intelligence Mission).

With all the MiGs crawling around the skies over North Korea in 1950, the days for USAF prop-driven bombers being used as strategic offensive weapons were numbered. It was far too dangerous to send these aircraft out; the Soviets has no scruples when it came to taking out a slow bomber.

The End of the Road

The USAF retired nearly all of their B-29s and B-50s when their newest weapon, the B-47 Stratojet, came into operation. Meanwhile, in 1955, the swept wing Boeing B-52 Stratofortress was moving in to replace the B-36 as the consummate bomber. The two main factors that contributed to the obsolescence of the B-36 Peacemaker were essentially very simple. First, the B-36 was not equipped for aerial refueling; the USAF had perfected that art form and needed to use it if they wanted to get deep into the Soviet heartland. Second, the B-36's slow speed made it vulnerable to the new Soviet jet interceptors, making long-range bombing raids over the USSR extremely dangerous; it was a long shot that they'd reach their target, let along return home safely. The scrapping out of the B-36s began in February of 1956, although there was work done by Convair to update the aircraft at their San Diego plant until 1957. By December of 1958, only twenty-two B-36s were still operational.

The variants of the B-36 Peacemaker are listed below:

> XB-36 prototype: used the R-4360-25 engines and only one out of all B-36s that used this engine.

YB-36 prototype: used a better cockpit canopy which gave better visibility.

B-36A: used for training purposes. Only twenty-two were built and all but one was converted to the RB-36E.

XC-99: the only large scale version of the cargo aircraft that was ever built

B-36B: used the R-4320-41 engine. Seventy-three were built and most were converted to RB-36Ds or B-36Ds. This aircraft was using ordnance.

RB-36B: there were thirty-nine B-36Bs using camera installations

YB-36C: production version of the B-36B and used the R-4360-51 engine using the tractor propellers. This was never built.

B-36C: became the production model of the YB-36 and ended up as B-36B.

B-36D: the B-36B was fitted out with the first of the J-47-GE-19 jet engines, two under each wing pod. Twenty-two were completed and sixty-four were converted from the B-36B.

GRB-36D: equal to the RB-36D and was built to use in the GRF-84F parasite program as part of the FICON project; ten were modified.

RB-36F: same as the B-36D, however these were adapted to six 3,800-hp (R-4360-53) engines and four J-47-GE-19 engines; thirty-four were made.

RB-36G: this was a reconnaissance version with twenty-four modified. These had an increased fuel capacity.

RB-36H: seventy-three of this strategic reconnaissance version were made.

The YB-36C, a production of the B-36B with six 4,300-hp (R-4360-51) engines. It utilized the driving tractor gear. (*National Museum of the USAF*)

The B-36 being led by its variant, the XC-99 Cargo. This was one of the largest existing cargo aircraft, and was the only example ever built. (*National Museum of the USAF*)

The Convair YB-60, originally designated as the YB-36G. The aircraft was the result of a project to build a jet-powered, swept-wing version of the B-36. Due its differences to a standard B-36, its designation was changed to YB-60. (*National Museum of the USAF*)

B-36J: this aircraft had the strengthened landing gear and an increase of the fuel capacity. However, armament was concentrated to tail guns and a lower crew numbers. Thirty-three were made.

YB-60: This was selected from the YB-36G (#49-2676 and #49-2684). It was supposed to be for a jet powered, swept wing version, but due to the drastic design changes the name was changed to YB-60.

The National Security Act of 1947 and Two New Services

The United States gained two new services between the close of the Second World War and the start of the Cold War. On 18 September 1947, after a long, vicious battle to gain their independence as a military service, the National Security Act of 1947 (Public Law 253) finally gave the US Air Force the autonomy it craved. The USAF was now independent, with its own Secretary and Chief of Staff and its own funding. This National Security Act also dispensed funds to the Navy and the Army. The Secretary of Defense was the one to coordinate all efforts for all the services and the Air Force Secretary would be accountable to him.

The new Public Law 253 came with another surprise in its creation of the Central Intelligence Agency. The formation of the CIA and the USAF completed the National Security Act of 1947, creating civilian secretaries for all of the armed services (i.e. USAF, Navy, Marines, and Army). There was no love lost between the CIA and the USAF; it was a turf war and the lines drawn were simple: the USAF wanted control of the skies and aerial reconnaissance, which they felt had been usurped from them by the CIA's aircraft reconnaissance program. It was not making the USAF happy, especially since they had to service and supply those aircraft. They fought bitterly for years until the USAF finally regained control of aerial reconnaissance, at least for a time.

2

Jet Bombers: The New Air Force

The Convair B-36 was leaving the hangar for good. Her service was up and it was time to look for a new intercontinental bomber. Plans for the Boeing B-47 arose from an informal request by the USAAF for a jet-powered reconnaissance bomber, sent out to aviation companies interested in jet engine research. Boeing and several other companies took the bait and started working on designs for the Air Force. The concept for the B-47 was essentially a long-range bomber capable of carrying nuclear weapons to targets within the USSR.

In December 1944, North American Aircraft Company, Consolidated, and Glenn Martin Company joined the proposal team for the new long-range bomber. Each of the companies was hard at work on their design, but. Boeing already had the edge. They had designed the unrivalled B-29 Superfortress and were going to use that aircraft to build from. The initial design from Boeing was called the Model 424, a scaled-down version of the B-29. The first wind tunnel tests showed that the Model 424's problem had to do with the drag from the placement of the jet engine just forward of the leading edge of the wing. Boeing then redesigned the aircraft and came up with the Model 432. This model used four jet engines built right into the forward fuselage to help reduce drag. All of this was to change when the USAAF gave the study contract to all four companies. The USAAF asked that North American Aircraft and Convair work on the four-engine design, which became the B-45 and B-46. Boeing and Martin were asked by the USAAF under the new contract to build a six-engine aircraft known as the B-47 and B-48. The powerplant for this new bird would be the General Electric TG-180 turbojet engine.

The New Wing Design

George Schairer was a Boeing Company employee since 1939 and went on to become chief of the technical staff and one of the most loved and admired of

The first B-47 (tail number 46-065) completed its first flight on 1 December 1947, forty-four years after the first Wright Brothers flight. (*National Museum of the USAF*)

the Boeing hierarchy. As the Second World War was coming to a close in the Spring of April 1945, Schairer went to Germany with a group of US scientists to find out just what the Nazis had been working on. Schairer was looking through a mass of wind tunnel documents that were left behind in haste when he found something so unique he couldn't believe his eyes. Nazi scientists were working on a revolutionary new aircraft design called the swept wing, which could only work with one thing—a jet engine. Schairer knew gold when he found it—he wired home to Boeing, 'Stop the bomber design!' and with that wire, the B-47 was reconfigured to a swept wing design. A Boeing analysis engineer, Vic Ganzer, another of the Boeing top engineers, suggested a swept back angle of 35 degrees. It would work perfectly. Boeing made the modifications to Model 432 to include a 35-degree swept wing, and then added a vertical tail which was enough to give the model a new configuration now called, Model 448. This configuration allowed for the four TG-180 engines to be placed in the forward fuselage and two more in the rear fuselage. This completed the requirements for the USAAF contract. The plans were presented to the USAAF in September 1945.

The Boeing Model 448 wasn't exactly what the USAAF wanted. They were not pleased about the rear fuselage engine idea; because of the flush-mounted air intakes for the rear fuselage, the engines were insufficient. The fact that the engines were literally built into the fuselage could be a possible fire hazard.

A flight crew next to their B-47, waiting to be deployed. (*Boeing Corporation*)

It reminded the USAAF too much of the engine issues that they had with the B-36. Boeing removed the engines from the fuselage. The engines were placed in pods underneath the wings, which resolved the USAAF's concerns. This led to the next Boeing configuration, Model 450. The USAAF was happier with this configuration. This model had the TG-180 jet engines in a twin pod mounted on a pylon, about a third of the way outboard of each wing, with another engine at each wingtip. The USAAF liked this new idea, but asked Boeing to refine the design just a bit by moving the engines inboard to three quarters of the length of the wingspan. The idea for the pod engines came from another of the Boeing superstars, Ed Wells, who would have a large role to play in the creation of the legendary Boeing B-52.

A small problem showed up in the wings: they provided no room for the wheels to retract into the fuselage. The 'bicycle landing gear' type was attempted, with two main landing gears arranged in the tandem configuration and the outrigger struts fitted to the inboard engine pods. The landing gear now made rotation impossible. The landing gear was again redesigned so that the aircraft could land and sit comfortably on the runway.

USAAF Chooses Boeing for the New Jet

Boeing made the changes that the USAAF wanted to the Model 450, and in April 1946, the USAAF ordered two prototypes, designated XB-47. The assembly of the prototypes started in June 1947; the Boeing Corporation could not have been happier as they felt they were on the edge of an aeronautical breakthrough. The first XB-47 was rolled out on 12 September 1947, a few days before the USAAF became the USAF on 18 September 1947. The first flight for the XB-47, a jet no less, occurred on 17 December 1947, the 44th anniversary of the Wright Brothers' first flight (to imagine that there was just a negligible forty-four years from the first powered flight to the first jet flight of a bomber of this magnitude is astounding). Test pilots Robert Robbins and Scott Osler flew the prototype up from Boeing Field in Seattle to Moses Lake airfield in central Washington State in a momentous twenty-seven minute flight. It wasn't all perfect, however: Robbins had to pull up the flaps with the emergency hydraulic system and the engine fire warning lights were falsely lit, but other than this, Robbins reported no problems and excellent flight characteristics.

The Boeing Corporation rolls out their new XB-47 Stratojet on 12 September 1947. (*Boeing Corporation*)

Malfunctions and More Testing

With every new aircraft, there is always something that goes wrong, and the XB-47 was no different. In a test flight on 11 May 1949, the canopy blew off at high-speed, killing pilot Scott Osler with a direct hit to the head. Flight test chief John B. Fornasero, who was traveling along as an observer, managed to lift Osler out of the pilot's seat while co-pilot Jim Fraser brought the aircraft home safely. Osler had been a test pilot for Boeing for some time. 'There is no measure for our appreciation of what Osler did for us,' said Wellwood E. Beall, the vice-president of sales and engineering. N. D. Showalter, who was the assistant chief engineer and a very close friend of Osler for many years, said:

> Those of us who knew Scott Osler personally had the greatest admiration for his integrity and straightforward personality. His friendship has always been held in the highest esteem, and the loss of this friendship is keenly felt by all his close associates. His professional contribution to our flight test and engineering problems has been an outstanding service.

In a conversation with Boeing archivist Mike Lombardi, Rob Robbins admitted that Scott Osler's untimely death in the XB-47 accident had really 'traumatized' him to the point that he stopped flying. However, nothing could take away the fact that Scott Osler and Robert Robbins were the first men to fly a jet bomber. That was a magnificent achievement and the two men deserved the honor.

The loss of Osler prompted the redesign of the canopy and a new chief test pilot, 'Tex' Johnson, was brought on board.

The second prototype XB-47 took off on its first flight on 21 July 1948. She was equipped with a much more powerful engine, the General Electric J47-GE3 turbo jet, packing 5,200 lbs of thrust. The J47, or the TG-190, was a redesigned version of the TG-180/J35. The first XB-47 prototype was later fitted with these new engines. The flight tests were carried out carefully and systematically since the design of the new jet bomber was breaking new ground in so many ways. The prototypes suffered from a 'Dutch roll', an instability that causes the aircraft to weave in, causing widening 'S' turns. The problem was fixed with the addition of a 'yaw damper' control system that applied the rudder mechanically to damp out the weaving motion.

Even before the tragic disaster which led to Scott Osler's death, Rob Robbins had been very skeptical about the XB-47, saying that before the first flight, he had 'prayed to God to please help me.' The aircraft was a mystery and he just didn't know if it was going to make it. In early 1948, the newly formed USAF ordered chase planes from Muroc Field (which is now Edwards Air Force Base) in California, to aid in calibrating the bomber's speed system. Robbins was back in the pilot's seat and this time there was a superstar among test pilots to contend with. Robbins reported:

> The chase plane was a P-80 [Lockheed Shooting Star developed by Kelly Johnson] with Chuck Yeager as the pilot. He did not like bombers and civilian test pilots. Yeager called me on the radio and said, 'Bob, would you do a 180?' I felt that Yeager was playing with me. 'Hey, Chuck is smart (I thought to myself). He just wants to stay reasonably close to Moses Lake. He doesn't have as much fuel as I do.' Well, I turned around, got stabilized, looked for Chuck, he was not there. Finally, I got on the radio and said: 'Chuck, where are you?' Yeager replied, 'I can't keep up with you, Bob.' Therefore, Yeager had to admit to a civilian test pilot [to Yeager, the lowest of the low] that in flying a bomber that he couldn't keep up with me. That was something!

Yeager later flew the XB-47 while it was still in development. Years later he said that the aircraft was so aerodynamically clean that he had big problems with putting it down on the runway. In his autobiography, Yeager's co-author Leo Janos wrote:

> General Albert G. Boyd (who was head of the flight test division), knew the prototype of the Boeing B-47, the first swept wing, six engine bomber capable

A P-80 takes off in chase of a B-47E. (*National Museum of the USAF*)

of delivering an atomic bomb to its target with the speed of a fighter, was a new aircraft still being felt out. He had Boeing engineers brief Yeager on the systems and he personally checked Yeager out on flying it. The bomber had two-seat tandem positioning, under a canopy. Boyd sat behind Yeager while he took off. Yeager did fine up until landing came around, He lined up with the lakebed, put down the landing gear, but the 200,000-lbs bomber refused to land. It was so clean aerodynamically that there was no drag to slow the aircraft down. Yeager floated some fifty feet over the landing field while he attempted to figure out what to do. Meanwhile, Boyd was right behind him, watching. Boyd was laughing to himself because he knew this was going to happen and wanted to see how the 'star' Yeager would handle it. 'Christ,' he said, 'this thing is like a hot air balloon.' 'So I noticed,' Boyd answered. 'But how about putting us down on the deck while it's still daylight?' Yeager finally fought the bird and taught it to sit down, but only after he ran out eight miles of the lakebed to do it. Boyd gave him the test program after that flight. For the next six months, and in between other test programs he was already working on, Yeager worked on the B-47. He did all the stability and control testing on the B-47, while flying with the engineers and filling out all the 'cards' on the take-off altitudes and heavy-bomb loads. Yeager was teased with 'The next time there's a fight at Pancho's (the infamous Pancho Barnes—Happy Bottom Riding Club) between the fighter jocks and the bomber pilots, I expect you to stay neutral.' Yeager replied, 'Bullshit, it'll take more than a couple of rides in the forty-seven to make me one of you bastards.' Hence, the 'love' of Chuck Yeager for bomber pilots.

Operational Flying

As the XB-47 became operational a year later, Yeager had more time flying the B-47 than anyone else; his vast experience as a top fighter pilot gave him a different outlook as to how to fly the bomber in a combat situation. Basically that mean that as a fighter pilot, he now saw the handling of a bomber in a new light and brought some of his vast knowledge of fighter flying to the handling new bomber. Flying in formation was second nature to Yeager, and SAC used his skills to teach the new KC-97 tanker crews, who would serve the bomber, to fly with precision. According to Yeager:

> Civilian test pilots (and there were a number of civilian test pilots working for the various aircraft manufacturers) were barely able to stay in the sky flying the new high-performance jets. They lacked the background and experience of military pilots.... They could not fly in formation. They had no background or military training.

While there may have been some truth in this, many civilian test pilots took offence to his statement. They were hanging it out over the line as much as any military test pilot and deserved the respect for that, even if Yeager felt differently.

Design

The first Boeing XB-47 (#46-0065) Stratojet was completed on 1 December 1967. The XB-47 was a sleek, gorgeous, highly advanced aircraft. The 35-degree swept wing was mounted high on the shoulder of the fuselage with twin inboard turbojets mounted in pods and the outboard engines tucked under the wings, just short of the wingtips. It is amazing to note that future airliners would soon use a similar layout. The aircraft's maximum speed was limited to 489 mph which would avoid control reversal. Anything faster that this would cause the wings to twist and produce a roll in the opposite direction to that desired by the pilot. Aileron inputs by the pilot would be needed to correct this twist. The wings were fitted with a set of 'Fowler' flaps (the upper surface of the main segment of the flap is drawn to the rear, so that the flow is sufficiently directed and the essential slot effect is preserved throughout the range of settings) which extended well behind the wing, allowing lift at slow speeds. Most of the concerns about the XB-47's handling were unfounded.

The XB-47 held a crew of three in a pressurized forward compartment. Both the pilot and co-pilot had a tandem seating arrangement. This allowed for the long, fighter-type bubble canopy, and a seat for the navigator in the nose. The co-pilot, also played the roles of the tail gunner/navigator and bombardier. The bubble-type canopy pitched up and slid backwards, but the cockpit was high off the ground, and the aircraft entrance was through a door and a ladder on the underside of the nose, which also allowed space for maintenance. The extreme front of the nose was glazed for visual navigation and bomb sighting. However, it was soon covered over with metal and all the production revisions required the metal nose and no longer had a window. The K-series bombsight offered incorporated radar and visual navigation with the optical segment extending through the nose of the aircraft in a small dome.

Engine

The TG-180 was the first axial flow (straight flow) compressor engine. It was a basic engine that had an 11-stage, axial flow compressor and single stage turbine. An afterburner that could sustain 7,400 lbs thrust was added later. The TG-180 was first tested in April 1944, only one year after the initial drawings were made. However, since there really was no place for this engine at the time, General Electric began work on the TG-180-J35. It wasn't until much later in February 1946 that the engine was actually flight tested with an XP-84 built by Republic Aircraft. The J-35 was used in the first version of the XB-47. The record of crossing the US in three hours and forty-six minutes in 1949 belongs to the TG-180-J-35.

The first prototype engines flew with the GE-J35 turbo jets, and the production version of the TG-180 could produce 3,970 lbs of thrust. Early jet engines did not develop good thrust at low speeds to help a heavily loaded bomber to take off. The XB-47 prototype had provisions for fitting eighteen solid fuel take-off (RATO) rockets, each with 1,000 lbs of thrust. The fittings for nine units were built into each side of the rear fuselage, arranged in three rows of three bottles each to help with take-off.

The performance of the Model 450 was said to be so good that the bomber would be as fast as a fighter. This allowed the design of defensive armament in the form of a tail turret, which carried two .50-caliber Browning machine guns directed by an automatic fire control system. The two XB-47 prototypes were not fitted with tail turrets.

In the early designs of the B-47 there was a problem with the altitude where the turbojet compromised the speed even though it did help with fuel consumption. There was a very small space between what would be maximum Mach speed and stall speed. It was a big issue. It left no room for error. This problem really showed itself when the B-47 would make long transoceanic flights. The simple autopilot system was virtually useless to the pilots. They would spend the long hours maintaining the airspeed manually so that they didn't meet up with the ocean below, in essence, crash. The fuel had to be balanced so critically that the CG (center of gravity) remained balanced in flight.

The later TG-190 or J-47 turbo jet was an axial flow turbine was designed in 1946 and flew first in 1948. The J-47s had one problem that had to do with the compressor rotor instability in the early models. General Electric solved the problem in a unique way. Engines are usually manufactured in the horizontal position. To solve the compressor rotor instability, they manufactured the J-47 engine vertically. This solved the issue and assured that the engine build up was totally stable. The vertical assembly also resulted in a more efficient and cheaper production. The USAF loved that feature. Production greatly expanded for the engines, used not only with the B-47 but with other USAF aircraft when the Korean War broke out in July 1950. It was the most produced gas turbine engine in history; 35,000 were produced by the time the production line was closed in 1960. According an article in a 1947 edition of *Aviation Week & Space Technology*, 'it was the most widely specified American Jet Power plant.'

The J-47 was a General Electric success. It had a longer lifespan than most engines, which saved the USAF almost $200 million. It was the most produced gas/turbine engine in history and was responsible for many innovations. The J-47 was derived from the GE TF-180, and after ten years in production, 35,000 had been produced. It was a true victory for the B-47, General Electric, and the USAAF.

Drag Chutes

There was one problem with the engines. When it came to landing, the pilot throttled down on landing approach. It would take almost twenty seconds to throttle them back up to full power, if needed. This would be an issue if an approach was missed, and a go round was needed. The big bomber could not easily do a touch and go landing. A small 'approach chute' (drogue parachute) provided enough drag so that the aircraft was flown at approach speeds, with the engines throttled at ready, to spool back up to medium power at least. The pilot had to increase his landing speed in order to cut down on the amount of runway used to land. Air Force test pilot Major Guy Townsend suggested the addition of German-designed 32-foot 'Ribbon drag chute' jet engine thrust reversers, but that was in the future. Consequently, the B-47 was the first mass-produced aircraft that had an anti-skid braking system.

The B-47 Operations

When the final number was released, there were 2,032 of the B-47 jet bombers produced. When delivered to the Air Force, most of the crews were excited about getting the hot new bomber. The B-47 performance was closer to a jet fighter—a very big jet fighter—than a bomber like SAC's late B-36. The B-47 certainly has speed on her side. In her early days she broke speed records, and she handled well in flight. The large bubble canopy for the pilot and co-pilot gave the aircraft that fighter look and feel. It also afforded enhanced vision, but the design made it difficult to control the environmental temperatures for the three-man crew.

The USAF finally declared the B-47 operational in 1953. The aircraft was slow on take-off, and too fast for landing which was not a great combination. Should a pilot come in on a bad angle, the B-47 would 'porpoise', meaning that it bounced on take-off for another go around. If a pilot did not touch and go for another attempt at landing, unsteadiness would cause the bomber to skid on one wing and cartwheel. Both wings and control surfaces were flexible and bent in flight. Low attitude speed constraint were needed to ensure good flight controls. Better training led to better safety records. As always, some crews loved the bird, others hated it. The workload in the cockpit was high and with only three crewmembers to keep the aircraft in good formation, it was a tough load to carry for the crew.

Training and Problems

The B-47's reliability and service record was good, there was no denying that, but the reliability of the avionics was poor. At the time, there were no printed circuit board electronics; everything ran on old vacuum tubes, which made it necessary to have a pressurized crew compartment in order to keep systems from winking out. Work was done to improve the avionics, yet they remained a problem throughout the B-47's service life. In the 1950s, several models of the B-47 included a fuel tank inerting system. Inerting was a process where oxygen was removed from the tank by the use of a more modern method of pumping liquid nitrogen into the tank with the fuel, thereby 'safing' the tank and making it less able to explode due to too much oxygen in the empty tank space. This process was used with the XB-70 Valkyrie bomber and the SR-71 blackbird. In this case with the B-47, dry ice was also changed to carbon dioxide vapor while the fuel pumps ran or while in-flight refueling was ongoing. The carbon dioxide was pumped into the fuel tanks and the rest of the fuel system, ensuring a low level of oxygen in the fuel system and therefore reducing the possibility of an explosion. There were ten carbon dioxide tanks and heaters, which were used to reduce the risk of static electricity discharges during in-flight refueling.

With the B-47 now in SAC's 1958 inventory, the aircraft was training in low altitude missions for nuclear bomb release. The operations were putting a great amount of strain on the aircraft and it was showing up as metal fatigue and stress, and in some cases even crashes. In order to alleviate some of that metal fatigue, a program by the name of 'Milk Bottle' was instituted. This program used very large connecting pins that were replaced in the wing root of the aircraft. However, the low altitude training missions were concluded even with Milk Bottle in place.

SAC's B-47 bomber was the world's first swept wing bomber. Initial missions included the use of nuclear weapons. Training for this mission imposed high stress on the aircraft; the airframe lifetime was limited by metal fatigue and that maneuver was eliminated.

The B-47's Top Years

By 1956, the SAC/USAF had twenty-eight wings of the B-47 bomber, five of which were of the RB-47 reconnaissance version. The bombers were always first up for the United States' strategic nuclear deterrent operation—in short, the bombing run. Included were forward bases in the UK, Morocco, Spain, Alaska, Greenland, and Guam. With a third of the operational aircraft available, they sat and waited for the call on the hard stand or on alert ramps. This was called 'one third alert.' Adjacent to the runways, the aircraft and crews were loaded with fuel, nuclear weapons, and nervous energy, sitting on standby, ready to attack the USSR at very short notice. It was boring and nerve-wracking work.

The B-47 crews were also trained to perform 'minimum interval take-offs' called (MITO). One bomber following the other into the air at periods of fifteen seconds apart, to launch all bombers as fast as physically possible. MITO could be hazardous as bombers left turbulence in their wake, the dense black smoke of the engines blinded the pilots taking off behind.

Production of B-47s stopped in 1957, but the aircraft remained the backbone of the USAF and SAC into 1959. It went through many modifications, changes, and rebuilds. Operational practice for the B-47 bomber at that time was changed from high-altitude bombing to low-altitude strikes, which were judged more likely to break through Soviet defenses. Bomber crews were trained in 'pop up' attacks, coming in at a low altitude and then climbing quickly near the target before releasing a nuclear weapon. It was a tricky and deadly maneuver.

The 1960s: the B-47s Start to Wind Down

B-47 out of Homestead Air Force Base, Florida, took part in a simulated combat exercise against an F-86 in 1958. The B-47 was carrying a brand new 7,600-lb Mark 15 nuclear bomb, with the warhead unarmed. The F-86 fighter collided with the B-47 bomber, leading the F-86 pilot to eject and the fighter to crash. The B-47 took on substantial damage, including the loss of power in one outboard jet engine. After trying to land three unsuccessful times at Hunter Air Force Base, the bomber pilot 'safe' soft dropped the Mark 15 bomb off the coast of Savannah, Georgia, near Tybee Island. The bomb was ditched and the aircraft landed safely. A nine-month search for the Mark 15 bomb was futile. This was known as the 'Tybee Island' crash.

Reconnaissance Duty

The only time that a B-47 ever really faced something akin to combat was when she served on reconnaissance duty. The first flights over Soviet territory occurred on 15 October 1952 when an RB-47 out of Alaska, paid a clandestine visit to the USSR airfields in Eastern Siberia. The B-47 pilots were caught in situations which they survived only through speed, evasive tactics, and basic guts. At least five RB-47s were fired on and three were shot down. The RB-47s fired back with tail turret guns, but no one knew for sure if they racked up a kill. Those were the only shots fired in anger by an RB-47.

On 8 May 1954, after a top-secret reconnaissance run on the Kola Peninsula, a 4th Division, 91st Strategic Reconnaissance Wing RB-47E flew west from the USSR. She was flying at a high altitude, out of reach of the Soviet MiG 15 fighters that were always looking for something to kill. However, unknown to the USAF at the time, the MiG 17s (a newer USSR fighter aircraft) were stationed in the area and were ready to intercept anything in their territory. The RB-47E was chased by three MiG17s over Soviet/Finnish air space in a nasty shoot out. She managed to escape over Sweden, and get back home to RAF Fairford, Gloucestershire, but not without sustaining damage. The superiority of the Soviet jets in top speed and combat radius made the difference—a serious one for the much slower reconnaissance/bombers of the USAF. This mission was the first time a jet aircraft equipped with modern photo equipment had been used for US military reconnaissance. The incident was kept quiet to all parties.

Other interceptions were not so lucky. In another incident, an RB-47 out of Alaska was scouting the Kamchatka Peninsula. On 17 April 1955, the reconnaissance aircraft was jumped by a MiG 15 in international airspace. The RB-47 disappeared from radar, presumed to be shot down.

Between 21 March and 10 May 1956, sixteen RB-47Es and five RB-47Hs, operating out of Thule Air Force Base in Greenland, made a total of 156 flights over Siberia under 'PROJECT HOMERUN.' The Soviets filed a very angry complaint with the United States, who added the flights up to 'navigational problems.' The USSR did not give up on trying to catch the United States out over their property. In the fall of 1958, flying over the Black Sea, a MiG jumped an RB-47E flight on three occasions. On 31 October, it happened again over the Baltic Sea, and again on 7 November, and once more over the Sea of Japan on 17 November 1958.

While a few RB-47s worked in Vietnam relaying ELINT data from drones, they were replaced by the RC-135. In December 1955, the final fifteen RB-47s were fitted with more equipment: the AN/APD 'Side Looking Airborne Radar' (SLAR) system and equipment to sample the air for nuclear fallout after tests. These modified aircraft were given a new designation, RB-47K. They were used for weather reconnaissance station work and carried Dropsonde weather sensors that were released at various checkpoints along the aircraft's flight path. Data was radioed back from the Dropsonde sensors and logged using equipment operated by the navigator in the RB-47K. These aircraft stayed in service until 1963, whereas the last RB-47H was retired on 29 December 1967.

Variants

Just like the B-36, there were many variants of the B-47:

XB-47: Of the two prototypes built, the first flight came with model 450-1 (46-065) and was powered by six Allison J-35-GE-7 turbo jet engines. The second model 452-2 (# 46-065) and the rest of the aircraft were built with GE-J-47-GE-3 engines retrofitted to the first XB-47.

B-47A: The B-47A bomber was called the 'fastest aircraft in the world.' It left the Boeing production plant in Wichita, Kansas, on 11 August 1950. Designated B-47A, the first ten aircraft were strictly evaluation models. The first of these aircraft were delivered in December 1950. The design of the

B-47A was close to that of the initial XB-47 prototype. However, they were fitted with J-47-GE-11 turbojet engines and could throw the same 5,200 lbs of thrust. The engines also featured the built-in RATO (rocket assisted take-off) bottles that were used for take-off only.

B-47B: The B-47B was the product of many negotiations before the sign off in November 1949. This occurred before the first flights of the B-47A. The Air Force had already ordered eighty-seven B-47Bs as a first operational alternative. The USAF was anxious to get the B-47 up and flying as fast as they could. The first of the new B-47Bs flew on 26 April 1951. The final contract called for 399 to be built. Lockheed Aircraft Corp. was signed on to help build the aircraft, as was Douglas Aircraft. This was not an unusual practice in the aviation industry. Those aircraft built by Lockheed were designated LM for Lockheed Martin, and those built by Douglas Aircraft were designated DT for Douglas, Tulsa. The Boeing production part of the order was designated BW for Boeing, Wichita, except for the plant bases in Seattle. XB-47s and the B-47As carried the BO suffix for Boeing Seattle.

The initial run of B-47Bs counted out at eighty-seven. They featured the same J47-GE-11 engines as the B-47As, but all subsequent productions featured the uprated J47-GE-23 turbojets with 5,800 lbs thrust. Early production aircraft were retrofitted with the improved engines. They all featured the built-in RATO (Rocket Assisted Take-Off) system used on the XB-47 and B-47A. The K4A used a periscope bombsight fitted into the tip of the nose of the aircraft; the transparent Plexiglas nose cone of the XB-47 and B-47A was replaced with a metal nose cone, along with four small windows on the left side of the nose and two on the right. Another visible change from the earlier models was the B-47B, which had a vertical tail with a squared off top rather than the rounded top of the previous versions.

A B-47B could carry a larger bomb load of up to 18,000 lbs. All B-47Bs carried the tail turret with twin 20-mm cannons and the B-4 radar-guided FCS (Fire Control System). This system proved rather troublesome, and in some B-47Bs it was replaced with the N-6 optical sight. The co-pilot could swivel his seat around to face backward and sight guns directly. The fuel capacity of the B-47 was not enough to give the USAF the range they wanted. In fact, there was a substantial prejudice against the type among the senior USAF leadership because of the limited range of the initial B-47. The solution to this issue was a high priority and so the in-flight refueling (IFR) receptacle was fitted in the right side of the nose for 'boom' style refueling from the KB-50 and the KC-97 tanker aircraft. This was the main reason for the removal of the Plexiglas nose cone for the bombardier/navigator.

The B-47B was fitted with jettisonable external tanks that were carried between inboard and outboard engine assemblies. The external drop tanks were larger with a 1,780-gallon capacity, and the B-47B was therefore a lot heavier than the A model. To reduce the weight, the ejection seats were taken out and a windbreak panel was fitted to the aircraft main door to make escape possible. Some sources claimed that a fatal ejection seat accident in a B-47A added to this decision. Whatever happened, it was not popular with the crews as a method of getting out of the aircraft at altitude.

YRB-47B: The Air Force had considered building a specialized RB-47B reconnaissance variant to compliment the B-47B bomber version, but as it turned out, schedule slips and the like ensured that the RB-47E was the first of the reconnaissance variants to be produced. As an interim measure before the RB-47E went into service, ninety-one B-47B bombers were fitted with a heated pod that held eight cameras stowed in the forward bay—these aircraft were designated YRB-47B. They could handle daylight reconnaissance only, and when the RB-47E was delivered they returned to the bomber role.

TB-47B: The first group of eighty-six non-combat B-47Bs were re-designated RB-47B in 1953 by the USAF. This change assuaged logistical problems that were occurring due to the problem of different engines and internal systems. Most were used as trainers and some were modified for Air Training Command by Douglas Aircraft Co. in Tulsa, Oklahoma, under project 'Field Goal.' This simple modification added a fourth seat for an instructor and took out the tail turret. In 1956, under project 'Ebb Tide', these aircraft were upgraded to the latest B-47E standard. They were also joined by four more of the earlier built aircraft, also named TB-47B. These aircraft gave crews valuable training through most of the 1950s.

MB-47B: The introduction of the hydrogen bomb had the USAF contemplating converting a small number of B-47Bs into MB-47B drones—essentially, huge cruise missiles that carried the 'H' bomb. The program was known as 'Brass Ring.' Under closer examination, the plan was deemed impractical and 'Brass Ring' was canceled on 1 April 1953.

YDB-47B: The AGM RASCAL missile was being used in many of the flight tests in the 1950s, using the B-47B as the launcher. This B-47B would become the YDB-47B RASCAL launcher. Although seventy-four B-47Bs were modified into DB-47B RASCAL launchers, the RASCAL program was politically problematic and never became operational. The waste was in converting seventy-four B-47Bs into DB-47B RASCAL launchers while the program was dumped.

WB-47B: In 1956, a single B-47B was converted into a WB-47B weather reconnaissance aircraft. It was run by MATS (Military Air Transportation Service), making it one of the few B-47s that SAC did not control. The aircraft remained in service with the Air Weather Service of the Military Airlift Command (MAC) until the mid-1960s.

KB-47G: In 1953, two RB-47Bs were modified for testing the probe and drogue refueling system. The tanker was given the designation KB-47G and known as 'MAW' by the flight crews. It was fitted with a British-built tanker kit. The refueling test aircraft was given the designation YB-47F and was known as 'PAW', though other aircraft (including the YB-52 prototype) were also used as refueling targets. The program was canceled in 1954; as it turned out, the KB-47G simply could not carry enough fuel to make it a successful tanker. The idea of fielding a B-47 tanker conversion came up again in a few years, but its probable cost was unclear and the program closed out in 1957. Around the same time, the RB-47 tanker prototype was being tested. Boeing tested its aerial refueling equipment using the Dash 80, which evolved into the KC-135 Stratotanker, and had a great fuel capacity.

Canadair CL-52: The Canadair CL-52 was an RB-47B loaned in 1956 to the Royal Canadian Air Force to test the new Orenda Iroquois turbojet for Avro's Canadair CF-105 Arrow. The Canadair contractor attached the Iroquois engine to the right side of the rear fuselage near the tail due to the large exterior diameter of the engine; no other location was feasible. Flying the CL-52 was a full-blown nightmare. After the secretive Arrow project was canceled in 1959, the CL-52 was given back to the United States with only around thirty-five hours of engine flight test time. The CL-52 was the only B-47 to be used in foreign service.

YB-47C: The B-56 was a four-engine variant of the B-47 YB-47C proposed by Boeing in 1950. It was to be powered by four Allison J-35A-23 turbojet engines, giving 10,000 lbs of thrust in place of the six GE J-47s. However, the Boeing B-52, which was being developed simultaneously (first flight took place in April 1952) had priority for this engine, and the B-56 was canceled in December 1952 before conversion was started. The donor fuselage that would have been the basis of the XB-56 prototype was then used as a ground instructional airframe.

XB-47D: Starting in 1951, two XB-47Ds were modified from B-47Bs as purely experimental platforms with a big Wright YT-490-W-1 turboprop engine with a huge four-paddle propeller, replacing each of the two inboard jet pods.

Difficulties in engine development delayed the first flight of the XB-47D until 26 August 1955. There really wasn't much of a change in the performance level of the aircraft and the USAF didn't go for the program.

B-47E: The designations B-47C and B-47D were applied to special variants that never went into any form of production and so the next production version of the B-47 was the definitive B-47E. The first B-47E flew on 30 January 1953. The four 'blocks' or 'phases' of the B-47E were built while incorporating refinements on the previous blocks and sometimes featuring production changes within a block. Other blocks were brought up to specification of later blocks as they were introduced. The B-47 also incorporated the production model with the radar controlled near the tail turret.

The early production of the B-47E carried the J-47-GE-25 turbo jet with 5,470 lbs of thrust. The new engine featured the hugely beneficial water-methanol injection—a mixture of water and methanol (the latter acting as an anti-freezing agent) which was added to the engines at take-off to increase the mass flow, temporarily pushing thrust up to 7,200 lbs and therefore reducing take-off distance. The engines left a cloud of black smoke behind when the water-methanol injection was used. Jet-assisted take-off (JATO) modifications were made to early B-47Es; eighteen were fitted with built-in JATO bottles but this system was quickly exchanged for an external 'split V' or 'Horse Collar' rack which was fitted under the rear fuselage and could be jettisoned by the pilot. The rack carried thirty-three JATO bottles in three rows of eleven. The built-in JATO system was discontinued because of concerns about having the JATO bottles so close to full fuel tanks, and in any case once the rocket bottles were exhausted they were dead weight. The racks were dropped over specific range areas after take-off.

As a weight saving measure, the internal fuel capacity of the initial production B-47Es was cut to 14,627 gallons. This was acceptable because of the use of big external tanks and reliable mid-air refueling, which was now standard practice and cost efficient.

One change to the B-47E relative to the B-47B was the return of the ejection seat; the USAF senior leadership thought again about the earlier decision to remove them. The two .50-caliber guns in the tail turret were replaced with twin 20-mm cannons which provided more firepower. These were backed by the A5FCS (Fire Control System) in early production and the MD-4FCS in later production. A final change in the B-47E was the removal of most of the windows in the nose, with only one remaining on each side. Many images of the B-47E show a full set of windows used on the B-47B; whether the number of windows varied throughout B-47E production or whether there were B-47Bs updated to B-47E specifications is not clear.

This excellent image shows the full effect of the B-47's take-off with JATO (jet-assisted take-off). (*National Museum of the USAF*)

B-47EII: The B-47EII had only minor changes from the late production model B-47EI. The B-47EIII featured the ECM (electronic countermeasures) suite consisting of a radar jammer which appeared as a bulge under the fuselage. There was also a chaff dispenser and improved electrical alternators.

B-47EIV: The B-47EIV was a more substantial update, with stronger landing gear and airframe, and greater fuel capacity. The bomb bay was once again shortened because of the new compact nuclear weapons. Another improvement was the introduction of the MA-7A BNS, which was a big step up from its predecessors. The MA-7A included the AN/APS64 radar with a range of up to 240 miles. The AN/APS-64 could be used as a long-range 'IFF' (Identification Friend or Foe) transponder interrogator to allow a B-47EIV to find a tanker or another B-47. It could also be used as a high-resolution ground-targeting radar. The B-47EIV retained the optical bombsight though it was rarely used.

There were 1,341 B-47Es produced—Boeing built 691, Lockheed built 264, and Douglas built 386. Most of the B-47Bs were rebuilt up to the B-47E standard. They were given the designation B-47II, though it appears that they were simply B-47Es. In 1955, a hundred B-47Es were modified to carry two removable external probes, one mounted on either side of the bomb bay, with each pod containing four AN/ALT-6B jammers. The pods were known as 'Tee Town pods' because they were from Forbes Air Force Base in Topeka, Kansas. These aircraft were known as 'Tee Town B-47s.'

EB-47E: The Tee Town B-47s led to a specialized ECM conversion of the B-47E, the EB-47E. The initial EB-47 conversion had a set of sixteen jammers in a removable cradle stored in the bomb bay, plus radar warning receivers and chaff dispensers. They were known as 'Phase IV' or 'Blue Cradle' EB-47Es. The more advanced 'Phase V' EB-47E had a pressurized module that was stowed in the bomb bay with thirteen jammers under the control of two 'Crows' (crewmembers who dealt with electronic countermeasures). While Phase IV jammer systems were 'broad band', covering a wide range of frequencies to jam radars operating somewhere within that range, Phase V jamming systems could be turned to specific radar frequencies by the 'crow' crewmembers. A radar jammer tends to broadcast the presence and location by radio signals it emits; EB-47E crews were perfectly aware that they were unlikely to return from a mission into the USSR. Yet, if they could cover for B-47 bombers, it was worth the sacrifice.

About forty B-47Es were converted to EB-47Es that did not carry bombs but had tail turret guns. B-47E #52-0410 and #52-0412 were converted to EB-47Es in the mid-1960s for service with the US Navy Fleet Electronic Warfare Support Group (FEWSG). On loan from the USAF, these aircraft were unlike the USAF EB-47Es as they had some of their ECM gear fitted into pods carried on external fuel tank pylons. They were used for Naval ECM systems and as 'Electronic Aggressors' in Naval and joint exercises. These two aircraft were the last B-47s in operational service, and #52-0410 had the honor of carrying out the last operational flight of a B-47. On 20 December 1977 this B-47 was flown to Pease Air Force Base and put on display in their museum.

EB-47E (TT): Three B-47s were converted to highly specialized EB-47E (TT) 'Tell Two' configuration to be used for 'telemetry intelligence', picking up radio signals from Soviet missile tests and space launches. The 'Tell Two' was the precursor to the RC-135s 'Rivet Ball' and 'Cobra Ball.' The EB-47E (TT) featured a 'Crow Capsule' in the bomb bay, locked in with the appropriate gear and two ECM operators (known as 'crows'). Also featured were distinctive antennas just below each side of the cockpit. All three of these aircraft operated out of Turkey and were in service until 1967. The antennas on the nose of the aircraft attracted a good deal of attention from the base personnel and crews, who made up some ingenious stories about them. One of these stories claimed that the antennas were part of a 'Return to Fighter' (RTF) defensive system that would cause Soviet air-to-air missiles to loop back towards their fighter and shoot them down. In reality, they were specialized receivers used for intercepting telemetry signals from the Soviet space and missile launches. However, the RTF story was a good tale to tell those who were not supposed to know what the antennas were to begin with.

ETB-47E: The B-47B and a few of the B-47Es were converted to trainers. A fourth seat for an instructor was added and the designation was changed to ETB-47E. These aircraft served until the 1960s and were used to replace the TB-47Bs that were 'too long in the tooth.'

DB-47E/YDB-47E: Two B-47Es were converted to YDB-47E to support the GAM-63 RASCAL stand-off missile program, and two more B-47Es were converted to DB-47Es in preparation for the operational introduction of the missiles before the program was closed. These two DB-47Es were used as drone controller aircraft.

JB-47E: Several B-47Es were assigned to specialized test duties and given the blanket designation of JB-47E. One was used in the later 1960s to test 'fly by wire' control system concept.

JTB-47E: Two B-47Es were fitted for a secret flight experiment in the early 1960s and given the designation JTB-47E. A third even more mysteriously modified B-47E was given the name JRB-47E. They appeared to be test plan forms for ECM experiments.

QB-47E: Fourteen RB-47Es were converted to QB-47E drones in 1959 and 1960. These aircraft were radio controlled and included some interesting features such as self-destruct charges and arresting gear to help with landing on aircraft carriers. They carried pods mounted on the external tank pylon to help in scoring weapons tests. Most of the missiles fired on them were directed for a near miss. The QB-47E were cut down to only two survivors and retired in the early 1970s.

RB-47E: A typical reconnaissance route was from Thule Air Base (Greenland) to the Soviet Union, flown by RB-47E crews. The B-47E was the basis for a number of important long-range reconnaissance variants and these were the B-47s to see combat. They operated from almost every airfield that gave them access to the USSR and often crossed into Soviet airspace.

The Boeing Wichita plant built 240 RB-47E reconnaissance variants; they were similar to the B-47E but with a nose stretched by 34 inches, giving these aircraft the more elegant appearance than the bomber variants of the B-47. The long nose was used to carry up to eleven cameras, which included: O-15 radar and forward oblique cameras for low altitude work, the K-17 Trimetragon (three-angle) camera for panoramic shots, and the K-36 telescopic camera. The navigator who controlled the cameras becoming a 'navigator photographer' instead of a navigator/bombardier. The RB-47E could also carry photoflash flares for night reconnaissance. It was refueled in flight, and its fuel capacity was increased to a total of 18,400 gallons.

WB-47E: The single WB-47B weather reconnaissance conversion took place in the early 1960s. Thirty-four aircraft were converted by Lockheed into WB-47Es. These aircraft were stripped of combat gear, including the tail turret guns. They were fitted with cameras in the nose to take pictures of cloud formations and carried a special meteorological instrument pod in the bomb bay. Assigned to the Air Weather Service of the Military Air Transport Service (MATS), they became part of Military Airlift Command (MAC) when that organization was established. The last WB-47E was flown on 31 October 1969.

RB-47H/ERB-47H: Thirty-two RB-47Hs were built for electronic intelligence (ELINT) missions, as well as three more specialized ERB-47Hs. These aircraft featured blunt rounded noses and had blisters and pods for intelligence gathering antennas and gear. They were designed to probe enemy defenses and then collect data on radar and defense communication signals. The bomb bay was replaced by a pressurized compartment, which accommodated electronic warfare officers known as EWOs or 'crows and ravens' (both blackbirds), a reference to Black Operations. There were three 'crows' on board the RB-47H, but only two on the ERB-47H. A distinctive bulged radome fairing was replaced by bomb bay doors. The only difference between RB-47H and ERB-47H was that the ERB-47H had a small, distinctive antenna fairing under the rounded nose.

The first RB-47H was delivered in August 1955 to Forbes Air Force Base in Kansas. The ELINT B-47s proved so valuable that modification 44 was installed in the 'Silver King' update program in 1961, giving the aircraft an upgraded electronic system. 'Silver King' aircraft could be recognized by a tear drop shaped pod for ELINT antennas attached to a pylon mount under the belly and offset to one side. A pylon-styled antenna under each wing beyond the outboard engine was also visible. It is not listed as to whether all RB-47Hs were updated with this program.

RB-47H and ERB-47H were great aircraft, but the Electronic Weapons Officer (EWO) compartment was not only cramped, it also had poor noise insulation and climate control. This made twelve-hour missions entirely miserable. It was said that the 'crows' also had to deal with fuel leaks. On occasion, not even a successful downward ejection (cutting through the belly radome) was possible on or near the ground. The crows were seated bob-sled style on the pilot compartment floor for take-off and landing. They had to dress in arctic clothing and wear a parachute, and getting to and from their compartment along an unpressurised maintenance shelf during temporary level off at 10,000 feet was not easy.

Operations with the RB-47H and the ERB-47H were often classified secret, with ten-hour missions flown at night. When the crews were asked what they were doing, the common answer was 'Classified.' When asked what the blunt, black nose was for, crews said it was a bumper for air refueling. There were many on the base that bought that answer, while others came to their own conclusions. These were the Silent Warriors who never divulged their mission, even to their families. If they died in service, it would be years before their mission became declassified, and some missions will never be declassified.

When the final RB-47H (#53-4296) was retired from service on 29 December 1967, it was sent to Davis Monthan Air Force Base to be used in avionic testing for the F-111 in the TFX program. A single B-47E was converted to an MA-2 BNS for the B-52 and given the designation YB-47J. Other B-47Es were also apparently used in MA-2 testing but not given a designation.

RB-47K: This was a photoreconnaissance variant based on the RB-47E. They were generally used for weather reconnaissance missions carrying a load of eight dropsonde weather sensors that were released off checkpoints in the aircraft's fight path.

The last flight of the B-47 was in 1986. B-47E #52-0166 was restored and ferried to the Castle Air Force Base Museum for static display.

The B-36 Peacemaker and the B-47 Forge the Path for the B-52

From the beginning of the Second World War to the start of the Cold War, the US Air Force was busy trying to build the best Air Force in the world. It cost time, money, and energy, but they did create two of the largest and strongest aircraft ever—the B-36 Peacemaker and the first jet bomber, the swept wing B-47. As the programs for both of these aircraft grew during their service, they forged ahead with different varieties and jobs that were assigned to them. If it was not bomber work, then it was a redesign to carry the new compact nuclear weapon. If not that, then they were turned to reconnaissance work ranging from the usual ELINT to crossing over into denied territory to look for traces of nuclear testing. Those working the reconnaissance variants very often did so in silence, and no one except their commanding officers really knew the extent of their service. They stood a real chance of being shot down, and even in the event of this happening, their relatives never got the real story of what had happened to them. These crew members knew that would be the case, and they flew regardless.

Both these aircraft paved the way for the B-52 to come into service. The Air Force needed an intercontinental range bomber, one that would be big enough and tough enough to handle all sorts of issues. While the B-36 and the B-47 never fired a shot in anger, this would not be the story for the B-52. She would enter war after war. She would serve with valor and distinction and she would survive some sixty years of service. Her crews were the best and they only flew the best. While her nickname BUFF stands for 'Big Ugly Fat (which is what we will politely use here) Fella', she was and is a beauty and one of the best aircraft that Boeing have ever turned out; she is a warrior queen and deserves better than BUFF, regardless of tradition. However, I want to make it known to the many BUFF airmen that have served with her in whatever year or war, and the many BUFF fans that I respect your nickname for this wonderful bird. At this point, we will leave the B-36 and the B-47 and see what it took to come up with the giant of a bird, the true 'Iron Eagle' and Warrior Queen, the B-52 Stratofortress.

The XB-70 Valkyrie and What Could Have Been....

The B-36 and the B-47 programs where both institutions at this point in time. However, in the backroads of the Pentagon, as always, there was another bomber that was being looked at to replace the B-52. While the B-52 was on the drafting table and working to get funding, the USAF was already looking for a replacement; it was the way the USAF did business—always one step ahead.

Now is a good time to discuss one of the best research and development aircraft ever built, the North American Aviation XB-70 Valkyrie. She was meant to be a replacement bomber for the B-52, but although that never happened, her considerable offerings to aviation development should not go unsung.

In October 1954, General Curtis LeMay, then the head of SAC, wrote a secret letter to the Pentagon outlining what he thought should be the next set of parameters for a follow on to the B-52. As we know, the Pentagon works in strange ways; this new bomber would replace the yet-to-be-built B-52. LeMay wanted a bomber with a 6,000-mile range, no in-flight refueling, and Mach 1+

cruise speed. His ambitions at the time were restricted to 600 mph and a dash speed of 1,000 mph. LeMay was known as being 'rather determined' in his quest for the ultimate bomber, and his motto was 'Tomorrow's weapon must be designed yesterday.'

Boeing and North American Aviation began work on proposals to the USAF for the new bomber competition; they were allowed just six months to complete them. To say the designs when they came in were futuristic is an understatement; they were also fantastically heavy at 1,000,000 lbs. North American Aviation won the bid and set about creating this futuristic bomber, but LeMay's dream was becoming just that, a dream. The extraordinary weight of the winning design issue LeMay was having to fight, he was also fighting opposition to this wonder bird in the Eisenhower administration.

Eisenhower was just coming out of the Korean War and he inherited Truman's policy of giving in to every political and military doomsayer within earshot. He did not, however, inherit Truman's penchant for giving the military everything they wanted. Eisenhower was afraid of another Pearl Harbor. He believed the defense of the nation was not a matter of funding for a single date in the future, but instead a matter of establishing appropriate protection to be projected into the future as actions and purposes of other countries. He wanted to make sure that all his bases were covered and that meant one thing—intelligence, no matter how he had to get it.

In the mid-1950s, while the B-52 was just about to enter the USAF inventory, North American Aviation had this futuristic aircraft just waiting to be born. The XB-70 was to be a very high altitude, triple-sonic replacement for the B-52. By the end of the 1950s, the new bomber system WS-110A (the name for the XB-70 program) was well under way. The question was whether it would have the chance against all the politics and budget mongering that was going on in Congress.

The XB-70 was getting project funding in the late 1950s, but the financial planners saw the aircraft as too expensive to satisfy the Eisenhower administration's desire for thrift, and in 1959, the project was canceled. Even with the full-scale mock-up completed in 1960 and shown in an issue of *Aviation Week* magazine, the reason for the cancellation was political as well as budgetary. The cancellation broke the hearts of the thousands that had already started working on the Valkyrie. It was a battle scene in Congress, with both houses fighting and the Pentagon protesting against the cancellation of the XB-70. The arguments were so strong that advisors in the mid-1950s for Eisenhower recommended that perhaps minimum funding would have been better, just to quiet the hysteria until Eisenhower got out of office and left the problem to the new Kennedy administration. In the end, Kennedy inherited the problem.

The USAF knew it wanted and needed an intercontinental bomber and fought the new Kennedy administration to have the XB-70 program reinstated. Senator Carl Vinson (D-GA) fought for the bomber as chairman of the Senate Armed Services Committee. There was the question of the 'Bomber Gap' between the US and the USSR. Kelly Johnson of Lockheed brought a resolution of sorts to the issue with his latest aircraft, the U-2 Dragon Lady. She was the first of high altitude reconnaissance aircraft that had the ability to photograph the areas in contention and show images of exactly what was going on. Under the auspices of the CIA, program 'Dragon Lady' brought back information from the USSR which showed the bomber gap was a fallacy. However, this information came at great cost: on 1 May 1960, the U-2 was taken out by a SAM missile. The missile exploded behind the fragile aircraft and she broke apart; Francis Gary Powers, the civilian pilot, managed to parachute to ground, but he was captured by the Soviets, initiating a political nightmare for Eisenhower, and thus ending the flights over the USSR. By July 1960, Congress approved $75 million in additional funding for the XB-70, which brought its fiscal year 1961 total to $365 million. Congress later raised it to $190 million, but without any assurance the money would be spent on the XB-70 program.

Three months after Kennedy took office, the new Secretary of Defense, Robert McNamara, canceled the production program of the XB-70 and authorized the building of only three experimental research aircraft. McNamara was adamant against any acceleration of the program, and he believed it should be dropped after an alternative weapons platform had been selected as a follow on to the B-52. 'The [XB-70] program and its management needs a completed review,' he said. The $575 million requested for FY62 by the USAF for the B-70 was cut to $338 million by the Eisenhower budget and then to $220 million by Kennedy. What McNamara missed was the fact that the XB-70 was planned for just such a position; he did not understand what he already had in his hand. The other part of the B-70 program called for a strategic system and the delivery of conventional weapons. This system would look to the possible use of nuclear weapons and deterrent balance. Again, McNamara did not look beyond the numbers to see what the USAF had laid out for the XB-70; he just did not want to give the USAF the chance it needed to show what the XB-70 could do. McNamara just did not want to see it, hear it, or spend it.

In July 1961, the $365 million previously approved by Congress for FY1961 was reduced to $75 million. Although the plan called for 250 B-70s to start delivery by 1962, the program was cut to thirteen aircraft in production and then the final cut was made to three experimental aircraft. It was a nasty blow by McNamara not only to the research and development in high-speed aviation, but also to the value of a potential commercial SST (supersonic transport) which was already being designed by France and Britain. This was a commercial venture that McNamara did not understand and held the United States back on. He could not be persuaded that the 'noise' factor of hitting Mach 1 was irrelevant as the aircraft would hit this speed over the ocean, not over the populated land. He was simply not interested in anything except his TFX program. The debacle of the TFX program was truly McNamara's folly as he was determined via the TFX program (F-111 Aardvark) to use one aircraft for all the services, saving money by not producing an aircraft for each service, much like the F-35 Joint Strike Fighter today. One aircraft cannot be all things to all services. McNamara found that out but it was too late and it cost too much, leaving the USAF with an aircraft that really didn't fly well and the Navy with nothing at all.

The epilogue to this tale is that only two aircraft were completed, and the third was partially built. North American Aviation had started work on the third aircraft, but this was canceled after the accident with the AV#2 aircraft in 1966. During a photo operation session, an F-104 fell into the powerful vortices of the XB-70 and rolled over, striking her verticals. Pilot Carl Cross and NASA test pilot Joe Walker were killed. Al White, the commander of AV#2-20207, survived but suffered debilitating injuries. The USAF lost the program for good.

3

Building a Warrior Queen

On 23 November 1945, the Air Materiel Command of the USAAF issued the wants and needs for a new strategic bomber. This bomber would be 'capable of carrying out the strategic mission without dependence upon advanced and intermediate bases controlled by other countries.' This new aircraft would carry a crew of five or more gunners for the turrets and a six-man crew for relief. It needed to be able to cruise at 300 mph at 34,000 feet with a combat radius of 5,000 miles. The aircraft would carry 10,000 lbs of conventional weapons. As of 13 February 1946, the USAAF sent out the bid invitations for this new aircraft to Boeing, Consolidated, and Glenn L. Martin Company. All of them sent in their proposals. However, the story is not quite that simple. It is a complex, amazing, difficult, and phenomenal story that created one of the most durable, loved and dependable aircraft ever conceived by man.

As the USAF evolved its forces and developed the B-36 and then the B-47 into the aircraft that they wanted, the development phase never stopped for the Air Force. It was always thinking and changing. It had to stay on top of what the Soviets were doing and of course, there was the nuclear threat. While Eisenhower's administration was busy developing both satellites and reconnaissance systems like the U-2 Dragon Lady and the A-12 Blackbird of the Oxcart program, there was still a great need for a bomber that could carry her weight and be able to defend herself no matter what the situation.

As the B-52 concept developed on paper over a period of years, most of the USAF leaders at the time found themselves funding a very expensive design study that just did not quite make the mark for the aircraft. As always, the USAF waited for the engine to be designed first, so that the aircraft could be built around it. This was nothing new and was part of the world of aircraft design from way back. The B-52 was only a glimmer in the eyes of Boeing when the decision was made that the B-36 had to be replaced by the late 1950s.

Loading one of the capsules carrying the different reconnaissance configuration for the B-52. (*National Museum of the USAF*)

As we have already discovered, the B-36 was a Second World War design, which started back in 1941 and the main design did not see the light of day until 1946.

It took until 1948 for the program to be approved and for the construction of one hundred B-36 aircraft to be ordered. General George Kenney, head of SAC at the time, was against the intercontinental bomber program. General Carl 'Tooey' Spaatz, the USAF Chief of Staff, wanted it. General Lauris Norstad, the Deputy Chief of Staff for Operations, joined Kenny. The argument rolled right over into the early stages of the B-52 design program. In January of 1948, the engineering study for the B-52 was halted. The plans were changed to convert only a few of the B-36s into aerial tankers for the B-50 (which was an enhanced version of the B-29) and both Generals Kenney and Norstad got their way. No intercontinental bomber, at least not yet anyway.

Since the United States held the atomic bomb in its hip pocket, it made the chance for another world war very unlikely, at least until the Soviets got their A-bomb up and running. Besides, the United States was also developing the new ICBM (Intercontinental Ballistic Missile) that could carry a nuclear warhead. With the use of overseas bases for strategic bombers and the much cheaper B-50 to rely on, the USAF felt it was in a 'safe' corner, at least for the moment. Yet, as always, things were not what they seemed. In 1948, the USSR had showed its true hand with Communism and the fact that they wanted to promote it worldwide. On 24 June 1948, the Soviets blockaded West Berlin. It did not take the USAF brass too long to get together and decide on a plan of action. USAF Chief of Staff General Hoyt Vandenberg and the USAF Secretary, Stuart Symington, met and decided on the number for a fleet of B-36 bombers. At this point, Generals Kenney and Norstad jumped on board with the plan, because truthfully there was no place else for them to go. This made the decision undisputed.

With both the Cold War and the Soviet testing of nuclear weapons and the blockade of West Germany, it was certain that the USAF had to start moving. Boeing Aircraft Corp was already working on engineering studies for a straight wing, prop-jet aircraft. Their Model 462, which they started to work on in 1946, looked like the B-36 with a tractor instead of a pusher prop. The wingspan was 221 feet with a total weight of 360,000 lbs and a range of 6,200 miles. Moreover, the aircraft used the Wright X1-35 powerplant.

The USAF promptly decided this configuration for the B-36 would be too slow and heavy to be useful. Boeing got the bad news from General E. E. Partridge, Deputy Chief of Operations. The Boeing team cleared the drawing table for a brand new start. The next idea was for a four-engine aircraft, with specifications by the man himself, General Curtis LeMay, the Deputy Chief of Staff for Research and Development.

Boeing's next proposal was ready in December 1946 and had two concepts to show. The first concept was called Model 464-16 and the second, Model 464-17. Model 464-17 would have a 10,000-mile range with a 10,000-lb capacity, and the Model 464-16 would be a conventional bomber with a lighter range, bombload capacity of 90,000 lbs, cruise speed of 400 mph at a 35,000 feet ceiling.

The USAF rejected the proposals outright. The explanation given was that models were just too slow. They felt that an intercontinental bomber should have a of 25 percent speed below that of an enemy interceptor aircraft. The idea worked like this: With the enemy aircraft holding a speed gain of 25 percent or less, it could not reach the bomber force in time to stop it from accomplishing its mission (assuming that were was a thirty minute advance warning). However, the USAF did not see it that way and by the time the arguments had stopped, the USAF was left with the world's heaviest bomber, should it want to have the range and speed decided on. In February 1947, Boeing pocketed additional funding to study the Model 464-17 prop-jet. With nowhere else to go, the USAF had to agree to the funding grant. One of the reasons Boeing and the USAF kept working together was that the B-47 Stratojet, then under construction, still had issues that needed fixing. She turned out to be a swept wing beauty with a design weight of 125,000 lbs and six G.E. J-47 turbo jet engines of 5,000 lbs of thrust each, a speed of 600 mph, and a range of 3,000 miles. You couldn't ask for more for the first jet bomber.

Boeing's newest design 'baby' was called Model 464-25; it was shown to the USAF in March of 1947. This model proposed a bicycle-type landing gear close to what the B-47 had. The landing gear consisted of four dual wheels in tandem and one dual wheel as an outrigger on each wingtip. This design contained an extended dorsal fin and all new wings with a tapered leading edge. The next Boeing Model 464-29 was the next and newest design brought to the USAF in August 1947. All of the Boeing reports illustrated the history of the 464-29, but the USAF records do not have a record of it anywhere. Nonetheless, according to a Boeing memo, the Model 464-29 had become a much larger aircraft, using four smaller but more powerful turboprop engines. It did meet the USAF range needs, but it was still considered too large and too slow in view of what they already had on the table. Boeing had considered using the Wright XTBE-W-3 gas turbine engines. This design's gross weight, with external fuel, would have been at least 400,000 lbs. The wingspan consisted of 205 feet. Boeing was correct on holding this one back from the USAF.

As of 21 September 1947, Boeing was given a contract by the USAF for the Model 464-25, which stipulated that the studies, drawings, and the mock-up

Testing the B-52 airframe in an anchoretic chamber. (*Boeing Corporation*)

had to be prepared and ready by 31 January 1948. This was a big contract for Boeing and a very tall order. The concept would have to be defensively fortified, reduced to a one vertical tail and two .50-caliber guns in the turret and carry a bomb load capacity of 12,000 lbs.

The inspection of the wooden mock-up was carried out on January 1948, just as planned. Boeing's contract was canceled at that time, however, the Air Force was due to reissue the B-52 design directive out to the Aviation Industry again, pushing the entire project back to the beginning with a new contract proposal. The USAF felt this was necessary since Convair was applying pressure for another shot at the B-52 contract. Convair, Boeing, and Martin were the original contractors for the airframe, and they responded to the initial design proposal. The mock-up constituted one complete fuselage and the right half of the wing. Four additional mock-ups of the nose, depicting the crew configurations were also added. The USAF Board of Senior Officers said that while the mock-ups were useful, they found them frustrating and confusing.

Northrop was also involved in making the Boeing decision problematical for the Air Force. In 1947, several of the USAF Commands were looking at Jack Northrop's revolutionary XB-35 flying wing. She was a strategic bomber with stats much in line with the B-36. Jack Northrop had been working on the concept since 1929. The XB-35 first flew on 26 June 1946, with a Pratt and Whitney R-4360 Wasp Major engine of 2,500 lbs thrust. Nine turbojet versions of the XB-35 were built and designated YB-49; they ran on the Allison J-35 engines, each with 4,000 lbs of thrust.

The YB-49 made its first flight on 21 October 1947 and really looked like it this might be what the USAF was yearning for. However, two of the birds were lost in test flights. In the end, the YB-49s were closed out of test production in one of the saddest and most wasteful stories in aviation history. This was also one of the stupidest decisions ever made by the USAF. Due to contractual circumstances that involved Convair and the B-36, the YB-49s were destroyed literally to the last aircraft. It was a prime example of how the USAF's gross inefficiency and reckless politics could influence a potentially great aircraft.

There were objections galore to the B-52 contract from Generals Craig, LeMay, Partridge, and the Air Force Secretary Stuart Symington. Generals Vandenberg, Kenney, and McNarney were agreed, however, they approved for Boeing to go ahead with the design of yet another prop jet. The Model 464-35, with a range of 8,000 miles and a cruise speed of 500 mph at 35,000 feet. ceiling, was on the table. By February 1948, the approval was agreed upon with Boeing and the USAF. By March, more changes were added and the Model was again re-designated 464-35-0. On 15 December 1948, the XB-52 prop jet was locked down to a 280,000-lb Model 464-35-0 that was able to carry 10,000 lbs of iron bombs, 19,957 gallons of fuel, and had a range of

6,000 miles. With a speed of 513 mph, and a ceiling of 35,000 feet, this was sure to make the USAF proud. The crew consisted of five men. However, the only armament carried would be in the tail turret guns.

With a delivery date of February 1951, the Phase II contract drove the cost of the project to $29,418,373. This included the construction of the aircraft. This calculation would be a pittance today, but back then, on the tails of a very expensive war and the budget cuts because of that war, it was a vast amount of money. One of the reasons the USAF returned to Boeing with the contract was that it would have been exceedingly hard to tell Congress that the USAF just blew $4 million out the window with a cancellation. Albeit, today it would be a drop in the bucket as Congress spends that much in the blink of an eye.

The USAF asked Boeing to enlarge the B-52's performance to include installation of the new Westinghouse J-40 turbojet engine in May 1948. To do this would require a minimum of changes to accommodate it, such as adding an external fuel tank. It would also increase the weight aspect. This configuration would finally claim the Model 464-40 name. While there was less range, the USAF felt the high altitude ceiling and speed would be more than enough to keep the aircraft alive in action. More Boeing studies showed

Douglas-Tulsa Oklahoma received a contract to modify 117 B-52s. A B-52 is shown here alongside B-47 Stratojets and RB-66s on the flight ramp. (*Boeing Corporation*)

that at least 4,000 miles could be added to the propjet range, by using a pure jet engine. That could be accomplished by allowing for aerial refueling.

The Model 464-40 version of the B-52 kept Boeing busy with further studies. In 1948, the Models 464-46 and 47 were offered to the USAF. Later on in 1948, the Model 464-49 was drawn containing the installation of eight Pratt and Whitney J-57 turbojet engines, each with 10,000 lbs of thrust. Finally, there was now a driving force in an engine that was equal to the B-52. This is what the USAF was looking for from the start.

Boeing's New Baby

Ed Wells, then vice president in charge of the Boeing engineering staff, Art Carlson, Maynard Pennell, W. H. Washington, Vaughn Blumenthal and George Schairer were all part of the team for Boeing. What they were offering the USAF was a bigger, better version of the B-47. The wings were swept back 35 degrees, the range was some 8,000 miles, and the speed 550 mph. To add to that, this version had a high ceiling of 45,000 feet. The pilot and co-pilot sat tandem to each other beneath an elongated canopy on top of the nose, much like that of the B-47. On 26 January 1949, there was a meeting held by the Board of Senior Officers of the USAF. They issued a directive allowing Boeing to continue the existing contract with conversion and development of the Model 464-49 turbojet aircraft. However, with all this, there is another story on how the B-52 came to life.

The Hotel Van Cleve and the Birth of the B-52

In October 1948, a group of Boeing engineering executives arrived at Air Material Command Headquarters in Dayton, Ohio, for a special meeting. They had come together, with all their notes, files, and drawings to show the USAF a brand new long-range bomber that they would hopefully consider for production, if only experimental. The Boeing engineers had some reservations regarding how this bomber would go over, but they weren't ready for the slap down they got from the USAF. According to the story, Colonel H. E. Warden of the Air Materiel Command said, 'In spite of previous indication, we no longer believe that this type of airplane can be counted on to do the job we now have in mind.' Boeing had been working the project for some two years and AMC (Air Force Materiel Command) was behind them with support, so they thought. The Boeing engineers had gone to Wright-Patterson Air Force Base, Dayton, Ohio, ready to show the USAF what they had developed—a turbo-prop aircraft that would deliver exactly what the USAF wanted. Yet, they were also ready to show that the engine and prop manufacturers would not be able to deliver the engine by the time needed; this would obviously affect the aircraft they were hoping to sell. While at face value all this looked bad for Boeing, they were up to the challenge Colonel Warden was giving them.

Colonel Warden explained, 'What we're interested in, as of now, is a look at what can be done in the way of a long-range bomber powered by a pure jet.' Warden then went on to show the evidence of a new turbojet engine, the J-57 created by Pratt and Whitney. The J-57 was not new to the Boeing crew, and they had already made some studies using it. They conferenced with Pratt and Whitney on the future development of the engine, and made suggestions. Warden continued to explain, 'What can you do with this in the way of a

An image from the Dayton Weekend reenactment. In October 1948, the Boeing team presented a turboprop design for the B-52 to US Air Force Colonel Pete Warden, who suggested that the team redesign the airplane into a swept-wing all-jet design like the B-47 Stratojet. It was a Friday, and he gave the team until Monday to come up with a new design. Over the weekend, the team of (left to right) George Schairer, Vaughn Blumenthal, Maynard Pennell, Ed Wells, Art Carlson, and Bob Whittington (not pictured in this photo) worked on the new design. Schairer made a balsa-wood model, and Ed Wells led the development of a thirty-three-page proposal. After seeing the model and the proposal, Colonel Warden said, 'Now we have an airplane: this is the B-52.' (*Boeing Corporation*)

specific bomber design?' The Boeing crew turned around and headed back to the hotel. On the next day, they called Warden and said, 'We'll come in Monday morning with a new airplane.' Hence the Dayton Hotel Van Cleve was soon to become the new drafting room for the Boeing engineers, at least for a weekend, anyway.

In that weekend, an aviation miracle unfolded. The B-52 Stratofortress was conceived and born in a hotel room in Dayton, Ohio. What happened was one of those weird things that occur when you are under enough pressure to sink an aircraft carrier—you find just what you are looking for. The Boeing engineers did just that. While the drafting was crude and unrefined, it was enough to make the B-52 a reality.

The Engineering Vice President for Boeing, Ed Wells, created the outline design of the B-52. Wells was also responsible for the 'pod' conception on the engines, an engineering miracle that would emerge further on in Boeing aircraft history. The senior project engineer, Art Carlson, and Maynard Pennell, then chief of preliminary design, went to work on breaking down the weight. H. W. Withington, the engine planner and aerodynamicist, and Vaughn Blumenthal wrote the estimated-performance report. George Schairer, who was then the chief of Boeing's technical staff, put out the design for a new type of sweptback wing. It was hand carved out of balsa wood bought in a local hobby shop along with the knife to carve it. It was an almost perfect model of the bomber that would grow up to be the B-52. With all this completed, the engineers decided to write a thirty-three-page document for presentation to Warden at AMC on Monday. It had been an extraordinary weekend.

When the B-52 took shape, there were hardly any alterations to the model engineered in the hotel room. Vaughn Blumenthal said, 'You have to look for fly specks to find the difference in appearance.' Ed Wells even admitted that 'The thing [Hotel Van Cleve] sounds unbelievable, unless properly qualified.' What needs to be explained is that the Boeing engineers that day did not draw up this new turbojet-powered bomber out of the air. They drew from their years of study and research, not to mention wind tunnel work on the high speed swept wing concept. They cut and tried the wings on both the heavy and medium bombers and used all the experience gained from the beautiful B-47. The previous summer, Boeing was so unhappy with the turboprop engine design that they went ahead, with Air Force approval, to delve into the possibilities of using a turbojet for the long-range bomber.

When the Boeing gentlemen got together in that hotel room, they had a ton of information already in their briefcases or a phone call away. They took all these things, brought them up to speed with the J-57 engine abilities and wrote the paper. This entire episode has to be on one of the strangest and most productive weekends in the history of aircraft construction. This was only the

A 5th Bomb Wing crewmember checks the warning lights under a B-52 at Andersen AFB, Guam. (*U.S. Air Force*)

beginning of the 'Incident in Dayton' as it is called. It brought the development of the B-52 and shaped it into the intercontinental bomber that had been talked about since the meeting between Roosevelt and Churchill in August 1941. The US was not yet in the war, but it was not looking good for Britain. If Britain and North Africa fell to Hitler, trying to counter-attack from North America would not be possible. We could not reach Europe from our shores. So, what happened in that hotel room as the Boeing team said, 'We will come in Monday morning with a new aircraft' was not something they just dug up; the foundation was there and they were the men that knew just how to make that magic happen.

The Boeing YB-52, XB-52 and 'a Helluva' Good Plane!'

According to a memo from the Boeing archives, on 29 November 1951 Boeing brought the XB-52, completely cloaked in tarps and hidden by the dark of night, out of the plant to Boeing Field for ground and taxi tests. These tests were the second stage of the ground-proving program for the huge eight-jet aircraft and this was all prior to her first flight of the second of the prototypes. XB-52 was treated as the second bird next to the YB-52, the other prototype. The taxi program included steering, braking, engine acceleration, and control surface action. The first XB-52 was returned to the plant for the installation of equipment that was not available at the time of the initial rollout. The first portion of the program, the Boeing memo went on, was a series of tests for the engines, functional systems, and equipment. When it was necessary to move the aircraft into a more exposed area for the start of the engine tests on 30 December 1952, a single photo was released, which did not give much in the line of detail. No additional photos were released during that phase of testing. While a complete equipment suite was being installed in the XB-52, the YB-52 was undergoing ground tests, and then was prepared to make her first flight.

The second of the two Stratofortress prototypes, the YB-52, rolled out of the Seattle Boeing plant on 15 March 1952. Designed to be a service test aircraft for the B-52A production models, the YB-52 was scheduled to undergo a series of ground tests before becoming the first to fly. As was the case with the first aircraft, the XB-52, which was rolled out of the Boeing hangar November of 1951, the pre-flight program included tests on the engines, functional systems, equipment, steering, brakes, and engine acceleration, along with control surfaces. Secrecy was as important as it was with the XB-52; the USAF 'desires that the press and public refrain from making any photos of the new YB-52 as they have refrained from photographing the XB-52 in order to prevent disclosure of any additional information at this time.' Boeing at that time also said that the second aircraft, the YB-52, was designated as such ('Y' denoted service test aircraft for production models while the letter 'X' denoted experimental aircraft). The Boeing memo closed by giving the following stats for the aircraft: 153 feet long, a 185-foot wingspan, and 48 feet to the tip of the sweptback tail. Other details of the 'new bomber' remained secret at the time the memo was written.

The YB-52 was first flown on 15 April 1952 by veteran Boeing test pilot A. M. 'Tex' Johnston with Lt Col. Guy M. Townsend of the USAF Air Research and Development Command as co-pilot. Townsend and Johnston, with Johnston in command, had the aircraft at a 5,000-foot roll on Boeing Field when she lifted off the ground, gear down, and made some gentle turns around the Puget Sound. Some forty minutes later, 'Tex' Johnston headed for Larson

The construction of the B-52 was no simple task, but Boeing always made it look easy. Here we see the wing mating for the aircraft. (*Boeing Corporation*)

The B-52 major test board is in full view of the Boeing worker on the catwalk, with the huge aircraft fuselage right behind him. (*Boeing Corporation*)

Air Force Base at Moses Lake in Central Washington. The YB-52 stayed in the air almost three solid hours. After landing, Johnston said, 'I am convinced that this is not only a good airplane, it is a helluva good plane!' It looked like Boeing had a hit on their hands; sixty years later, that hit is still going strong.

On 2 October 1952, the XB-52 made her maiden flight from Boeing Field. The aircraft took off at 5.56 p.m. 'Tex' Johnston and Lt Col. Townsend did the honors again. On the crew list for the 2 October flight was Arthur Curren, another Boeing test pilot, and Capt. William M. Magruder of the USAF Air Research and Development Command. After a flight of two hours and forty-two minutes, XB-52 returned to Boeing Field at 8.38 p.m.

The first XB-52 came through the test program with 'highly satisfactory results' according to a Boeing memo. More tests for both aircraft were made at Boeing Field. At the time of the memo, the quantity of B-52s to be manufactured was top secret. Both test pilots Johnson and Lt Col. Townsend were scheduled to put the XB-52 through some preliminary flights before turning the aircraft over to the Air Force for further flights. Lt Col. Townsend and Capt. William Magruder were the pilots for this phase of the testing. Arthur Curren, who was an alternate co-pilot on some of the flights, continued Boeing's advanced

Engineers are watching from the upstairs station as the workers below undertake a wing static test of the B-52. The work floor at the Boeing plant is intensely busy. (*Boeing Corporation*)

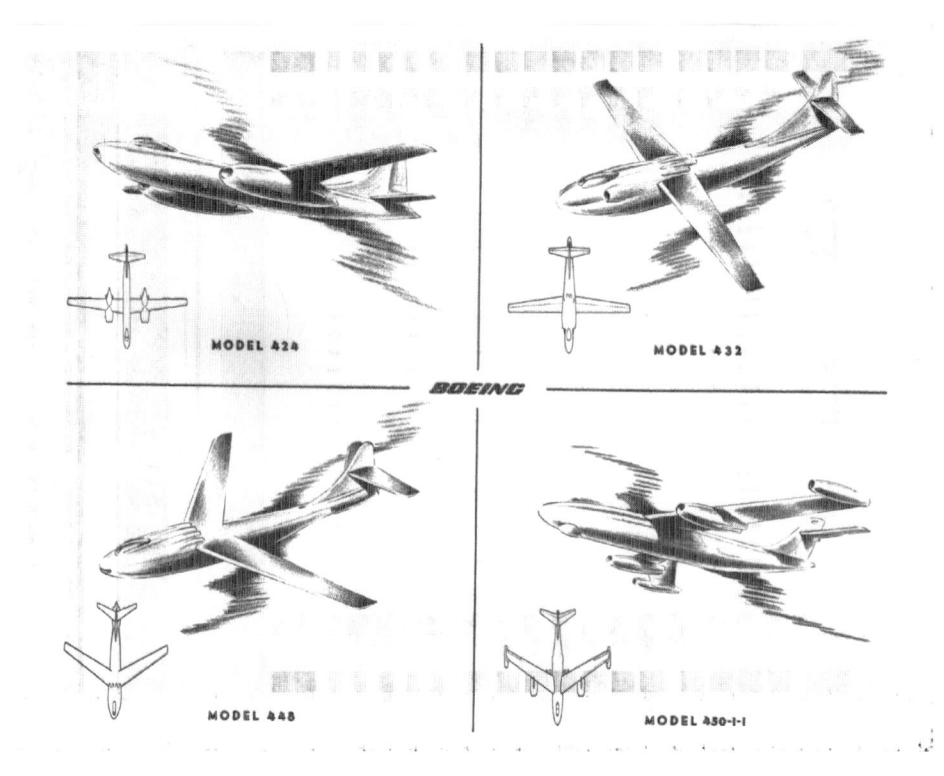

Above: The various design phases of the B-52, from Model 424 to Model 430-1-1. This image charts the changes that had been made and how the B-52 developed into the aircraft we know today. (*Boeing Corporation*)

Below: The final assembly area for the B-52 was an amazing sight to behold. (*Boeing Corporation*)

performance testing of the YB-52. Both aircraft were used in an accelerated program of 'Prove Out' on all systems, which intended to explore all of the aircraft performance characteristics.

The B-52 Problems and Learning Curves

The B-52 test program was among the roughest out there. SAC got the first deliveries of the B-52s they ordered some three years later. No B-52 was lost in the test program. However, there were three B-52s added to the test program in 1954. It was not all peaches and cream with the program and they did have problems. There was one aircraft that landed with one set of main wheels retracted. There was another test flight where one of the four main bogies was jammed at the full 20-degree inclined position, causing some heavy damage of the fuselage as she landed. There were tests for structural fatigue and load limits, which were done at the Seattle plant on a B-52 airframe. On 20 December 1953, there was a special concrete pad built for a load of 85,000 lbs at any point and enveloped by 500 tons of steel superstructure, which also allowed every flight condition to be tested along with many different configurations of flight loads.

There was also the issue of skin wrinkling. Technically skin wrinkling is explained as: 'monocoque shear stress upon the skin when the aircraft wings command a roll and the fuselage mass resists rolling forces.' This issue showed up a little later on in the program once the aircraft went into full service. The skin wrinkling was a baffling issue to everyone. If you first look at it, it almost looks like delamination. Delamination occurs when the skin separates from the longerons in a bubble form, sort of what the XB-70 has on her skin; it's not deadly and is caused from contraction and expansion in heat and cold. With the B-52, however, there is only aluminum. The skin wrinkles are caused by the weight of the forward fuselage, which is forward of the main landing gear. It's more pronounced in hot weather, which is why the B-52s in Vietnam looked like a mess and ready to fall apart. The wrinkles disappear when the aircraft is in flight. The skin for the B-52 is not laminated, just aluminum sheet metal. Many of the machinists who worked with the aircraft have also seen the wrinkles happen in the aft section behind the main landing gear. That section has also been seen with a 17-foot crack extending over the top, which was caused by a hard landing. An article in the 15 May 1961 issue of *Aviation Week Space Technology* said, Lt General Mark Bradley, Chief of Staff for Materiel, highlighted some concern regarding the condition of the skin wrinkling: '... there is terrific stress on the wing skin in the later models (G-H) which carry fuel in the wings. We are having trouble with the G's and

Perhaps the strangest sight of all. The B-52, completely shrouded, is being rolled out in the middle of the night to ensure that enemy spies can't get a glimpse of SAC's latest bomber. Even the tail was removed. (*Boeing Corporation*)

we predict trouble with the H's and it looks like we will probably have a modification program to keep them flying.' The B-52s did keep flying and the skin wrinkling continues today.

There were two years of 'torture' testing until the USAF was satisfied that it was getting what it wanted for the long wait and the money poured into the program. While the airframe tests were solidly performed and approved, the equipment tests were something else. As the program went on, so much attention was paid to the structural problems that the equipment did not get quite the same amount of testing. Later on in the program, many of those systems failed and aircraft were lost because of it.

Early Losses

In the winter of 1955, the first Boeing B-52 Stratofortress was lost in an accident. A second B-52 crashed in 1956, when a turbo alternator failure exploded in a fuselage fuel cell. There was an electrical fire that destroyed yet another aircraft in mid-September 1956. On 30 November 1956, a flight crew of six and four instructors died. December 1956, three other aircraft were lost to in-flight fires. During this extremely arduous time in the program, the B-52s were grounded twice, until a new alternator power system was found.

Even with this distressing period, however, there was a great advance with the B-52 main landing gears, which were set in tandem. The pilot could turn the landing gear 20 degrees on either side. The forward and aft bogies could be turned independently for ground maneuvering, or they could be synchronized to allow the aircraft to crab for a crosswind landing. The outrigger wheels on the outer wing panels (148 feet apart) pressed against the ground but only when the wing tanks were filled. This was before the 'G' model wet wing, which was a total redesign. A B-52 had numerous individual fuel cells in each wing, in addition to the external drop tanks. The flight control system for the B-52 had small flaps sandwiched between the huge Fowler flaps. Fowler flaps consisted of a flap that extended rearwards and in a downward deflection. The flap adjustment ranged from a simple rotation around a fixed point to a combined rotation and movements in which the leading edge of the flap moves near the trailing edge of the original profile. The upper surface of the main segment is drawn to the rear so that the airflow is evenly channeled and the slot effect is maintained throughout the range of settings.

Pratt and Whitney J-57 and More Modifications

The Pratt and Whitney J-57 engines were fitted to the first B-52s and produced approximately 10,000 lbs of thrust each. During the B-52's eight-year production cycle, from August 1954 to September 1962, the power for the engines increased. Only fifty-three aircraft were built by March of 1956. The B-52C model appeared with the new Pratt and Whitney J-57-P29-W engines, which were then rated at 12,800 lbs of thrust. The final installations were made to the 'H' model, which went into production in September 1960, with the Pratt and Whitney TF-33-P-1 turbofan engines, each bringing 18,000 lbs of thrust. At this time, the weight reached 420,000 lbs for the B-52B, to 490,000 lbs for the B-52H. The unrefueled range of 6,000 miles rose to 10,000 miles. This was before the installation of the turbofan water injection system, which was necessary for take-off at full gross weight of the aircraft.

Many other modifications were added before and after the B-52 production run was entirely over. There were three different types of bomb navigation systems. These were installed through the production period along with five different fire control systems. The increase in gross weight of the 'G' and 'H' models brought in an additional 60,000 lbs (10,000 gallons of fuel capacity). All the B-52 models had defensive armament in the tail only. The tail turret contained .50-caliber machine guns which were used up to the 'G' model, and a six-barrel Gatling cannon of 20 mm on the 'H' model. A tail gunner was moved forward to join the rest of the crew beginning with the 'G' model. From the start of the program, the tail stinger carried an optical sight for manned firing and search and tracking radar. When the gunner position was moved forward, a closed circuit television was added so that the gunner could get a view from the tail of the aircraft.

With the innumerable B-52 systems on board, there were innumerable problems to overcome. The pneumatic power system for the major accessories operation was first, and then there were problems with the plumbing. The air turbine used to turn the alternators led to another conventional system issue, starting with the B-52 'G' (#-0039), where shaft power from the engines directly drove alternators mounted in the nacelles and powered the hydraulics. These modifications added yet more weight to the aircraft. This is something every aircraft designer lives in fear of. It allowed for the elimination of most of the air ducts, which cleared the way for redesign of the wing for improved fuel capacity. The most obvious modification was the shortened fin and rudder of the 'G' and 'H' models. A 20 percent reduction in the area of the vertical tail was possible thanks to the success of the cross wind landing gear, which allowed for ground maneuvering of the aircraft.

The B-52 being serviced on a Seattle field in the dead of night. During the early part of the B-52's life the Cold War was in full flow, and Boeing and the USAF were concerned about Soviet spies. (*Boeing Corporation*)

The B-52 became the 'intercontinental bomber' that the USAF had dreamed of; an aircraft built for a service life of 5,000 hours at a cost of $5,857,962 each. That was cheap by today's standards. The modernization programs starting in the 1970s cost about $4 million for each aircraft and added some 7,000 hours to the airframe of the 'D' models in service, but included the offensive and defensive systems on the 'G' and the 'H' models, which used advanced technology. This included the following:

Quick Start: The installation of cartridge starters were applied on all eight engines of each B-52 'G' and 'H.' This allowed concurrent starting of all eight engines and made sure that an extensive number of the B-52s were available to get airborne before the arrival of incoming missiles which could include submarine launched missiles that had the lower trajectories which cut the warning times down to less than it would be with an ICBM.

Electro Optical Viewing System (EVS): Allowed some structural changes in the aircraft which to place sensors under the aircraft's chin. This included a FLIR) forward-looking infrared (sensor and (LLLTV). a low-light-level television The LLLTV supplied a TV picture of ground scenes under conditions approaching total ambient darkness. FLIR could see through a haze and even a heavily clouded area and anytime of the day, could give a good quality TV signal. Aimed laterally and vertically, sensors were coupled to an aircraft. Terrain avoidance radar, bombing and navigation systems, and flight direction images secured by FLIR and LLLTV were shown on a 10-inch TV monitor which was located by the pilot/navigator and radar operator positions.

Phase 6 Electronics: The electronic countermeasures system better known as ECM was also installed in the 269 'G' and 'H' models of the B-52. The cost of this addition was just about a million dollars per aircraft. This new ECM package included a detection jammer to counter any of the Russian pulse radars and an increased number of A-T-28 noise jammers and infrared deceiving flares. A reworked station for the electronics warfare officer also added a 40-inch tail extension along with two nose and two tail fairings, which held three microwave horns each. These horns formed a 360-degree radiation pattern around the aircraft, which aided in further confusion of the enemy radar.

Short Range Attack Missile (SRAM): This variation required hard points in the aft bomb bay to be repositioned with the ability to carry the eight-missile rotary launcher, much like that used in the B-2 today. Twenty SRAM missiles were carried with the addition of two on the under wing pylons and the related computerized hardware. The B-52 has the radar cross section of a barn so

A B-52 being towed across a street to the flight line at Boeing Seattle. This aircraft also carried a new test engine. (*Boeing Corporation*)

that makes her very observable, even though she has a low altitude ability and could fly under radar when possible.

Electronic Countermeasures (ECM): The B-52 carries a high-level electronic countermeasures ability. The ECM system counters the high observables, but their effect on the Soviet systems was a matter of debate. The beauty of SRAM was that it allowed the B-52 to be exposed to the Soviet air defenses. However, the cruise missile was a low observable on the radar screen and could be positioned in large numbers so that they could penetrate the advanced Soviet defenses. The SRAM was designed with the B-52 in mind. It is a defense suppression weapon made to support penetration missions; the short range would not allow for much else. The SRAM project team knew it was wise to bear up Air Force principles: 'The trick in any innovation is to balance the demands of the innovators with the political reality. We always took care to list modifications as "refurbishments" rather than as "upgrades". We kept everything as incremental as possible. It's a lot less threatening that way.' With this judicious method, the SRAM beat out the advanced Hound Dog missile, and went into full production in 1972.

Pacer Plank: An additional 7,000 hours of flight time was given to eighty cautiously chosen B-52Ds. They would carry Pacer Plank, which was a $1.6 million investment per aircraft. The replacement of the fuselage skin was incorporated with a new wing. 'Big Belly' aircraft that were previously modified to carry an amplified amount of standard iron bombs were known as the 'D' models of the B-52 .The 'Big Belly' carried 108 iron bombs (dumb bombs)—twenty-four of the 750-lb varieties on exterior wing pylons and eighty-four of the 500-lb type in the bomb bay.

The B-52 strategic strike force continued a limited standard bombing capacity while the B-52Ds had the potential for reconnaissance service. SAC's B-52Gs and B-52Hs were the nuclear bomb carriers and continued to represent one of the three United States' nuclear deterrents. According to *Defense News*, as of 2014 the Pentagon was looking to shrink the number of the bomber aircraft with nuclear capability. They were also looking to shrink the number of submarine ballistic missiles to meet the new START treaty with Russia. The Air Force will have to convert thirty of the B-52 bombers to just standard weapons carriers. This meant that no nuclear weapons were supplied to those aircraft. In 2010, Russia and the US signed the new START treaty, which has set a lower level for the number of deployed and non-deployed nuclear weapons. The non-deployed status means that the delivery system, be it a bomber, submarine,

The YB-52 and the B-47 side-by-side on the Boeing Seattle flight line. (*Boeing Corporation*)

or ICBM, is somewhere undergoing a series of maintenance checks and can't be in service. With the changes to the missiles, silos, and the submarines—not to mention the B-52s and other nuclear weapons carrier aircraft like the B-2 and the B-1—it will cost some $300 million over many years, with reductions to be completed by 2018. The issue illustrates how the B-52 remains a stronghold of this country's defense in terms of the conveyance of nuclear weapons. With the state of the world as it is, this reduction leaves the United States without much in the line of bargaining chips.

The Birds Are Out of the Nest

Three B-52As, the first production aircraft, made their first maiden flight on 5 August 1954. The 'A' model had a nose that was some 4 feet longer than that of the prototype, and it had a standard cabin with a side-by-side seating style for pilot and co-pilot, instead of the original tandem seating. These aircraft never saw operational service. Fifty B-52Bs followed the 'A' models. On 29 June 1955, the first delivery for SAC went to the 93rd Bomb Wing at Castle Air Force Base in California. The ferry flight was made with aircraft #52-8711 and flown by Brig. General William E. Eubanks Jr., commanding officer of the 93rd Bomb Wing. While everyone was thrilled with the new bird, this author seriously does not believe that those folks thought she would still be flying missions in 2015. If you consider the 1950s and 1960s, one look at *Aviation Week* magazine would show you the huge amount of technical advances that were being made every single week. We were going to the moon and yet the backbone of the USAF was this venerable bird, the B-52 Stratofortress.

The B-52 started as a conventional bomber with iron bombs dropped at high altitude, but she evolved into a glass cockpit, nuclear weapon carrier. This also shows that she was able to carry and deliver at low altitude and use the newer 1960s weapons like the AGM-28 and AGM-69 nuclear warhead missiles.

The main issue in the summer of 1951, was for the B-52 to be brought on line without too much fanfare. With the aircraft considered at the time to be complex and temperamental, it was going to be a tough job to train and maintain crews to handle it. Because of her huge size and bomb load, runways had to be prepared for her size; she weighed well over the standard weight of aircraft in the 1950s. There were also other issues that SAC had to deal with; logistically, they had to figure out how many B-52s they would eventually end up with.

In the summer of 1953, the USAF was working on the pretext of getting some 280 aircraft, which was enough to support seven bomb wings. That meant having about thirty aircraft per wing with manpower and materiel. In 1955, the procurement range went from about 400 aircraft way up to 600. By

The spectacular roll-out day for the B-52A. As can be seen from the crowds, she was welcomed in style. (*Boeing Corporation*)

September 1955, with a proposal from the Air Force Council to attain at least 516 aircraft, SAC had a more motivated idea. They were thinking about a total of eleven bomb wings, each with forty-five units established in three different squadrons. By December 1956, the defense budget was set for eleven wings and a total 603 aircraft.

SAC eventually ended up with just three squadron groups. These three squadrons were converted to the B-52. The newly formed 93rd Bomb Wing had one real issue to overcome—the crew and the aircraft needed to start talking to each other. In essence, communication between the aircraft and the new crew would create the basis of the newly formed wing. Without that communication, the B-52 and her crew would be at odds with each other. The three tactical squads (328, 329, 330 Bomb Squads) had to be ready for combat by 12 March 1952. A unit establishment was of thirty aircraft, made up of the B-52Bs and a bomber/reconnaissance version, the RB-52B. Just a couple of months later, an additional forty-five aircraft to came into the wing. However, they were not combat ready, and the wing lost operational status until June 1957.

The 93rd Bomb Wing suffered its first loss during a training mission on 16 February 1956. B-52B (53-0384) took off from Castle Air Force Base early in the morning of 16 February on a routine test flight. Just about half way through the mission, the aircraft caught fire. The fire got worse in almost no time at all and the B-52 lost control, going into a steep dive. She broke up into several sections at 10,000 feet. Of the eight crew members on board, only four could get out by parachute; the other four perished when the aircraft broke up. The crash investigation showed that the alternators were at fault. This was an issue in the B-52 'B' and 'C' models; twenty B-52Bs that were fitted with that same alternator were immediately grounded and there was a hold up on the deliveries of the other B-52s until the middle of May 1956 until Boeing made sure the problem was fixed. It was not until 1957 that the problem was finally resolved.

There was yet another setback that resulted in the grounding of the B-52, which occurred in July 1956. This time it was the hydraulics. While it was not as serious as the alternator issue, it caused difficulty in training schedules for SAC's 42nd Bomb Wing at Loring AFB, Maine. The 42nd Bomb Wing was also one of the first of the B-36 wings that were in transition to the B-52. They started to take out the B-36H by the start of 1956 and started accepting the B-52C on 16 June 1956. What a shock it must have been to go from the huge B-36H to the new B-52C! Both are large aircraft, but yet so diverse.

The RB-52B reconnaissance aircraft was congruent with the reconnaissance capsule, but its maximum take-off weight was higher: 450,000 lbs compared to the 420,000 lbs of the B-52B. The B-52C was also fitted with much stronger J-57-P-19W turbojet engines and had a couple of other new features. The most visible one was the thermal reflecting paint on the underside of the aircraft, which was not standard on the B-52B and the RB-52B models. The other was the extra fuel capacity with the outboard position of the J-57 pods.

Only thirty-five B-52Cs were completed and Boeing sent these to the USAF between June and December 1956. They were sent to the 42nd Bomb Wing in Maine. All aircraft were delivered to the USAF from the Seattle Boeing Plant. By 1953, Boeing declared that things would move a little faster and a second factory in Wichita, Kansas, was proposed. The next three versions of the B-52 that the SAC received were to come from Kansas. There was loads of floor space available at that plant since the B-47 finished production and the war was over.

After the 'B' version of the B-52s started to depart the plant at Seattle, they were followed by 35 'C' models, 170 'D' models, 100 'E' models, and 89 'F' models. These models also encompassed numerous changes. All of them now included the 'flying boom' system for aerial refueling. This would now give the aircraft unlimited range. The 'F' model was given the Pratt and Whitney J-57-P-43-W engines, which were also added to the new 'G' model. The last

The first of the B-52s to come out of the Boeing plant at Witchita, Kansas. (*Boeing Corporation*)

The roll-out of the beautiful and deadly B-52G. (*Boeing Corporation*)

models to be built were the 'G' and 'H.' There were 193 'G' models and 102 of the 'H' models, with the last delivery taking place on October of 1962. Of the eight B-52 production models that were built, the 'A', 'B', and 'C' editions were built by Boeing in Seattle, Washington, while the 'D', 'E', 'F' models were manufactured at both the Seattle plant and the Wichita, Kansas, facility. All of the 'G' and 'H' versions were built in Kansas. In total, the entire production amounted to 744 B-52s, 467 of which were assembled in the Kansas plant.

The Boeing plant in Wichita, Kansas was producing the first of its B-52s, with more than 12 million engineering man-hours spent on the aircraft as of October 1955. That was an unparalleled amount of work. In terms of the number of operational aircraft, the B-52 reached its peak in 1963, with thirty-eight wings available for service. At the start of the 1980s, there were eighteen B-52 wings, which equated to 350 B-52s available for duty.

4

LeMay's Greatest Wish

One of the greatest or worst things to happen to the USAF, depending on your viewpoint, was the successful career of General Curtis LeMay. Many people disliked his gruff, tough way of talking and bullying his way into getting the thing he wanted for his men. One person in particular that was not fond of LeMay was Secretary of Defense Robert McNamara. The reason was simple—LeMay was actually McNamara's boss in the Second World War. LeMay, who was a colonel during the war, was in charge of aerial bombardment policy, and McNamara was a captain who was crunching numbers in operations. LeMay and McNamara did not seem to agree in anything. When it came to the decision whether the USAF and the Navy would each get separate fighters, they bumped heads like two bulls in a pasture. LeMay knew what the USAF needed and he wasn't convinced that trying to build one fighter for both services was the right way to go. LeMay was right, and McNamara was most assuredly wrong. The TFX F-111 was a disaster from the start. This wasn't the first fight that these two strong-willed men got into. The XB-70 Valkyrie bomber for the USAF, which would have replaced the B-52, was a huge sore point. McNamara didn't see the reasoning behind the XB-70 when the Mach 3 bomber came up for budget issues. It burned LeMay that the B-52 was being cut back at the same time the B-70 was not being funded. However, missiles were really McNamara's favorite mode of mayhem, but they were not LeMay's. McNamara believed heavily in MAD (Mutually Assured Destruction) while LeMay was more in favor of a method that could be recalled if needed at the last moment. You couldn't recall a missile, and besides that would put more of LeMay's bombers and airmen out of work, not to mention bases. These two fought all the way down the line until LeMay was finally forced into retirement. He fought for the B-70 tooth and nail, but it just wasn't to be. The B-70 was relegated to two aircraft with a third almost built. LeMay gave his heart, literally (he suffered a heart attack during the B-70 fight), and soul to his Air Force. He was a man in a million. Many of his policies are still laced throughout the USAF in various forms today, and LeMay's spirit is still with the airmen coming in today.

One day in the mid-1950s, General Curtis LeMay was walking down a flight line with his trademark cigar between his teeth when he passed a B-52. He decided to take a closer look and found a young crewmember to show him the bird and perform a bomb bay inspection. The young man looked at LeMay and took his life in his hands. 'General,' he said, 'you can't smoke in the aircraft.'

'Why the hell not?' LeMay barked back.

'Because, sir, the plane might explode.' LeMay removed the cigar from his mouth, looked at the crewman and said, 'Son, it would not dare.' That was the typical LeMay, a man that many came to either love or hate.

LeMay took command of SAC in October 1948 and did much to improve it. When LeMay took over, the morale of SAC, which was created on 21 March 1946, was at its lowest. He transformed it from a collection of Second World War leftover aircraft into a powerful strike force of modern bombers, fighters, and tankers, despite the many problems he faced. With his bulldog strength of will and determination, he created an organization that served the Air Force well. LeMay was known for his inflexibility when it came to his rules and commands. He was a pilot, navigator, bombardier, and observer. He knew the heart of the aircraft and the heart of the Air Force. He ran an organization that was not only tight, but his officers knew how to tow that line, when to ask questions, and when not to. He was the quintessential leader when it came to aircraft and airmen. In 1948, SAC already had some 52,000 personnel with 837 aircraft when he started out. When he left, SAC's inventory had grown to some 224,000 airmen and 2,700 aircraft, which included 127 B-36, 1,500 B-47s, and 243 B-52s. That was quite an expansion. By 1957, the mid-air refueling techniques were now established and SAC maintained a stable of tankers that were now part of each bomber wing. The KC-97 tanker would soon be replaced by the newer KC-135. LeMay loved to have things up to date. As he was fond of saying, it was necessary to create the weapons of tomorrow, yesterday.

One of LeMay's many improvements was to move the SAC headquarters to Offutt Air Force Base in Nebraska, which was the geographical center of the United States. He also ordered the command to prepare for global operations and to be able to counter-attack at any time. LeMay personally saw to it that SAC personnel enjoyed the best of everything that he and the Air Force could offer. Across the military, the best food was always served in the Air Force mess. That food was on the table every day. Also, LeMay made sure that SAC families were comfortable. Doing that made for a happy and more comfortable

General Thomas Power was SAC's third commander between 1957 and 1964. In this photo, he is discussing 'Reflex Action' in the underground command post at SAC headquarters. The chart shows the SAC program to deploy B-47s at bases in Morocco, Spain, and the UK. (*National Archives, Still Pictures Division*)

The official USAF portrait of General Curtis LeMay, the driving force behind SAC. His Air Force career was magnificent from the Second World War onwards. He was retired early due to his intense dislike of Secretary of Defense Robert McNamara.
(*US Air Force*)

crew. Fewer worries for crewmen about wives and children meant greater attention to the job. LeMay was asking for a lot from his crews and he knew it, but he knew it would pay off in the end. He believed that 'Loyalty begets loyalty,' and pride in one's job is a super morale booster. He was determined to give his people the absolute best he could get for them, and hell or high water, he made sure he got it.

LeMay also founded the NCO (Non-Commissioned Officers) Academy, which allowed enlisted men to get up to speed on their positions. He also had a lead crew school, which was a great training ground for the standardization of the SAC methods for airmen doing their jobs. It also allowed LeMay to weed out the washouts and push ahead those who could prove to be the best material. LeMay's policy for awarding spot promotions for outstanding performance resulted in a high percentage of SAC personnel in rank—significantly higher than any other part of the service with equal time. A seventy-two-hour duty watch was not unusual, and each man was expected to pull his weight. There was no backsliding in LeMay's SAC. When the Korean War broke out in the summer of 1950, SAC's B-29s quickly destroyed strategic targets in North Korea, but they were denied the authority to hit the true source of aggression—the Red Chinese, who were running a tactical game until the shooting finally stopped.

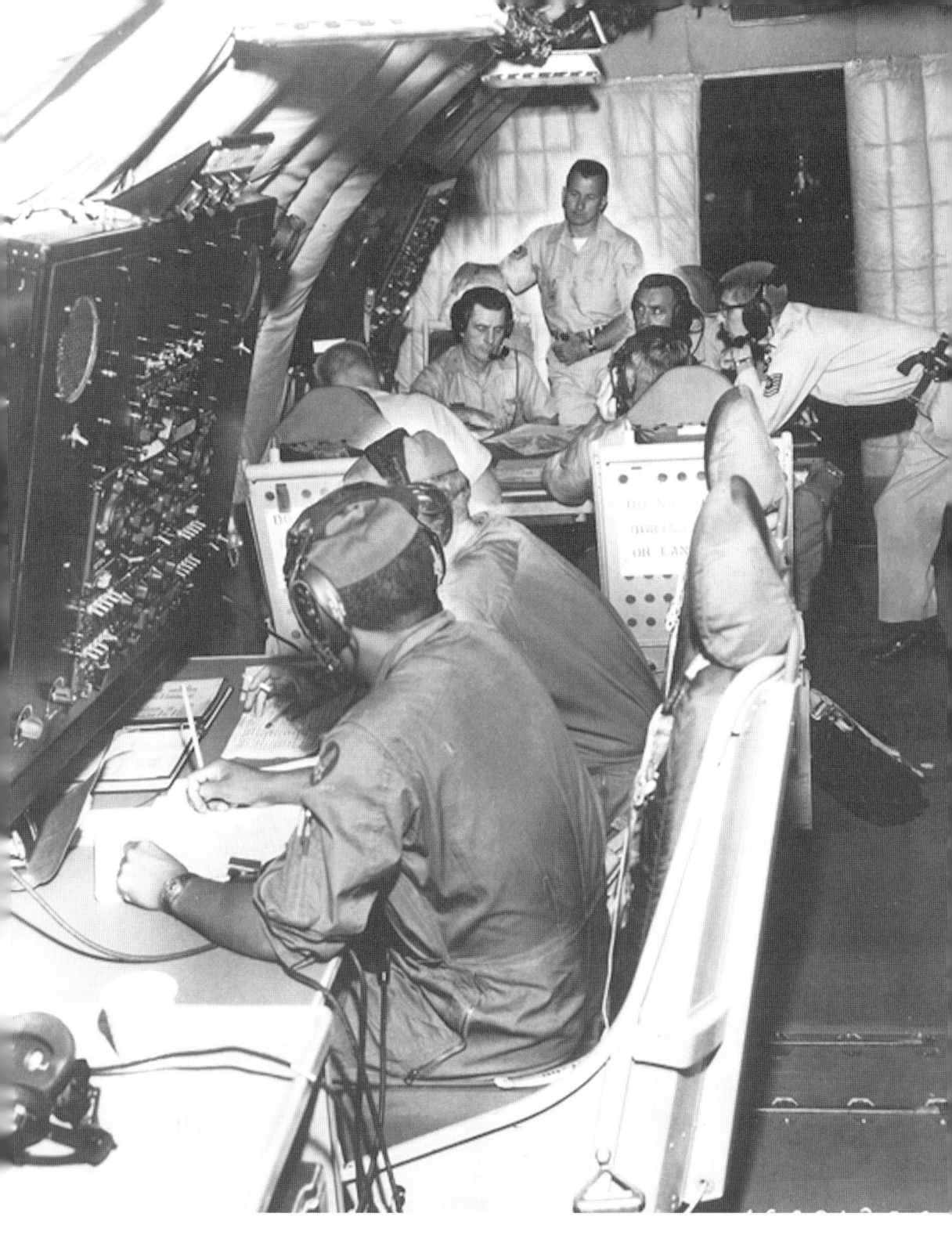

An early 1961 image of the Airborne Command Post, which was capable of directing all of SAC's aircraft and missiles. There were five specially equipped KC-135 tankers converted for airborne command purposes, with a general in charge in case the control center was hit by a missile. (*National Archives, Still Pictures Division*)

This red telephone (pictured in June 1959) was the primary alert system at SAC headquarters, and it was placed on the desk of senior controllers. The telephone connected the controller to every SAC command post in bases all over the world. (*National Archives, Still Pictures Division*)

By the time the B-52 was delivered to SAC in 1955, aerial refueling was an everyday occurrence, so SAC was able to continue using the bombers that were available. There were 1,200 B-47s and a total of 3,000 assigned aircraft: B-36, RB-36, RB-50s, KC-97s, KB-29s, B-24s, and FRF-84s. By the end of the 1950s, a portion of the B-52s would be on a fifteen-minute ground alert while various dispersal concepts and an airborne alert were tested to ensure a manned nuclear response to even the briefest warning of attack.

LeMay made sure that SAC was all he wanted it to be before he left in 1957 to become the Vice Chief of Staff and later Chief of Staff in a short four years. He was replaced by General Thomas S. Power, whom LeMay had chosen to be his vice commander some nine years earlier. Power was also responsible for beefing up the US missile force. Strategic Air Command knew that while the B-52 had cost much and gone through many changes, SAC had the sharpest blade in the force. The B-52 was destined to become a legend and that she became. It did not take that long for her to get started either; General Curtis LeMay made sure of the B-52's place in SAC.

SAC—The USAF's Sword in the Sky

21 March 1946 was the official date on which Strategic Air Command came into being. The USAAF, which the Air Force was still called at that time, consisted of three different commands:

TAC (Tactical Air Defense Command), SAC (Strategic Air Command) and ADC (Air Defense Command).

TAC (Tactical Air Command) was established the same date as SAC and its position was to control the air defense, tactical air and air reserve forces. TAC would control the fighters and ground support for what SAC might need in the event of an attack or a call to arms. December of 1950 TAC was returned to a major command status and remained there until deactivated on 1 June 1992.

ADC (Air Defense Command) organized missions and administered all of the integrated air defense system of the Continental United States known as (CONUS). ADC was in charge of direct control of all the active means of defense and to co-ordinate all passive means of air defense. It was deactivated right before the start of the Korean War on 1 July 1950, but was reactivated in another form on November 10, 1950 with a new mission, which entailed 'the Air Force which had approved activation of a separate Air Defense Command [from CONAC].' By 1968, it was then reorganized and re-designated Aerospace Defense Command (ADCOM). After a few more changes that led to Aerospace Defense Command on 1 October 1979, ADCOM's atmospheric defense resources (interceptors, warning radars, and associated bases and personnel) were transferred to Tactical Air Command, being placed under Air Defense, Tactical Air Command (ADTAC). ADCOM became a specified command. It later was known as NORAD (North American Aerospace Defense Command).

SAC's main mission was to mount a strategic nuclear strike and to maintain that ability twenty-four hours in the day and night, whatever the weather, whatever the conditions. General George C. Kenney was in command and by the time that Kenney established the SAC headquarters initially at Bolling Field, Washington D.C. and then moved operations to Andrews Air Force Base, Maryland, on 20 October 1946. The already five-year-old B-36 program was revitalized while the B-52 program went to look for proposals from aircraft contractors to build it. Kenney was given 36,000 men, eighteen active bases and 600 aircraft to play with. Two hundred and fifty of those aircraft were bombers that included the B-17, B-29 and B-25. Kenney's main objective was to create a professional and highly trained organization that could respond to a call in a moment's notice and also establish a peacetime deterrent to any form of attack against the United States. SAC also controlled the infrastructure which encompassed tankers to fuel the bombers and until 1959, the fighter escorts.

The mission statement for SAC was delivered by General Carl 'Tooey' Spaatz, Commander of the USAAF:

The Strategic Air Command will be prepared to conduct long-range offensive operations in any part of the world, either independently or in co-operation with land and naval forces; to conduct maximum-range reconnaissance over land or sea, either independently or in co-operation with land and naval forces; to provide combat units capable of intense and sustained combat operations employing the latest and most advanced weapons; to train units and personnel of the maintenance of the Strategic forces in all parts of the world; to perform such special missions as the Commanding General Army Air Forces may direct.

SAC remained in effect after the USAAF became the USAF on 18 September 1947. On 9 November 1948, SAC moved its headquarters to Offutt Air Force Base, Bellevue, Nebraska. On 19 October 1948, Lieutenant General Curtis LeMay became the commander of SAC and went about making the changes he felt were necessary. With his background of planning the US attacks on mainland Japanese (i.e. the firebombing of Tokyo and other Japanese cities), LeMay firmly believed in a strong strategic bombing policy that included the destruction of the enemy's main cities and industrial complexes. The birth of the atomic bomb solidified LeMay's belief that the only answer to ending battlefield warfare was a tough bombing strategy. Thanks to his determination, his ideas became the rock upon which the USAF's strategic policies were built. The Soviets were the new target and LeMay was determined to keep them at bay. By 1962, there were 217,650 airmen, 28,531 civilians, and 38,542 officers in SAC.

SAC's motto was 'Peace is our Profession.' According to LeMay, that meant having a bomber loaded to the gills and ready and waiting to take off at a moment's notice. With the 'Missile Gap' and the 'Bomber Gap' floating around, even though the intelligence was tainted at best, LeMay conceived the plan that SAC should be ready to run a fast pre-emptive strike and a crushing attack on the Soviet Union before the Russians had a chance to get off the ground. Within the next two years, SAC grew to 1,000 aircraft. There were many 'Goodwill' training missions flown to Europe and the Arctic region, including countless US cities.

LeMay's Greatest Wish 93

This December 1958 image shows the nerve centre of SAC. The three-story administration building was connected by underground ramps to a three-story control centre buried 45 feet underneath the ground. The roof of the central wing is a 'snifter'—an electronic device capable of detecting any kind of radioactivity within 50 miles. (*National Archives, Still Pictures Division*)

This is the underground command post in 1961, featuring a new visual display that could expedite any information SAC needed. The large screens gave information on weather, force deployment, aircraft and missiles. (*National Archives, Still Pictures Division*)

In 1967, B-52s are lined up on the flight line on alert duty, armed with AGM-28 Hound Dog missiles. A crew is getting ready to board the aircraft. (*National Archives, Still Pictures Division*)

The heart of SAC, General Curtis LeMay, died on 1 October 1990. He didn't live to see the end of the Cold War that he had fought for so long. The USSR dissolved on 25 December 1991.

SAC would be later disbanded on 1 June 1992, and all the men, equipment, and histories would be rolled into the new Air Combat Command of today. It was quite a legacy that LeMay left the Air Force and the men of the USAF that he loved.

5

From 'A' to 'H': The B-52 Comes to Life

The production history of the B-52 is long and varied. There are so many different versions of this aircraft and although it is amazing, at the same time it can be very confusing. From the first flight of the YB-52, which actually was the second aircraft made and the first to fly to the Vietnam War, the B-52 has shown that it could be just about anything that it needed to be; sixty years after her first maiden flight, it is continuing to be used in new ways. The production history is a list of the improvements and basic refinements to a design that later resulted in eight different versions. All this happened before the aircraft production line closed in autumn 1962. Most military aircraft have one or two different versions, and that is usually just a reconnaissance version or maybe, as in the case of the Navy's F/A 18 Hornet, a fighter/attack aircraft. The 744 B-52s that were produced had many variations:

Model	No. produced	Design initiated	Out of assembly	First flight	First USAF flight
XB	1	10-48	11-51	10-2-52	N/A
YB	1	10-48	3-15-52	4-5-52	12-53
B	23	2-51	5-16-55	7-7-55	11-9-55
RB	27	4-52	7-14-52	1-25-55	3-3-55
C	35	12-53	12-23-55	3-9-52	6-14-56
D (S)	101	12-53	7-12-56	9-28-56	12-1-56
D (W)	69	12-53	12-2-55	5-14-55	6-26-56
E (S)	42	5-53	8-12-57	10-3-57	10-7-57
E (W)	58	5-53	8-7-57	5-14-58	6-14-58
F (S)	44	11-54	3-17-58	5-6-58	6-1-58
F (W)	45	11-54	2-18-58	5-14-58	6-14-58

G	193	6-56	7-14-58	8-31-58	10-31-58
H	102	1-59	10-7-59	3-6-61	3-9-61

(S): Seattle
(W): Wichita

The Cold War and the doctrine of Mutually Assured Destruction (MAD) were in full bloom by the mid-1950s. SAC was ready for the worst and ready to respond to it. The B-52s were now coming off the production line and assigned to various wings and squadrons. The first of the B-52s to go operational were the 'B' models that were built in Seattle's plant. These aircraft were delivered between June 1955 and February 1956. Squadron service began with the 93rd Bomb Wing stationed at Castle Air Force Base in California. Crew training started and the new crews were initiated with the 4017th Combat Crew Training Squadron also stationed at Castle Air Force Base. The B-52s were being delivered and the 'C' models were starting to roll out of the Seattle plant. Now at the Wichita, Kansas, Boeing plant, the B-52 'D' models were also on the production line. The first of the 467 B-52s ('D' to 'H') models were also being worked on and would come from the Wichita plant. Forty percent of the B-52 airframes were subcontracted. Approximately 65 percent of the construction cost of each aircraft was shared by twenty companies; among the companies involved were Goodyear (for the fuel cells, side panels, and wing stub structures) and Aeronca (for the rudder, ailerons, elevators, and wheel well doors). Fairchild handled the outer wings, rear fuselage, and mating of components, which were built to a maximum tolerance of 0.02 of an inch. Even the paint film thickness was carefully controlled, because 275 lbs were added for every single 0.005 inch of paint that was applied to the monstrous 185-foot wing. Paint would always be a problem for the B-52; the crucial reason for painting the aircraft was that the aluminum and magnesium alloys used were susceptible to corrosion, which would lead to considerable structural damage if not controlled.

In the 1970s, Lockheed finally managed to devise a paint primer; the company had vast experience in holding weight down on aircraft such as the A-12 and SR-71 Blackbirds. The primer was still effective after five years of testing on an active B-52. The savings that were promised with the new epoxy primer were (happily) in the millions, due to the fact there would be less structural repair to deal with and an extended time between paint jobs. The painting of the B-52s, as well as all the modifications for refurbishing along with major overhaul, was handled by the Boeing Wichita, Kansas, plant. This was near the McConnell Air Force Base and Air Materiel Centers at Tinker Air Force Base, Oklahoma City, and Kelly Air Force Base, San Antonio, Texas. Some engine overhaul work was done by Pacific Automotive. The original B-52 engines were geared for 500 hours between each major overhaul; however, 4,000 hours between engine changes was not an unusual custom.

The B-52 Missiles, SRAM, and Armaments

During the 1950s, the manned bomber was the only US weapon that was geared for the delivery of nuclear weapons. By 1962, however, there were 126 Atlas ICBMs ready to field in eleven sites through the United States. There were also twenty Minuteman missiles and the first of the Titan missiles. The US Navy's new Polaris missiles had just entered service, with twenty-two operational out of a planned forty-one in 1964. At the time, the US planners felt that missiles and manned bombers would complicate any Soviet attack plans against the US. In the 1960s, the United States was under the impression that both the deterrent and retaliation forces had corrupted and deteriorated in comparison to those of the USSR. With the B-52 coming on line, there had been no serious discussion of its planned successor—at least not just yet. Of course, the XB-70 was being worked on, along with the Lockheed YF-12 interceptor. When the XB-70 was written off, the B-1 bomber was the next down the line. Through all of this, the B-52 remained on the flight line, holding down the fort.

The B-52 was now armed with cruise missiles and this was a major problem for the Soviets. They were in uproar over the deployment of the ACLM (air-launched cruise missile) that would jeopardize the newly signed Salt II Treaty. If the B-52 would continue to be a restraint to nuclear warfare into the 1980s, it would have to be armed with the right missiles, and the answer to this was the SRAM. The SRAM, or short-range attack missile, was effective, but the Soviets were building more interceptors and radar to counter it. If the B-52 was to stay in the game, it would have to be more maneuverable. It would need the SRAM, a missile of greater range. The SRAM went operational in 1972 with the 42nd Bomb Wing at Loring Air Force Base in Maine, and by the end of the 1970s, the B-52 crews were finding new ways to use the systems. The SAC crews said that by reprogramming the SRAM's computer, it could be now be used against attacking enemy aircraft. In defense suppression, the SRAM could hit enemy radar and SAM missile sites, which would allow the B-52 to penetrate to its primary target, which it could attack with the remaining SRAMs in the rack, or use of gravity bombs. The SRAM was powered with the Lockheed LPC-145 restartable solid propellant two-pulse rocket engine, a lovely product from the folks at Lockheed.

Another missile that was destined for the B-52 in the 1960s and '70s was the AGM-28B or 'Hound Dog' missile. These was carried in pairs externally under the wings. This 1,200-mph missile had a 500-mile range and was powered by a Pratt and Whitney J-52 turbojet engine. It was 42 feet in length, 28 inches in diameter, and had an inertial guidance system.

Another more precise instrument was the Skybolt missile. It was similar in range to the Hound Dog missile and was built the 1960s for the B-52 fleet; the British also wanted to use it for their Vulcan bomber. However, Skybolt was brought down by the unfathomable politics that were characteristic of the Kennedy and Johnson administration. At the time, Secretary of Defense Robert McNamara was responsible for many viable programs being tossed aside with no comprehensible reasoning other than his accounting spreadsheet.

Another missile was the AGM-86A, also known as the SCAD (subsonic cruise armed missile), which was canceled in 1974. The research funds generated by this cancelation went into the ALCM (air-launched cruise missile), a more viable product. Indistinguishable on radar from a B-52, the SCAD was an air-breathing decoy missile with a radar signature that could fool the enemy. The SCAD could deliver a nuclear warhead and fly maneuvers similar to the B-52, yet its effective range was only a few hundred miles. The SCAD could be carried in the B-52's internal rotary launcher, much like the B-2 stealth bomber of today. The B-52 also carried regular gravity bombs—the B-28 and the B-61. The B-61 was available in various weights, and was even small enough to be carried in an F-111 Aardvark. The larger B-28 was only carried by the B-52.

The typical weapons mix for the B-52 on alert duty was a complement of four gravity bombs and six SRAMs, although this varied with the mission and target selection. Only a third of the B-52 'G' and 'H' group stood alert at any given time. All of the B-52D models were positioned at bases in the southern US and capable of delivering gravity bombs as a follow-on strike force.

The ADM-20 Quail decoy missile was carried for quite some time on the B-52. A tiny fiberglass jet could be air launched from the bomb bay as a counter measure. The self-contained ECM gear created a radar signature that was identical to that of a B-52. It carried a 'quick load' clip in packages with multiple Quail releases to decoy hostile air defense systems. In the inventory since 1961, the Quail had been largely superseded by more sophisticated hardware in the later 1970s.

Crews and their Training

During the B-52's early years of service, the crew training emphasized high-altitude penetration and bombing techniques, but in recent years the training mission has included the major in-flight decision points from take-off to target. This is what a crew had to look forward to in running a B-52:

Positive Control Turn Around Point: the point in the war situation at which the aircraft must have the 'GO' code to proceed with the mission.

Air Refueling Initial Point: the point in time and place where bombers on a strike mission rendezvous with their KC-135 tanker.

Weapons Release Check Test: at this point, the aircraft captain electronics warfare officer and radar/navigator co-ordinate acts that prepare the nuclear weapons for release.

Primary Entry Control Point: the point where the B-52 started to descend to a low level to avoid enemy radar.

Hypothetical Hour Control Line: the precise timing point *en route* to the target that can be reached within three minutes of scheduled time. In a war situation, it would intersect a radius line around the enemy territory.

Start Countermeasure Point: at this point the B-52 crew would activate the ECM or electric countermeasures, which would protect them from enemy radar tracking and decoy missiles and chaff to distract incoming missiles fired at them.

In the late 1970s, the average age of a B-52 crew was below thirty. Most crew members on a B-52 worked the aircraft for at least five years. No weapons were used on training missions and all the bomb and missile releases were tallied electronically. Each mission usually included both primary and alternate release techniques to ensure targets got hit no matter what. When the B-52 entered service in 1955, crew commissions took ten weeks to conclude; however, it could take up to five months with the transition from the B-36 to the B-52 operations. The flight simulator built by Curtis-Wright got potential B-52 pilots interested in the new bird. All the B-52Bs, along with some 'C' and 'D' models, went to the 93rd Bomb Wing at Castle Air Force Base, which had three squadrons and a total of forty-five aircraft. In the past, thirty B-36s made a bomb wing.

The 93rd Bomb Wing had set up a school called the 'Stratofortress College.' The 4017th CCTS (Combat Crew Training Squadron), which started on 8 January 1955, was up and running before the first B-52 hit Castle Air Force Base. This training was the biggest thing the squadron ever dealt with. The 4017th CCTS was responsible for all the training and ground instruction for three squadrons, which meant that each student crew had some thirty-five to fifty hours of flying time during the four-week training course; however, it was not all smooth. There were many problems to be faced, such as the leaks in the fuel cells and faulty water injection pumps, all of which made test flights a problem for the students. There were other issues along the line of not enough space and equipment for ground and aircraft training.

Quick Kick

In the fall of 1956, when the first 100 B-52s were delivered to SAC, training flights over the US ended with Operation Quick Kick, a record non-stop flight of up to 17,000 miles by eight B-52s. This was followed by a round-the-world flight in January 1957 by three B-52s. Five aircraft took off from Castle Air Force Base, but one landed in Newfoundland with engine trouble, and another stopped in England to show off the new aircraft to the RAF brass. The RAF team consisted of many senior officers, and members of the press were also present. The British were very impressed with the B-52, and there was marked interest in the automatic crew ejection seat. The aircraft shown to the Brits was the third from the last of the 'B' models produced. Her tail number was #53-0395 and her name *City of Turlock* (which is in California) was proudly painted on her nose. She was commanded by Major Gen. H. Clements of the 330th Bomber Squadron and 93rd Bomb Wing. Clements was a former B-17 pilot and had been stationed in the UK during the Second World War. The three aircraft that continued around the world were back in California after a flight of forty-five hours and nineteen minutes, averaging 525 mph for 24,325 miles, which included aerial refueling using KC-97s over the Atlantic Ocean, Saudi Arabia, and the Philippines. The three aircraft in the flight landed some eighty seconds after each other. Long-distance B-52 flights were almost routine within the next five years.

By November 1957, six B-52s flew a non-stop round trip between Plattsburg, New York, and Buenos Aires, Argentina. In December 1958 a Boeing Wichita crew remained in the air in a B-52G for eighteen hours and 9,000 miles without an aerial refueling. As time went on, records continued to be broken by the new aircraft. In January 1962, a B-52H of the 5th Bomb Wing from Minot Air Force Base, North Dakota, flew 12,519 miles non-stop from Kadena Air Force Base in Okinawa, Japan, to Torrejon Air Force Base in Madrid, Spain. It took twenty-one hours and fifty-two minutes and set eleven distance speed records without refueling. These were impressive flights during the B-52's first ten years in operation, and despite a number of systems failures and the loss of several aircraft by 1964, SAC had the lowest accident rate in the USAF, which worked out to 1.4 incidents per 100,000 flying hours. After some ten years of service, the B-52 fleet averaged 3,500 hours per airframe; the first B-52 delivered, serial number #52-004, was still operational in the 7th Bomb Wing at Carswell Air Force Base in Texas with 5,640 hours flying time.

The KC-135 tanker was the primary limiting factor of the US manned bomber fleet; the issue was that it needed to have tanker support to be globally effective. SAC had to maintain two KC-135s for every three B-52s, and tankers needed to be dispersed as the manned nuclear carriers were. The whole concept of a manned global force rested on the backs of those KC-135 tankers. Tanker support requirements were one reason the B-47 could not remain in service alongside the B-52—it would have needed a lot more tankers at a lot more bases worldwide.

Once the B-52s were in place, a total of eighty B-58 Hustlers were needed to replace 1,200 B-47s. The same quantity of the FB-111s was needed to replace the B-58 Hustlers. Officially, the FB-111s would have replaced the early B-52s that were retired, and had Secretary of Defense Robert McNamara remained in office, all B-52s would have been dumped—with the FB-111s as the sole remaining bombers. He did, after all, push through the TFX program, which was a disaster. The FB-111 is not a strategic bomber. General LeMay characterized the FB-111 as a 'jury rigged ... stop gap weapon system!' Originally, the F-111 was supposed to be a tactical fighter; the design was modified to serve the USAF and Navy, but the Navy refused to compromise with the results. In an effort to justify his highly publicized 'cost effective' approach to the acquisition of defense weapons, McNamara said that the 'new' fighter (which was a disaster in all of the design specs) was to be used in both tactical and strategic roles by the USAF.

McNamara also closed many USAF air bases, dumped the XB-70, and said he did not believe in the manned bomber concept. It is ironic that he was forced to call upon SAC and the B-52 for support in his 'Flexible Response Theory' limited war in Vietnam. General LeMay, USAF Chief of Staff, strongly disagreed with McNamara and his theories and refused to keep quiet about it, despite being ordered to do so by McNamara. As was likely to happen with anyone who crossed McNamara, he got rid of LeMay; the general was retired as of 1 February 1965. LeMay was of the old school that believed in the strength of the military and the fact that civilians should leave military work to the people who knew it best, but McNamara disagreed. He believed that he knew better on how to spend the defense budget, and that the military should adhere to his policies unquestioningly. That was never going to happen with LeMay.

Early on, the Defense Reorganization Act of 1958 had reaffirmed SAC's position as a specified command and the US Department of Defense defined the line of control from the President through the Secretary of Defense to the Commander in Chief of SAC, with Joint Chiefs of Staff acting as the executive agents for the Secretary of Defense. The act was passed to firmly re-establish the principle of civilian control of the US Military (influenced by McArthur's resistive attitude to White House orders during the Korean War) for reasons such as efficiency. This principle cannot be questioned. That is the way it might be, although inherent in it is the trust that no president or Secretary of Defense will ignore advice from his best military minds. However, that is not always the case—much as we see today in the Obama administration.

From A to H: The Variations of the B-52

The production history for the B-52 is truly amazing. As the aircraft were produced on the factory line, improvements were added in as they were developed. Refinements to the design were made daily, which resulted in some eight different models with many changes to each variation along with many sub variations. Many of these changes came from lessons learned during the manufacture process; some were the consequence of improvements that involved component parts like the engines or the avionics packages right down to the electronic warfare or ECM packages. Others were due to the development of different weapons systems like the Hound Dog missiles. All of this went on from the beginning of production in 1951, all the way to 1962. A total of 744 aircraft were built and completed by the two assembly lines in Wichita and Seattle. These production quantities relate to aircraft as they were built, but that was not the original plan. The completion of the first thirteen B-52As was initially expected, but modifications to the contract resulted in the ten aircraft to come out of the Seattle plant being RB-52Bs—reconnaissance versions—instead. An increase in the size of SAC in late 1956 meant that the batch of B-52Gs purchased in the fiscal year of 1957 would actually turn out to be B-52Es. These changes seemed to happen throughout the entire production run of the B-52s.

The XB-52A on her maiden flight in April 1952. (*National Museum of the USAF*)

B-52A

The B-52A rolled out for the first time from the Boeing Seattle Plant on 18 March 1954. The first B-52A (52-0001) made its successful maiden flight on 5 August 1954. The B-52As were delivered to the USAF in the summer of 1954; these aircraft were returned to Boeing in a bailout program via the USAF and put on flight test duties as actual production versions. They used the Pratt and Whitney J-57 water injection engines and had no equipment as far as armament or avionics; they also never saw service with a unit. The unmistakable change in these versions was the forward fuselage section when compared to the XB-52 and YB-52 prototypes. The original (and rather monstrous) bubble canopy and tandem seating for the pilot and co-pilot were removed thanks to General Curtis LeMay; his dissatisfaction carried a lot of weight, even though he was not the only one resisting the tandem seating. Boeing redesigned the forward compartment to make LeMay even happier, ending up with a 21-in. extension that allowed for some extra equipment and an extra crew member position.

The pilot, co-pilot, navigator, electronic warfare officer, radar navigator, and tail gunner made up the contingent for the B-52. The tail gunner was separated from the rest of his crewmates by almost the entire length of the fuselage. The redesign on the B-52 was more inventive and looked more welcoming, balanced, and aerodynamically adept. Another change to the B-52A was in the engines; Pratt and Whitney engines (with the J-57-P-1W) had already been used in the B-52A program, being fitted as standard equipment. This edition was already more powerful than the engines fitted in the prototypes, but the provision for water injection brought added benefits. This was a process that allowed for significant increases in thrust; if the engine was operated in the 'dry' output, you could depend on 10,000 lbs of thrust for output. If the water injection system was using the 'wet' rating, the thrust was brought up another 1,000 lbs to equal 11,000 lbs thrust. However, the water injection could only be utilized for a limited time; the extra bump in thrust came in especially useful in hot weather, when any extra help to get that heavy, bomb-laden B-52 off the runway and into the air would be a happy addition. Use of the water injection did carry a slight penalty in terms of fuel; the capacity of the B-52A was less than that of the prototype aircraft. The fitting of 1,000-gallon auxiliary tanks outboard of the outrigger wheels was almost equivalent, allowing the tank to balance out. While this system could be installed on the prototypes, the B-52As did not use them. The benefit of being fitted with an in-flight refueling receptacle would soon be a standard for all B-52s.

The B-52's defensive military capability consisted of the A-3A Fire Control System (FCS), which supported a search-and-tracking radar antenna that could consistently aim and fire a battery of guns that were in the tail barbette.

To allow for manual operation, the tail gunner was also able to utilize a periscope gun sight. No 'bomb/nav' system was installed, and many other mission-defined objects (such as avionics) were also not installed in the three B-52A aircraft since they were only used for testing and research.

B-52B/RB-52B

The first of the production aircraft in the B-52 line to enter service with SAC was the B-52B. The delivery of the RB-52B went to the 93rd Bomb Wing at Castle AFB, California, in June 1955, which was six months after the maiden flight. The maiden flight took place in Seattle on 25 January 1955.

Fifty aircraft were completed. Twenty-three came from the Seattle plant as a pure bomber configuration, while the remaining twenty-seven were completed as reconnaissance versions called the 'RB-52B.' The weight, fuel capacity, and unrefueled radius of these two versions were indistinguishable from the B-52A. The J-57-P-1W Pratt and Whitney engines were delivered to about half of the B-52Bs and the RB-52Bs, while a lot of work went into improving the reliability of the water-injection system that allowed for more thrust. This work was expected to lead to the next type of engine, which was the J-57-P-9W; this employed the first titanium compressor blades, allowing weight to be reduced due to the use of the lighter, stronger metal. However, there were many flaws in the manufacturing development; the problems were severe, and Pratt and Whitney had to return to using steel components on both the J-57-P-29W and J-57-P-29WA. Until late 1956, before the problems were found with the titanium components, those engines were installed in the production aircraft. This was just in time to allow another version of the Pratt and Whitney engine to be fitted into the final five aircraft coming off the production line—the J-57-P-19W, which also employed the titanium components. Regardless of the many differences in the designation thrust ratings for the 19W, the 29W and 29WA engines were one and the same, with 12,100 lbs of thrust.

There were problems with the bombing, navigation, and fire-control systems. It was anticipated by SAC that the MA-2 system would solve many of the issues, but during development problems were found that proved difficult to fix. SAC was quite obstinate in that it did not want another system that was untried in flight testing; it was decided that they would use an earlier production aircraft that had the K-3A system installed. The K-3A Avionics package was not the best system available at the time as it was built to work at the low altitude of 35,000 feet. The B-52 spent the majority of its time in the air at altitudes as high as 45,000 feet, which was too high for the K-3A package. Operating the avionics at this level led to poor resolution and a

The RB-52B reconnaissance version of the B-52B. (*National Museum of the USAF*)

loss of definition, making it impossible to identify targets with any certitude. The Philco Corporation built a temporary fix for the system, helping to clean up some of the problems, but it was still not an ideal solution. The updated version of the K-3A system (the MA-6A) eventually became available, and it was installed during the production of the B-52B models.

Efforts were focused on attempting to fix the problems with the FCS component of the B-52's defense system; this led to two different units being installed in the B-52B and RB-52B models. One of the early RB-52Bs (#52-009) was fitted with the MD-5 Fire Control System (FCS), which used different ordnance such as the M24A-1 20-mm cannons. The M-5FCS twin cannon was installed as standard equipment on seventeen of the RB-52Bs and sixteen B-52Bs, which reverted to the original defense setup of four machine guns and a version of the A-3A.

Bomber or Reconnaissance?

There were earlier disagreements on the nature of missions for the B-52. The Air Staff's October 1951 directive stated that the B-52's mission should primarily be that of reconnaissance, with its bomber duties taking a back seat. This did not go down well with General LeMay at all. The decision was not reversed for some time, with the result being that the first B-52s manufactured were constructed to handle reconnaissance work first and foremost; by the end of the century, this would be unthinkable. In January 1955, two weeks after the maiden flight of the first B-52, the USAF did an absolute U-turn and decided that the B-52's future responsibilities would be that of a bomber.

Meanwhile, SAC were struggling to operate the half of the B-52Bs that had been configured for a reconnaissance role, while all of the B-52Cs could have been allocated the job. However, since the RB-52Bs were already amplified for a reconnaissance role, the RB-52B crews were increased by two more mission-specialist personnel; they would occupy a pressurized capsule inserted in the weapons area of the fuselage.

The reconfiguring of the aircraft was quite a straightforward process, and it was done in just under four hours. The equipment was revamped for intelligence work of a different category, integrating a long-focal-length and panoramic camera in addition to photo flash bombs for all types of mapping radar receivers, photographic reconnaissance and recorders for electronic reconnaissance (ELINT). Weather reconnaissance was also part of the job.

All of the B-52Bs and RB-52Bs from the 93rd Bomb Wing at Castle AFB were used in testing and development. Many of the aircraft from these units stayed on until the 1960s, but most of them were sent on to other units like the 95th Bomb Wing, Biggs Texas, and the 22nd Bomb Wing at March AFB, California.

The B-52Bs were all ready for retirement by 1965–66, except for one that was redesigned by NASA for use as the mothership of the X-15 rocket plane experiments. Aircraft 52-0008 was now called 'NB-52B *Balls 8*', and the example served alongside the sole NB-52A as the mothership for the X-15 and Lifting Body programs for NASA at Edwards AFB, California.

SAC ended up with a group of units that operated as a full three-squadron group with conversion to the B-52. At this point, the 93rd Bomb Wing had to get the crew and aircraft 'talking to each other'; this communication would help create and solidify the wing. The three tactical squads (328, 329, and 330 Bomb Squads) had to be ready for combat by 12 March 1956, with a total of thirty aircraft (including the B-52Bs and the RB-52Bs). A couple of months later, the wing grew to forty-five aircraft; however, these additions were not combat-ready, and the wing lost operational status until June 1957.

On 16 February 1956, during a training operation, the 93rd Bomb Wing suffered its first loss. B-52B 53-0384 took off from Castle early in the morning on a normal routine, undergoing test flights. About halfway through the operation, the aircraft caught fire. The flames took hold rapidly, and the aircraft lost control, going into a steep dive. The B-52 broke up into several sections at 10,000 feet, and of the eight crew members on board, only four could escape by parachute; the other four perished when the aircraft broke up. The crash investigation showed that the alternators were at fault, and there was an immediate response by the wing; the grounded twenty B-52Bs were fitted with the improved alternator. Once knowledge of the failure reached Boeing, they held up deliveries of the other B-52s until mid-May 1956 in order to remedy the problem. Issues remained in the B-52B and B-52C models, but they were finally rectified in 1957.

The B-52 was also grounded in July 1956. This time it was not the alternators giving the headache but rather the hydraulics; these problems weren't as serious as the alternator issues, but they did cause disruption to training for SAC's 42nd Bomb Wing at Loring AFB, Maine. The 42nd BW was also one of the first B-36 wings to transition; they started to remove their B-36Hs in early 1956 and began accepting the B-52Cs on 16 June 1956. It must have been shock to move between the two types; they were both big birds, but so different.

The RB-52B did end up using the reconnaissance capsule, but the addition pushed up the weight of the aircraft from 420,000 lbs to 450,000 lbs. The B-52C was fitted with the much more powerful J-57-P-19-W, which held more features; the most perceptible of these was to do with the thermal-reflecting paint on the underside of the aircraft (which was not standard on the B-52B and RB-52B models). Another noticeable feature was the extra fuel capacity it offered via the outboard position of the J-57 pods. The RB-52 was equipped with the K-36, the K-38, and T-11 reconnaissance cameras. Twenty-seven aircraft were reconfigured to carry this reconnaissance compartment.

B-52C

Of all the B-52s built, the 'C' model was of in shortest supply. The first of the B-52Cs flew on 9 March 1956, and thirty-five more were completed over the next three months. The 'C' models entered service in the 42nd Bomb Wing at Loring AFB, Maine.

Similarly to the RB-52Bs, all the 'C' models carried the twofold bomber-reconnaissance role, with the reconnaissance capsule present in the bomb bay. However, this similarity was not reflected in the latter aircraft's designation; there were also several subtle variations compared to previous models. Two features set the B-52C apart from the B-52B when she rolled out on 7 December 1955:

1. An increase in the capacity of the auxiliary fuel tank (compared to that in the B-52A and B-52B) from 1,000 gallons to 3,000 gallons.
2. The external finish of the aircraft (adapted from the 'B' model and then set as the standard for all B-52 models). The natural metal finish was retained,

but the undersides of the fuselage and wings were covered with a glossy, white, anti-flash paint that would reflect thermal radiation from a nuclear bomb blast.

With the extra fuel and new paint finish, the maximum take-off weight of the 'C' model had risen to 450,000 lbs, with no compensation in the engine thrust. The B-52C used the same J-57-P-19W or the J-57-P-29WA engines as used by the late-production B52Bs.

The avionics were again updated for the B-52C, but the changes to the bomb and navigation system were not as drastic. At a later date in production, just as it was being inducted into the B-52D task force, the B-52C acquired the AN/ASQ48 package. Defensive equipment was comprised of four .50-caliber machine guns. All but one of the B-52Cs required the 'improved' A-3A FCS that was mounted on the last seven of the B-52Bs. The effort to address the issues of the A-3AFCS had not yet achieved the needed results, and the meager levels of reliability meant those constructing the B-52C had to utilize yet another type of FCS—this turned out to be the MD-9 package. While similar in appearance to the earlier packages, this version succeeded in giving the B-52 a dependable defensive aptitude.

The B-52C with Pratt & Whitney J-57-P29-W engines, which were then rated at 12,800 lbs thrust. (*National Museum of the USAF*)

As one can imagine, it was a 'catch as catch can' situation when it came to the acquisition or replacement of new equipment on the next B-52s to come off the line. The change in avionics required the 'B' models to be retrofitted, and the 'C' models lasted only until the 'D' models came into play with more improvements. Only thirty-five B-52Cs were completed between June and December 1956, and these were then sent to 42nd Wing in Maine. In 1953 the strain had been taken off the Boeing plant in Seattle with the assurance of the second factory in Wichita, Kansas; from 1956, the next three versions of the B-52 to be received by SAC would come from the second factory. There was copious floor space there since the B-47 was out of the production and the Second World War was over.

The 99th Bomb Wing served for many years. The B-52C task force served until 1971, when these aircraft were retired to the boneyard at Davis Monthan AFB, Arizona.

B-52D

The first of three B-52Ds were built at both of Boeing's factories (Seattle and Kansas). The Kansas plant had the honor of rolling out its first aircraft (#55-0049), and the B-52D's first flight occurred in May of 1956. SAC signed off on the model in June 1956, and 170 of the 'D's were completed by 1957, making the model second to the B-52G in the number of aircraft actually completed. As for the original plant in Seattle, the major contribution to the fleet was made here, with 101 aircraft being built, rolling out into the damp northwestern air—sixty-nine were completed in Kansas.

Since flight testing had been completed before the B-52D entered service with SAC, it took a while for the aircraft to transition to full working members of the organization. As the aircraft started to reach the various bomber wings (such as Loring AFB, Maine, and the 42nd Bomb Wing), they were still working on bringing the 'C' models up to scratch. The 42nd Bomb Wing started to change out the 'C's as fast as the 'D's came in, and the 'C's moved on to the 69th, 70th, and 75th Bomb Squads. By 1957, everyone was using the B-52D models.

The 93rd Bomb Wing at Castle AFB, California, began to get their training school up and running. The 90th Bomb Wing had given up their B-36s at Fairchild AFB, Washington, in late 1956, and they had moved to a new home at Westover AFB, Massachusetts, by September 1956; the first of their B-52Cs arrived in December from the 42nd Bomb Wing. Meanwhile, the 99th Bomb Wing brought in aircraft as quickly as they could, soon ending up with 'C' and 'D' models; there were two squads of B-52Cs and one squad of B-52Ds.

The B-36 Peacemaker was quickly being shuffled out of service and into the boneyard, while the B-52D was replacing two wings of B-36s by 1957. By June of that year, the 28th Bomb Wing from Ellsworth AFB, South Dakota, were also showing off this new bird. SAC was happily filling up the Bomb Wings with new B-52s; they had already taken on 250 B-52s of various models, and there were five wings already flying with them. However, only three of these were considered to be combat-ready, while the others were just getting up to speed. It also wouldn't be long before the next version—the B-52E—would be making her debut in October 1957. The pace of change was also reflected within SAC itself; the large unit wings that were used in the Second World War had disappeared, with hundreds of B-17s lined up. SAC now looked to condense their wings towards a smaller, more concentrated outfit that would be easier to move and command.

The later-production B-52Ds got into the air no earlier than 28 September 1956. In its original production, the 'D' was basically identical to the 'C' in terms of structure, equipment, and appearance; by the time it was released, any doubt over the mission nature of the B-52 was settled, with a firm decision taken to concentrate on its bomber capabilities.

B-52E

The Boeing plant in Kansas took over as the leading source of the B-52E, delivering fifty-eight aircraft—Seattle delivered forty-two. The maiden flight for the new version took place in Seattle on 3 October 1956, and the first SAC delivery took place in December. Wichita's first B-52E took her maiden flight on 17 October.

From the outside, these birds were identical to their predecessor; however, the B-52E did diverge in several important ways that could not be seen by the casual observer. The internal equipment changes were driven by SAC's plan to utilize a new strategy in the event of nuclear war with the USSR. The level and capability of the USSR air defense network was high and marked by intensity, and this meant that a US bomber would be significantly vulnerable to attack from USSR fighters and missiles even at a high altitude. SAC knew that the days of exclusively high-altitude bombing could be over; times were changing, and SAC had little option other than training crews in the challenging and potentially more perilous low-level penetration campaigns. This approach changed airborne warfare in general, and necessitated the implementation of a more complicated set of bombing and navigation avionics (such as the AN/ASQ-38 system) on the existing B-52s and their later models.

The B-52D waiting to be serviced and declared ready for duty, with her crewman alongside. (*National Museum of the USAF*)

The B-52E's maiden flight took place in Seattle on 3 October 1957; the first delivery to SAC took place not long after, in December 1957. The first B-52E from the Wichita plant took her maiden flight on 17 October. (*National Museum of the USAF*)

This change in avionics seemed hypothetically viable, but it turned out to be more difficult to pull off—especially while the new system suffered from performance troubles. There were also maintenance difficulties, and although these were fixed over time, the adjustments that had been added to AN/ASQ-38 were certainly not inexpensive. The codename for the refit for previous models of B-52s was 'Jolly Well.' The program was completed in 1964, with B-52Es to B-52Hs being 'fixed'—totaling some 480 aircraft.

By this stage, some of the earlier B-52s were exhausted, and they were retired in 1967. The majority of the B-52Es were phased out of SAC and put into long-term storage at Davis Monthan AFB storage in 1969 and 1970.

B-52F

The B-52F was the last B-52 to be produced at Seattle. The maiden flight of the model occurred on 6 May 1958 from this plant, and the first flight of a Kansas example occurred eight days later. The B-52F was also the last of the 'tall tail' models. Seattle completed forty-four aircraft, while Wichita completed forty-five. All eighty-nine aircraft were delivered to the USAF between June 1958 and February 1959.

The B-52F had key differences compared to earlier versions, mainly to do with the installation of the much more powerful J-57-43-W or J-57P-43WA engine, which were now fitted as standard. These engines had a typical military rating of 11,200 lbs of thrust, but all three versions of the J57-P-43 were able to manage 13,750 lbs with the help of a water-injection ignition process for take-off. A prominent feature of these new engines were new alternators that supplied electrical power to the aircraft; these were connected to the left-hand side of each of the pod braces of engines, replacing the very testy air-driven turbine and alternators situated in the fuselage of earlier models. The alternators did necessitate some redesign of the engine cowling cover, and this changed the exterior of the aircraft—creating a bulge on the lower left-hand side.

The implementation of even more modifications gave the B-52F potential for an increased conventional warfare payload. The B-52F would in fact be the first model to see combat; aircraft from the 7th and 320th Bomb Wings were sent to hit targets in South Vietnam in June 1965. They were replaced by B-52Ds in the spring of 1966, and did not play any further role in the Vietnam War. Several of the more-exhausted aircraft were retired from service over the course of 1967–68, but the majority continued in service until they were taken to retirement at Davis Monthan from 1969 to 1973.

B-52G

Perhaps one of the best of the B-52 versions is the B-52G. The first flight for this version occurred on 31 August 1958; 193 were produced by the Kansas Boeing plant between 1958 and 1961. The B-52G differed from her earlier sisters in areas such as her structural weight, but her maximum take-off weight also increased to 488,000 lbs. This increase in weight was something that no aircraft manufacturer wanted to see. A large part of the increase came from an extended fuel capacity, extending from 41,533 gallons in the B-52F to 48,030 in this new model; this had a large impact on the unrefueled range statistics for the 'G.'

A reduction in weight was partially accomplished by the use of alternative materials in construction. Aluminum alloy gave the best results by far, but the redesigned wing structure was put under additional stress in similar flight routines to earlier models. There were some serious fatigue problems with this wing; SAC enacted a number of flight limitations on the B-52G (and the 'H', which would also use this wing) until there was a suitable 'fix' for the issues. This came in the form of an adapted wing box created from aluminum of increased durability, alongside some other changes to augment the wing's strength. This modification—known as 'Engineering Change 1050'—was made in May 1961, and upgrade work immediately began on the entire Air Force's fleet of these models. The cost of the upgrade was covered by a $139 million supplement from 1962 to 1964. The aircraft affected were mostly rebuilt with modified wings as they came in for a routine inspection called an 'IRAN' ('inspect and repair as necessary'). The last eighteen production B-52H aircraft were constructed with pre-modified wings at the Wichita plant.

The revamping of the vertical fin to a smaller size also reduced some weight; this was the most visible of the changes, but it was not the only one. The 3,000-gallon auxiliary tank could provide some weight loss as it could be dumped when dry; its capacity was also reduced to 700 gallons. Some of the other weight-saving changes came from a decision to move the gunner position from the extreme rear of the aircraft to a new position, just alongside the electronic warfare officer (EWO), in the forward fuselage.

The FCS was altered to adopt the newer Avco-Croseley AN/ASG-15 unit. Like the earlier systems, this featured a radar for search-and-track functions, and it also featured a small TV camera. This equipment was later replaced by the ALQ-117 ECM. Meanwhile, the aircraft's ordnance capacity remained much the same. The stowage location for the 44-foot-diameter braking chute was moved to the furthest aft fuselage section of the aircraft.

There were 193 'G' models and 102 'H' models. All of the 'G' and 'H' models were built in Kansas. Out of the total built (744), 467 B-52s were assembled in Kansas. (*National Museum of the USAF*)

The new and improved wing gave the aircraft a range characteristic that was far better than the earlier versions in terms of offensive basics. The B-52G was the first revision of the series to have what is known as a 'standoff' ability; this was due to the use of new weaponry such as the GAM-77 Hound Dog missile, one of the early cruise missiles, later to become the AGM-28 Hound Dog. The first group of the B-52Gs was unable to carry these new missiles; it was not until later, with the production of the fifty-fifth aircraft on the line (#58–0159), that it actually became part of the armament supply. Post-production modifications resulted in the 'Hound Dog' being added to the first fifty-four of the B-52Gs, as well as some of the early birds.

The B-52G also carried the GAM-72 (AGM-20), also known as the 'Quail.' This was a decoy missile that produced the same radar image as the B-52, managing to confuse any enemy aircraft looking to attack the aircraft. While the Hound Dog was an external missile, the Quail was carried internally, and at least four were part of the aircraft's inventory. However, not all B-52 wings were able to carry either of the missiles.

The 5th Bomb Wing at Travis AFB, California, accepted the new B-52G on February 1959. The last aircraft was delivered to the 5th Bomb Wing in February 1961. There were plenty of Gs to go around, being delivered to some eleven squadrons. No aircraft left its wing until May 1989, and this was simply due to the model being worn out.

B-52H

The B-52H was similar to the 'G' model, but it enjoyed increased power due to new engines. Compared of the J57, which was notable due to stupendous black clouds on ignition (due to water injection) and enough noise to rival the loudest rock band in history, the new engine was definitely more ecologically aware. The new Pratt and Whitney TF-3-P-3 turbojet engines produced some 17,000 lbs of thrust, and their performance was spectacular. The engine was cleaner, quieter, and wholly more efficient—not to mention much cheaper to run. It supported a better mission profile, with the ability to carry a 10,000-lb load and run over a range of 4,176 miles—beating the B-52G by 626 miles.

Air refueling was now part of SAC's everyday operation. The organization was prepared to show the world that the 'H' could go a lot further even without aerial refueling; on 10 January 1962 Operation Persian Rug began with B-52H #60-0040 (from the 4136th Wing at Minot AFB, North Dakota) creating a new distance record for a straight-line flight with no refueling. She flew some 12,532 miles from Kadena AFB, Okinawa, to Torrejon, Spain.

The B-52H. The increased gross weight of the 'G' and 'H' models brought an additional 60,000 lbs (with 10,000-gallon fuel capacity). All the models had defensive armament solely in the tail, which contained .50-caliber machine guns in the 'G' model and six-barrel, 20-mm Gatling cannons on the 'H' model. (*National Museum of the USAF*)

The engine changes were the least of the alterations in the B-52H. Studies of the vertical tail ensured that the defensive armament was improved from earlier versions, with the new Emerson AN/ASG-21 system installed and set as standard equipment for the 'H' model. Alongside this, the .50-caliber gun pod was discarded, and in its place was the new General Electric M61 multi-barrel Gatling-type gun, with a 20-mm rotary cannon. This new weapon held an amazing 1,242 rounds of deadly ammunition, and its awesome power gave the B-52H added punch for defense.

Another of the basic systems in the B-52H was the radar subsystem, which carried out the search and tracking for the fire control system and could only go after one target at a time. As with the B-52G, the gunner seat was now in the crew compartment, forward of the wing, next to the electronic warfare officer. The main offensive weapon in for the model was supposed to be the GAM-87 Skybolt air-launched ballistic missile, which was also known as the AGM-48; it had been developed in 1962 and was capable of carrying a nuclear warhead. However, the Skybolt program had been canceled, and this meant the B-52H maintained the same weapons as the B-52G. The B-52H later received the AGM-69 short-range attack missile (SRAM) and the AGM-86 air-launched cruise missile (ALCM). Boeing had built the AGM-86 in the hope of increasing the effectiveness and survivability of the B-52H.

The new model was fielded out to various SAC wings; the 379th Bomb Wing at Wurtsmith AFB, Michigan, received the first of the new production aircraft on 9 May 1961. The fall of 1962 saw the last production line shut down forever on the B-52H and all previous versions; the last of the birds arrived home at the 4136th Strategic Wing, Minot AFB, North Dakota.

Escalating the SAC Force—Contracts and More Contracts

By the end of 1957, SAC had heavily built up the B-52 force, with three different models in the air. The fourth version—the B-52E—would soon roll out. The B-52F was also expected, and the B-52G design (due in 1960) was well on its way.

However, as is often the case with government contracts, the agreed plan and the finished result did not entirely match. The difference came about mostly due to how SAC decided to distribute the aircraft as they left the factory floor. There were so many follow-on contracts written between 1958 and 1960 that the number of aircraft to deliver went from 603 to 744—not to mention the array of B-52 variants that were being developed as the others were being built. SAC created a new group on 10 December 1957, naming it 4123 Strategic Wing (SW), and assigned it to Carswell AFB, Texas. This finalized the end of the Second World War big wing units for SAC and the USAF. Another thirteen smaller Strategic Wings were added by 1958, and eight more were added to those by 1959.

The Missile Gap

The missile gap was one of the biggest fallacies of the Cold War. SAC had its reasons for going with smaller, more precise wings instead of the huge wings of the Second World War; they thought that the Soviets were building massive amounts of ICBMs, and US ground intelligence was faulty at best in 1957. It was felt that a big wing (comprising of forty-five bombers and twenty-plus tankers) would be a perfect target for an ICBM, and SAC wanted to make life more difficult for the Soviets by splitting up the forty-five bombers into three squads of fifteen each. However, the 'missile gap' was discovered to be based on faulty information; nevertheless, SAC had still ended up with a more effective way of arranging their bomber wings. This allowed them to get into the air faster and protect their assets more effectively; this became the 'Ground Alert' program of 1958, SAC's next phase.

Wings and Squadrons Abound

B-52s, B-47s and other aircraft were ready to get airborne at a moment's notice, eliminating the chance of leaving a group of 'sitting ducks' on the runway for the Soviets to take out with a missile. The movement of wings and various other bases and equipment (along with their reconfiguration) precipitated the building of the B-52F; the first few completed examples were brought for training to the 93rd Bomb Wing, Castle AFB, in February 1959. Meanwhile, the 7th Bomb Wing at Carswell AFB, Texas, was just about to be readied for operations.

The 11th Bomb Wing at Carswell was in the process of shedding its B-36s for B-52s, adding two operational squadrons from June 1958—the 9th and the 492nd Bomb Squadron. However, the 492nd left Carswell for the 4228th Strategic Wing at Columbus AFB, Mississippi, on 15 June 1959. The 436th Bomb Squadron was still with the 7th Bomb Wing when it received its first B-52F in June 1958.

The 72nd Bomb Squadron of the 5th Bomb Wing (Travis AFB, California) also received B-52Fs during 1958. These B-52s started to fly before the main unit— the squadron was ready to go. The 5th Bomb Wing transferred to the 4134th Strategic Wing control on 1 July 1958, and they received the B-52 at Mather AFB, California, in October, just a few months later. The newly completed B-52Gs were flown from the Wichita plant from August 1959 to February 1961; the first 154 aircraft were within the fiscal appropriations of the 1957–58 fiscal year, and were under the original contract. The last thirty-nine examples were funded in the 1959–60 fiscal year due to cuts to the B-58 Hustler program.

The B-52Gs flew with the 2nd Squadron Wing (which controlled the 23rd and 31st Bomb Wings until October 1959) for a short amount of time in 1959. The 31st Bomb Squadron was transferred to the 4126th Strategic Wing, but the squad did not leave their home at Travis AFB to go to Beale AFB until 18 January 1960, when the 5th Bomb Wing was shut down for good.

The 72nd Bomb Wing, based at Ramey AFB, Puerto Rico, gave up the B-36 in the fall of 1958. This allowed three squadrons to receive the B-52Gs. The 73rd Bomb Squadron went to the 4241st Strategic Wing at Seymour Johnson AFB, North Carolina, on 5 January 1960, and the 301st Bomb Squad came into the 4135th Strategic Wing at Eglin AFB on 17 June 1960.

The 4135th Strategic Wing worked with the Air Research and Development Command's (ARDC's) air-proving ground to help with Category-III testing of both the Hound Dog and Quail missiles. The B-52G was finally delivered to the 72nd Bomb Wing in August 1959. The 95th Bomb Wing (Biggs AFB, Texas) also had its B-36s changed over to B-52Gs; they had B-36s in their inventory as of 1959, representing the last of these aircraft that SAC were holding on to.

They were officially removed on 12 February 1959. The last B-36J left Biggs AFB to be rebuilt as a drone, going on static display at Fort Worth.

The 95th Bomb Wing did not receive all brand-new B-52s; their aircraft were the 'gently used' B-52s from other units. The 335th Bomb Squadron left the 4130th Strategic Wing for Bergstrom AFB, Texas, on 15 January 1959, and it took only a few days before they began to take on B-52Ds from Loring AFB, Maine—where the 42nd Bomb Wing was taking on the B-52G. The 335th unit could not have been that happy to receive these older versions.

As aircraft and units were shuffled, restarted, shut down, re-equipped, and moved all over the continental US, B-52s of various models were brought into SAC's 'dream team.' The B-52 program was blooming with the delivery of an additional 141 B-52s, adding to thirty-nine B-52Gs and 102 B-52Hs that were fully operational in June 1960. Three more wings were added to the roster, providing nine extra squadrons that were ready to take over the B-52H. All of the previous B-36 wings were now filled with B-52s, and SAC had to also look at the B-47 wings like the 97th Bomb Wing—this became three of the nine added squadrons.

A second base came from Florida—Homestead AFB. In the late 1950s the 823rd Air Division also took care of the B-47 wings, made up of the 19th and 379th Bomb Wing, which had forty-five aircraft each of the bigger B-52 units, with four bomber squadrons instead of three. This also included tankers, such as the KC-97 of the 19th Bomb Wing. This carousel continued until SAC had finally completed its shift to an all-B-52 bomber force.

MAJCOM

The big-wing concept of the Second World War had now been officially abandoned by SAC, including the air refueling wings. However, two new groups were added—MAJCOM (Major Command Control) and AFCON (Air Force Control).

MAJCOM consisted of four-digit units (the 4135th Wing, for example) that were given to individual USAF commands. SAC retained numbers 3900 to 4399, and any units under these numbers were under SAC control. MAJCOM was a temporary measure to consolidate the control of certain units and also 'parent' AFCON squadrons.

AFCON consisted of squadrons and wings with one to three numbers, and operated according to different principles. The control of any AFCON organization could be switched from one command to another, which also meant that the history of the unit could also be transferred; this allowed them to keep some of the inactive Second World War units alive, which is what SAC wanted.

Ground Alert Operations

An important part of the B-52 legend was is the 'Ground Alert' scenario. After the 'bomber gap' and the 'missile gap' were shown to be fallacies, the large-scale development of the B-52s in the late 1950s and the plan SAC had for bringing in new aircraft and systems (in addition to other new policies and plans) were shown to be an overestimation of the perceived Soviet threat. As such, SAC gave serious consideration as to how they would find ways to improve the survivability of their bomber and tanker forces. The decision was made to introduce a system where a number of armed bombers and their tankers were maintained on alert at major SAC installations in the US and overseas. The name of this initiative was 'Ground Alert', and SAC were ready to ensure the USSR knew that the US was ready for anything.

The crews and resources were ready to be airborne within fifteen minutes of an alert; this was a major stepping stone to staying on top of a missile attack. Fifteen minutes was considered to be an adequate margin of response in the event of a surprise enemy missile attack; while it did not involve an overwhelming force, the ground alert system would certainly be quite capable of launching a damaging punishment on any aggressor.

A number of test trials were set up by SAC from 1956 to 1957, after which the project would be extended to the rest of the Air Force. There were three evaluation programs—Tryout, Watchtower, and Fresh Approach. These programs included the B-47 and the KC-97 tanker aircraft in the US, and sought to show where reorganization would be needed in the event of implementing the ground alert initiative. The necessary refinements discovered were carried out in the US and certain overseas bases by SAC from 1 October 1957, with other bases later joining the effort.

Alert forces in the US already had many questions and concerns, but the problems were far worse at overseas bases (such as those in North Africa and the United Kingdom). Until 1958 these bases supported SAC's rotation training program, where combat-rated groups would go on sixty–ninety-day tours of duty. This often meant wing movements, and since a typical B-47 Stratojet wing was made up of three squadrons (forty-five B-52s and a supporting KC-97 tanker, alongside another twenty aircraft and several hundred crewmembers), deployment was a harried mess at best. Oversea transport was a particularly complex issue; the incoming unit needed to relieve the outgoing one, and this meant, for example, that a single rotation to the UK would need ninety bombers and forty tankers traveling across the Atlantic.

The spring of 1958 saw SAC's training policy end with the 100th Bomb Wing's tour of England. A few months earlier in French Morocco, a new plan of bases and bombers was enacted, using the B-47 as a guinea pig. This was known as 'Reflex Action'—a system where smaller numbers of aircraft were sent overseas to stand on ground alert duty over the course of a three-week tour. In this test, a total of twenty bombers were drawn in equal numbers from four US wings. 'Reflex' consisted of a continuous rotation, with one third of the aircraft wing (and its personnel) were replaced by fresh aircraft (and personnel) every three weeks. However, the changeover did not occur until the new bomber crew and staff presented themselves for alert duty, with nuclear weapons loaded and locked.

Since the responsibility for 'Reflex' was handed to the B-47, the introduction of the project had a huge impact on the medium-sized bomber. The division also supported the air-refueling needs of all US Military agencies operating in or travelling around the region. The concept of 'Reflex Action' was not a big deal in the late 1950s, and in 1963 an effort to update it with the B-52 and B-58 Hustler in Europe was abandoned.

In mid-1958 the entire SAC wing deployment to Guam was replaced by an 'Air Mail' alert program, whereby several B-47 wings in the US maintained a specific number of B-47s and KC-97s at Andersen AFB, Guam, to meet both routine and alert requirements. April 1964 saw the switching of the division from 'Air Mail' B-47s and KC-97s to 'Reflex' B-52 and KC-135 forces at Andersen AFB. The aircraft and crews were again deployed from US-based SAC wings. In the US the alert status began on 1 October 1957, and the early aim was to keep at least one third of a bomber and tanker force ready for immediate action.

Whether the alert status was at home or overseas, the lack of action became mind-numbing for the crews, with only 'no-notice' test drills to liven up the situation. These could be called at any time, day or night, and were designed to keep the men sharp. Attendance was mandatory. The exercises would occur at least once during a regular tour of duty, and began with a bomber or tanker starting up, charging to the runway, and getting into position before receiving stand-down orders. Many times this resulted in a minimum take-off (MITO) departure that was stopped literally seconds before the aircraft went into the air. The idea was to ensure the aircraft could get off the ground in fifteen minutes; the engine started within two minutes, and bombers were moving to the runway ramp within five minutes. Considering the size of a B-52 and that of a KC-97 or KC-135 tanker, five minutes was an impressive timing. At SAC bases in Alaska, aerial tankers were refueling SAC bombers to help keep them on alert for as much as twenty-four hours each time. One KC-135 carried a complex array of black boxes alongside a ranking SAC general and his staff of controllers; they flew a pattern that continually circled the headquarters at Omaha, Nebraska, with the base some 6 miles below them. The idea behind this was to preserve continuity of command in case of an incoming enemy missile hitting HQ and taking out the base.

SAC wanted to equal instant combat readiness. General Thomas Power was the head of Air Research and Development at the time, and he waited to see the need for an airborne alert; this came with the Cuban Missile Crisis. By utilizing an airborne alert system, SAC would ensure the survival of a higher number of heavy bombers in the case of a surprise attack. After insistent urging, Power was given permission to acquire an 'on-the-shelf' capability for placing and maintaining a portion of the B-52 fleet on airborne alert. The precaution paid off; it was possible to put enough B-52s in the air to maintain combat capabilities in the face of a missile strike from Cuba. General Power said that it was important to sustain the airborne alert for a full month, during which time the B-52 would be ready for immediate attack. The B-52s actually flew over 200 million miles without a single incident; this unprecedented operation involved over 2,000 bombers and tankers and sorties, with 50,000 hours of continuous flight. B-47s were also deployed to previously selected and prepared 'dispersal bases', including a number of civilian airfields. This dispersal increased the number of targets an aggressor would have to hit simultaneously in order to prevent an SAC counter-attack.

All alert B-47 aircraft operated out of SAC's southern-US bases. The crews were treated well by the civilian population, who loved seeing them in their local towns. The civilians understood that SAC's presence in their town meant that they were looking out for the entire country, and SAC's existence during this time served as the most effective deterrent to any aggression against the United States.

In most of the US bomber bases, air crews on alert duty passed the time in facilities they were specially built. General Curtis LeMay did his best to allow his crews some comfort from the tediousness by building these special facilities well away from the regular areas of the base and close to the flight line and hard stand areas. The facilities built for alert crews allowed for areas to take naps, watch movies, and play pool and cards. The crews were allowed to leave the area if they desired, but they had to stay together, and movement was restricted to selected areas around the base and close to the alert line. A crew could normally expect to be on alert duty on a monthly basis. However, some had shorter alert times that lasted for three to four days. They carried two-way radios so, if needed, they could be contacted immediately to go on their deadly, frightening mission.

In the event of a launch, special paths marked by flashing yellow lights existed on base to speed the crews back to the hard stands. This was the reason why the crews named the area 'the Christmas tree.' These lights directed non-essential personnel to pull over and let the crews through so they could get to their aircraft.

By May 1960 SAC hit its goal of keeping one-third of the fleet ready on the flight line. By March 1961, President Kennedy increased the line to include half of the B-47s and B-52s, and SAC implemented this by July. However, SAC were not always entirely honest about their exact state of combat-readiness; this was just part of the little game the USAF played to make sure they had all the assets they wanted.

By 1966 SAC tankers and bombers were already committed to the Vietnam War, which put a direct strain on their twenty-four-hour alert status. From 1968 onwards this became a stressed point, and in 1970 and 1971 there were more discrepancies in the SAC's reports on how many aircraft they actually had available. The biggest cut to their resources happened in 1972, when a call came for aircraft to support Linebacker II in Vietnam; this would cause the number of aircraft on alert to drop from 179 to forty-nine. Secretary of Defense Robert McNamara had really harmed the ground alert status and the Single Integrated Operating Plan (SIOP). Most of the problems had to do with the amount of ICBMs available, and the fact that these items could not be recalled once used (unlike the bombers).

In 1973 B-52s were heading back from Guam and Thailand to boost the alert numbers, but they would not arrive back until 1974. It was not until SAC lowered official requirements in 1974–75 that the numbers began to look better, and this meant that for the first time in almost ten years SAC could not meet its own requirements for alert-status aircraft. The number failed to rise above 100 aircraft until 1982, not counting the seventy-five B-52s that were retired over that period. Only a quarter of the force was on alert over this period.

Eighty B-52s were retired from 1982–83, and this brought the alert status down even further, to seventy-six bombers. By the end of 1983 this meant that the total force available was at 323 bombers. However, the dawn of the B-1 bomber did something to help the situation, but this did not represent an increase in the number of alert-status resources. The total number of aircraft available for alert duty was 411 at the end of 1988, and in 1989 the number of aircraft on alert dropped to sixty-three. The retirement of the B-52G brought even more reductions, with the number of alert aircraft dropping to just fifty-three by 1990. At the beginning of 1991 almost two-thirds of the B-52Gs were fighting in Iraq, while the B-1B was suffering problems—it had been grounded due to an accident resulting from a technical issue. As the bomber crews returned from Operation Desert Storm in March, everyone returned to regular duty, but this was no long haul; six months after returning from the conflict, the Cold War was over.

On 10 January 1964, a B-52H carrying a three-man crew and a Boeing civilian test pilot by the name of Chuck Fisher took the aircraft over the Sangre de Christo Mountains in New Mexico. The test was designed to test how well the B-52H would cope with vibration and turbulence at high speed and high altitude. After six hours of shaking around, the crew finally detached the vertical stabilizer; the test was a success. Chuck Fisher is the only person to have landed a B-52H without a tail. (*US Air Force*)

The End of the Cold War Alert Status

Gravity bombs and cruise missiles were removed from the B-52 and the B-1 on 18 September 1991, with the removal beginning in the morning and finishing by that afternoon. The rest of the armament (450 Minuteman II missiles) were taken down, and the SAC base commanders were informed that ground alert was finished. Thirty-four years of hardstands and tours of duty, and the accompanying boredom, were over. However, this did not mean that SAC relaxed in their approach to a nuclear war; the Peacekeeper and Minuteman II missiles were always at the ready. Since the Cold War had taken SAC out of the business of continual alert, the organization lost its place on the alert line and closed down for good in June 1992. This precipitated a total reorganization of the USAF, with SAC being transferred to the new Air Combat Command.

Operations and Upgrades

With all the B-52 variations coming off the production line in the late 1950s, SAC decided that the time was ripe to put a new operation into effect. Operation Chrome Dome started in 1960 and was one of the many USAF and SAC airborne global alert systems. Later in 1961, another programme was attached to Chrome Dome named 'Hard Head'; this consisted of a nuclear-armed B-52 flying a path around Thule AFB, Greenland, to keep an eye on the Thule ballistic-missile early-warning system (BMEWS) site, which consisted of a double-faced phased array radar located some 6 miles from the Air Force base itself. If the site was attacked, the B-52 on station would report it immediately to SAC headquarters by any means possible. This program was flown twice per day.

Chrome Dome itself was the creation of General Thomas Power, Commander of the SAC. He initiated many of the SAC's operations (such as Hard Head, Round Robin, and Giant Lance). His bombers hung around in airspace just outside the USSR to make sure that their first-strike capability remained just that. Of the missions flown for Chrome Dome, the first was a B-52D that flew from Sheppard AFB, Texas, across the US to New England and then over the Atlantic Ocean. Refueling over the Atlantic and then heading north to Newfoundland, the B-52's course then changed, flying northwest over Baffin Bay and towards Thule AFB in Greenland. From here the B-52D flew west, across the Queen Elizabeth Islands in Canada, on to Alaska, where she refueled over the Pacific Ocean before heading southeast and back to Sheppard AFB. This huge flight was successful, and spurred three other similar missions in 1966—heading from over the East Coast to the Atlantic, and then to the Mediterranean Sea before returning to Baffin Bay. The third flight took place over Alaska.

Operation Chrome Dome came into effect in July 1961, and brought an airborne alert program that encompassed the use of aerial tankers and bombers. In order to keep a bomber in the air for twenty-four hours straight, it was necessary to have a ready source of fuel. This was a well-designed and critical program, using several B-52s that flew alternating twenty-four-hour sorties along three routes. The northern route ran up the eastern seaboard, through Greenland, and then back towards Alaska, with the aerial refueling occurring just off the eastern US, around Cape Cod. The western route traveled along the west of the county, and there was also a southern route that went from the eastern coastline to the northwest corner of the Iberian Peninsula, underwent aerial refueling, and then traveled back to the base. The aerial refueling was carried out by the venerable KC-135 tankers that were stationed at Eielson AFB in Alaska. There were also other tankers stationed at Torrejon AFB and Morón AFB in Spain. The first aerial refueling was undertaken by KC-135s that called Griffiss AFB, New York, their home; however, this base was dropped in favour of having the KC-135s assigned all along the northeastern United States.

The USAF wanted the world to know it had the ability to keep aircraft airborne for twenty-four hours; the idea was that this would intimidate the rest of the world. The heart and soul of the program was the aerial refueling aircraft and their 'boomer' crews. Without their technical skills, Operation Chrome Dome would have been difficult to undertake; this is not to say it was any easier for the B-52 pilots that had to line their massive bird up with the tankers, hooking up a miniscule hose and nozzle to gulp up the thousands of pounds of fuel needed to keep the B-52 in the air. The refueling operation was no easy feat, and it took much practice from both sides to make it work. Even still, there were always problems; it could be that an electrical system shorted out, or that the engines had issues.

Chrome Dome gave SAC the edge that they wanted—the ability to go anywhere at any time, loaded and ready to do what was needed. SAC had their ace in the hole, and they were determined to hold on to it.

If there was one constant in the history of the B-52, it was upgrades. Despite the noise, the red tape, congressional arguments about budgets, stress, and other factors, upgrades were a way of life if you had a B-52 in your hangar. It was a pain, but a necessary one. In order to make the change, the aircraft had to come out of service, and this did not make many commanders happy because it meant their wing would be one plane short—and an aircraft was a valuable asset. The upgrades could be lengthy, and that irritated the crew chiefs. The absence of even one plane could markedly affect a mission and how it was flown.

The B-52 was on alert status for many years, and this meant that her and her crews were subjected to hundreds of individual improvements and changes. Various types occurred; they involved combat-readiness, better radar systems, or just adjusting a design flaw. This all added up to a substantial cost, but this seems worth it when considered against the B-52's longevity; she was still going when most of the other aircraft in the USAF inventory had already headed to the boneyard at Davis Monthan AFB.

There have been considerable changes to the weapon system of the B-52. The AGM-69A SRAM (short-range attack missile) and other conventional gravity bombs and nuclear-warhead bombs were part of the B-52's arsenal until the late 1970s; it was around this time that SAC decided that a bomber was perhaps not the best way to try and beat a Soviet defensive radar system. SAC looked for a way to bring the B-52 up to speed and update the weapons systems to help protect her. The initial system introduced was the air-launched cruise missile (ALCM), which had been developed in the late 1960s and early

The skies were full of history. The Boeing Dash 80 precedes the B-52 as they overfly the roll-out of the KC-135 tanker. (*Boeing Corporation*)

'70s. The ACLM system gave the B-52 the ability to deploy a deep-penetration weapon from a distance, in order to protect the aircraft and crew from attack while in denied airspace. It also allowed the B-52 to deliver a heavy weapon hit before going further into Soviet airspace and lining up gravity bombs on designated targets.

This new ALCM was a big-ticket item, and the aerospace contractors were all itching to fight for the privilege of building it. The contract was worth $1.4 billion. Boeing won the day with its AGB-86B after a fly-off between the competing companies in 1979. The B-52Gs from the 416th Bomb Wing, Griffiss AFB, New York, were the first to receive the new AGM-86, taking delivery in December 1982. Ninety-eight B-52Gs and ninety-six B-52Hs were fitted for the new ALCM, and the B-52Gs received a new leading edge wing root fairing that made them identifiable as missile carriers to satellites (a requirement of the Salt II treaty). This would cause problems later on. The B-52Hs were already quite identifiable due to their turbofan engines, which were used instead of turbojet engines. The B-52Gs were able to carry the AGM-86—twelve missiles carried under the wing—while the B-52Hs added eight additional missiles internally thanks to its new common rotary launcher (SCRL), a feature unique to this model.

Big Four

From 1959 a modification named 'Big Four' ('Mod 1000') was made to the B-52 in order to improve the aircraft's combat abilities. This was needed due to an operational change that moved the B-52s from high-level to low-level operations. All models of the B-52 except the B-52B were affected, although some B-52Hs saw this change during their pre-production phase. The changes consisted of: the capability to launch the Hound Dog AGM-28 standoff nuclear missiles; the ADM-20 Quail decoy, which was an advance ECM unit; and upgrades for all-weather, low-altitude interdiction missions that were based on the idea that the Soviet defenses were advancing at a fast rate.

The modification also included the AN/ALQ-27 ECM (electronic countermeasures) system on 572 of the B-52s; this change was limited to these B-52s due to the extremely high cost of the equipment ($1 billion in today's money). The change was made to the B-52Hs that were just coming off the line at Wichita, and also to some of the earlier models. Funding was the major factor in these low-level modifications, forcing Air Command to hold back funding in summer 1960 after consecutive costs rose from $192 million in November 1959 to $241 million and then $265 million in July 1960. The plan was eventually completed with the last invoice stating a cost

Above: The B-52 meets her ancestor, the horse and wagon. Quite a comparison! (*Boeing Corporation*)

Below: A B-52D getting ready to be serviced at Andersen AFB, Guam. (*Robert F. Dorr*)

The first of six B-52s taxies to its parking spot at Andersen AFB, Guam, after landing. These aircraft were fulfilling a rotational bomber force at Guam as ordered by Pacific Command. (*US Air Force/Staff Sgt Bennie J. Davis III*)

Along with the black underbelly and tail fin, the camouflage was chosen to avoid detection by searchlights in North Vietnam, where the optically guided anti-aircraft guns were a major defence factor. The new paint scheme added to the aircraft's fearsome reputation. (*Robert F. Dorr*)

A B-52G from Andersen AFB, Guam, dropping her bombs on the Viet Cong during Linebacker II. (*US Air Force*)

A mothership B-52 taking last-minute instructions from her crew chief as she prepares to take off for a Captain Hook mission, carrying a D-21 drone under each wing. (*USAF*)

Damage done by the B-52 during Operation Arc Light. (*National Museum of the USAF*)

The B-52D 'Big Belly' living up to her name. She could carry more ordnance than any other B-52. (*National Museum of the USAF*)

A B-52 lining up for a refuel from a KC-135 during Linebacker II. (*National Museum of the USAF*)

The day's bomb load is laid out for the B-52s during Linebacker II. The B-52 in the background had a black belly because the missions were flown at night. (*National Museum of the USAF*)

An incoming crew from Linebacker II. The wrinkles in the forward section of the B-52 fuselage, right by the wing root, can be clearly seen. (*National Museum of the USAF*)

The quintessential Vietnam image—a B-52 returning from a mission while a soldier stands guard by his bunker. (*National Museum of the USAF*)

This photograph was taken during the 1960s. An SAC B-52 crew heads to their aircraft, which is ready to go and loaded with Hound Dog missiles (one of which can be seen in the foreground). This crew was part of alert teams that were on constant guard during the Cold War. (*US Air Force*)

Maintenance staff of the 96th Bomber Wing sit in a rather unique position, taking care of this B-52's engines. This image gives a good indication of just how large the engine pods are. (*Department of Defense*)

A B-52H and his crew chief stand ready for trials in a rapid-response exercise at Minot AFB, North Dakota. (*National Museum of the USAF*)

A B-52 refuels from a KC-10 tanker, with an F-4 also in attendance. (*US Air Force*)

Where are AAA when you need them? Senior Airman John Myer hauls a tow bar underneath the nose wheel of the B-52H Stratofortress during a Red Flag exercise at Nellis AFB, Nevada. The B-52 blew out a tire on landing after a four-hour mission. Myer is assigned to the 2nd Aircraft Maintenance Squadron at Barksdale AFB, Louisiana. (*US Air Force/Staff Sgt Vernon Young Jr*)

An ordnance crew uses an MJ-1 bomb loader to fill a B-52 with Mk 117 750-lb bombs during Operation Desert Shield. (*US Air Force*)

A B-52 and a KC-135 refueling over the Pacific Ocean during the Tropic Fury exercise at Andersen AFB, Guam. This exercise was used to train crews in the use of different weapons systems. (*US Air Force/ Master Sgt Kevin J. Gruenwald*)

A B-52 with a drogue chute deployed lands at Nellis AFB, Nevada, after her trip from her home base at Barksdale AFB, Louisiana. The Red Flag war games involve realistic warfare training, involving the US Air Force and allies in some very gritty, serious exercises. This Red Flag exercise took place in January 2013. (*US Air Force*)

Above: The B-52 has not just worked on USAF projects; examples were also loaned out to NASA as the NB-52 mothership, which carried captive research vehicles so that they could be released at altitude. Here, the HIMAT sub-scale research vehicle is on the way to being released to free flight. (*NASA*)

Below: The NB-52 mothership also carried the M2-F3 lifting body, which was part of early space shuttle research. (*NASA*)

A more recent NB-52 mothership test involved the X-51 Wave Rider, which was an unmanned scram-jet. The nose of the B-52 was reconfigured by NASA. (*NASA*)

A B-52 at Minot AFB, North Dakota, lights up her engines very early on a January morning, with the temperature at -25 degrees Fahrenheit. This cold-weather test was being used to determine the differences between the JP-8 fuel and the new synthetic fuel; it was the last step in certification. (*US Air Force/Airman 1st Class Christopher Boitz*)

Above: A B-52 waits to be prepped for flight on a very cold 8 January at Minot Air Force Base, North Dakota. The base was suffering some very harsh weather, with sub-zero temperatures, no visibility, and wind gusts of up to 50 mph. (*US Air Force/Airman 1st Class Christopher Boitz*)

Below: Coming and going, B-52s take off and land at Edwards AFB, California, using a mixture of JP-8 and a new synthetic fuel. The aircraft taking off is the first flight to use the mix. Both B-52s are from Minot AFB, North Dakota. (*US Air Force/Senior Airman Stacy Moless*)

A B-52 displays her total armament at Barksdale AFB, Louisiana. The rotary launcher is directly in front of the aircraft; it uses the same method as the B-2 stealth bomber to launch munitions. (*US Air Force*)

Ghost Rider is towed from a maintenance area at the 309th Aerospace Maintenance and Regeneration Group at Davis Monthan Air Force Base, Arizona, on 11 February 2015. She is being regenerated for active service after sitting in storage since 2008, when she was sent to the 'boneyard'. (*US Air Force/ Master Sgt Greg Steele*)

Ghost Rider is up on the very early morning of 12 February 2015, being prepped for an early morning taxi test. She passed with flying colors. (*US Air Force/Master Sgt Greg Steele*)

The tow bar is removed while the crew wait—Air Force Master Sgt Steve Vance, 307th Aircraft Maintenance Squadron Crew Chief, and Tech. Sgt Jonathan Spears, 307th Maintenance Squadron Engine Specialist. (*US Air Force/Master Sgt Greg Steele*)

Ghost Rider is towed from the Davis Monthan boneyard for taxi tests on 12 February 2015. (US Air Force/Master Sgt Greg Steele)

Ghost Rider continues to be prepped in the early morning hours for taxi and engine tests. Soon afterwards she headed to her new home at Barksdale AFB, before being transferred to Tinker AFB. (US Air Force/Master Sgt Greg Steele)

of $313 million.

The Big Four project suffered with many technical problems. Moving to a low-level configuration failed to solve the B-52's previous issues with operating at this height, which were more complex than initially thought. This was partially to do with the many different versions of the aircraft; each model needed unique fixes. The existing set of avionics also needed fine tuning—the bomb and navigation systems, the Doppler radar, the terrain-clearance radar, and radar altimeters. The huge bomber also needed strengthening to manage the stress of the new Hound Dog missiles. Regardless of the depth of improvements needed and the issues they faced, Big Four was completed in 1963.

Blue Band and Subsequent Wing Leak Fixes

Blue Band was the first chance to fix the fuel leaks that had plagued the earlier models of the B-52 'B', 'C', and 'D' models. In September 1957 these repairs were completed—a fairly basic fix of a clamp in place of another device used to interconnect the fuel lines to the fuel cells in the wing. The modification was undertaken at the Wings' home bases.

However, Blue Band also faced problems; the CF-14 aluminum clamps were folding under stress. They were deteriorating some three months into service, with some very dangerous consequences. To fix this, another program was enacted—Hard Shell. Boeing took another deep look into the problem of the wing fuel leaks, replacing the C4-14 aluminum clamps with the new CF-17 stainless-steel clamps. Boeing and the USAF began a joint effort that was completed in January 1958, but it did not take long to see that the problem was not fixed.

The failure of the above led to another new program—Quick Clip. This modification added safety straps around the CF-17 clamps. It was started in 1958 and completed very quickly; B-52Fs being completed at the Wichita and Seattle plants were fitted with the new straps during production.

Hi-Stress

Force-wide structural repair was undertaken to help solve the problem of wing fatigue caused by high and low-altitude flights. This was initially meant to be included in Big Four, but it instead occurred during the supplementary three-phase program. The first two phases were completed in 1962, with the final one completed in 1964. Phase III was undertaken as an IRAN (inspect and repair as necessary) venture, involving early B-52s and dealing with wing cracks.

Hot Fan

The Pratt and Whitney RF-33 turbofan engines were not trouble-free, especially during their early years of service. By 1961, the problems were intolerable. The problems included throttle creep, hang and slow starts, flame outs, uneven throttle alignment, excessive oil consumption, turbine blade failure, and inlet case cracks. Hot Fan was created to alleviate these failures at a cost of $15 million, which was considered a bargain at the time. The two main goals were to increase engine reliability and remove the failure before 600 hours of operation. Work began in 1962, but the Cuban Missile Crisis put everything on hold because all B-52s were put on ground alert. The program restarted in 1963 and ended in late 1964 with 894 engines repaired.

ECP-1050

The Engineering Change Proposal (ECP) was a wing-structure upgrade for the B-52 'G' and 'H' models that was conducted between February 1962 and September 1964, costing $219 million. The program was undertaken because of the ruinous wing fatigue that was affecting the aircraft. This involve replacing the wing box beam with a new type that used a stronger, thicker aluminum and different steel taper back fasteners instead of the titanium ones used before. More brackets were used on the wing skin, and extra panel stiffeners with a new coating were used on the interior of the wing fuel tanks. Instead of taking aircraft out of service to make the changes, SAC undertook them during IRAN depot visit. Eighteen B-52Hs were rebuilt with new wings during this process.

ECP2126

This program affected B-52 'G' and 'H' models, bring the AGM-64A SRAM to them by the mid-1970s. It cost over $400 million, and included the addition of modified wing pylons and launch gears alongside a new weapons bay, rotary launcher, and avionics equipment. Labor work began on 15 October 1971, when the first B-52G arrived in Oklahoma City. She was sent to the 42nd Bomb Wing at Loring AFB in Maine in March 1972, and the wing became operational with SRAMs in August 1972. The Oklahoma AMA was also responsible for undertaking the procedures for the B-52H. Two hundred and seventy surviving B-52 'G's and 'H's received the SRAM modification, allowing them to carry twelve SRAM missiles under their wings and eight more internally.

EVS Modifications

The AN/ASQ-151 Electro-optical viewing system was selected after the mid-1960s, when Boeing's Chief of Flight Testing, Jack Funk, installed a Sony TV camera onto the fin of a B-52 during a test. This makeshift system showed good results, and it was offered to the USAF representative Colonel Rick Hudlow. Hudlow advised SAC that the idea was to explore the possibility of using visual sensors to improve damage assessment and strike potential, in addition to expanding the efficiency of terrain-avoidance equipment. It was initially planned that just the B-52G and B-52H would have the system; between 1971 and 1976, 270 aircraft were upgraded for this purpose at a cost of $248.5 million. The AN/AVQ22 low-light lead TV unit (LLL-TV) operated in starlight; at starboard, a Hughes AN/AAQ6 forward-looking infrared radar (FLIR) was utilized. Data shown on the pilot screens included overlaid terrain-avoidance profile trace from either TV or FLIR-mode alphanumeric symbology, incorporating radar altimeters and indicated airspeed as well as artificial horizon overlay.

Giant Fish

This modification was for the B-52H, and it added the ability to take samples of the atmosphere using a pod installed in the forward section of the weapons bay. The controls were located at the gunner's station. The pod had five forward-facing scoops which allowed for the trapping of particles and radiation samples. At least four B-52Hs were used in Giant Fish—#60–024, #60-033, #0051, and #0052. The last two aircraft were in the 7th Bomb Wing at Carswell AFB, Texas. They conducted sample-gathering missions after the 1986 Chernobyl disaster. At the end of the 7th Bomb Wing's operations, the aircraft moved on to Minot AFB, North Dakota, in 1994.

Jolly Well

There were ongoing troubles with the avionics systems, and these were addressed by the Jolly Well program. The AN/ASQ38 bombing and navigation systems (present on B-52s from the 'E' to the 'H' mode) were replaced, with 480 aircraft refitted by 1964.

MADREC

This acronym stood for the 'Malfunction Detection and Recording system. The modification ran across all B-52s in the first half of the 1960s, installing monitor equipment in the bomb and navigation pods and also implementing the autopilot systems, which would alert the aircrews to possible malfunctions. From 1961, MADREC was used to check out the AGM-28 Hound Dog missile; Phase I worked on the B-52 'B', 'C', and 'D' aircraft, and this was finished in 1963; Phase II worked on the later editions, and this was completed by 1965.

OAS Modification

The B-52G and B-52H received the AN/ASQ176-offensive Avionic system, which replaced the AN/ASQ-38 bombing/navigation equipment that was originally built into these models. By the mid-1970s it became clear that this updated system was malfunctioning, and it became an issue to fix this. The USAF began searching for a replacement in 1975, and this led to the OAS, which made use of new digital equipment. The OAS 'kit' was tested as a prototype on a B-52G on 3 September 1980; it was used to effectively launch an AGM-69A SRAM in June 1981. The system was found to be more consistent than the kit it had replaced, being calibrated for low-level use, and it performed well in the face of an electromagnetic-pulse effect. The updating process began during the first half of the 1980s, with the last 168 B-52Gs and ninety-six B-52Hs finished by 1986. The undertaking proved to be very expensive, with a final cost of $1.66 billion.

Pacer Plank

A total of eighty B-52Ds were involved with the ECP (engineering change proposal) at the Boeing factory in Wichita, Kansas. The fundamental plan was to cover the aircraft's conventional-warfare ability, also bringing about the repair of the lower wing skin by using new alloys with better resistance to fatigue. Pacer Plank permitted the redesign and substitution of the wing center panel, with new upper longerons and fuselage side skins substituted and a new pressure bulkhead added in the forward fuselage. Endorsement came in late 1972, and the work was finished in 1977. This was another expensive program, with the final cost coming in at $219 million.

Quick Start

The motive was this program was increasing the ability to launch alert bombers as quickly as possible. It was approved in 1974, and featured the addition of a cartridge start to each engine on the B-52G and B-52H. The work was completed by July 1976 at a cost of $35 million. Quick Start allowed instant ignition of the eight engines, reducing the time needed before each aircraft could hit the runway for take-off. Not every engine needed modification; in 1963–64, each B-52 had been fitted with two cartridges, and this had reduced reaction time by two critical minutes. This aided in the deployment of ground-start equipment.

Rivet Ace

Phase IV Electronic Counter Measure Defensive Avionics came under ECP (Engineering Change Proposal) 2519. This program involved the B-52 'G' and 'H' models and began in the 1970s. The most obvious change implemented was at the outermost aft fuselage section, which was extended by 40 inches to allow for extra equipment. The project cost was $362.5 million, but this extended to $1.5 billion on completion in the late 1980s. The final version of the AN/ALQ-172 (V2) came to the B-52H in mid-1988.

Rivet Rambler

Rivet Rambler upgraded the electronic warfare capability of the B-52D with an improvement known as the Phase V ECM, which was installed from 1967 to 1969. It added one AN/ALR-18 automatic receiving unit, one AN/APR-25 radar homing and warning system, four AN/ALT-6B or AN/ALT-22 continuous wave jamming systems, two AN/ALT-32Hs, one AN/ALT-32L high/low jammers, six AN/ALE-20 flare dispensers (with a total of ninety-six flares), and eight AN/ALE-24 chaff dispensers (with 1,125 bundles).

The B-52Gs assigned to Southeast Asia were also given the Phase V ECM; they received the AN/ALE-25 forward-firing chaff-dispenser rocket pod, suspended on pylons between the engine pods. Some of the Guam-based B-52Gs were seen with the AN/ALQ119 (V) ECM pods in place of the AN/ALE-25 pods during Operation Linebacker in 1972.

Captain Hook

This program belonged to the A-12 Oxcart/Tagboard project, the D-21 drone program; it involved the use of two B-52Hs (#60-0021 and #60-0036) during the late 1960s. The programme allowed for the captive carry or launching of the D-21 drone, which was initially carried on the M-21 (the modified A-12 Blackbird). After the loss of two test pilots in the first phase of the program, Kelly Johnson (creator of the Lockheed A-12 Blackbird) decided that the B-52 would be the best aircraft to carry the drones. Two specially fitted B-52Hs were modified to carry the D-21s on specially made pylons underneath their wings.

The B-52s were capable of sixteen hours of flight, allowing the D-21 a 3,000-mile range. This allowed the program to achieve the goal of reaching China. The test flights for Captain Hook started in 1968, with two control officers on board the B-52; a stellar inertial-guidance system was added, along with an air-conditioning system to keep the D-21 cool. The test flights left Hawaii, flew over the Pacific Ocean, and photographed Christmas Island and Midway Island. Over the course of fourteen test flights, there were two failures.

By the latter half of 1969, the CIA began recommending missions for the D-21 to the Committee on National Security, and these were then approved by Richard Nixon. The drones would go to Lop Nor, 2,000 miles inland from the Chinese-Mongolian border. Lop Nor was situated in a 2,000-foot depression, around 120 miles wide, on a 4,000-foot plateau; it was an area of key interest for US intelligence as the Chinese were conducting missile testing there.

A B-52H carrying two D-21s (one under each wing) left Beale AFB for the mission. When the bomber reached the designated launch point, it released the D-21s, which then flew beyond the range of the Chinese radar. The mission, however, bore no fruit. As Kelly Johnson explained, 'Damn thing came out of China, but was lost. It was not spotted or shot down, but it must have malfunctioned and crashed on us.' The Chinese radar never picked up the drone, and Johnson concluded that the drone's radar guidance must have been inaccurate.

Eleven months later, Nixon approved another mission to overfly Lop Nor. The flight went ahead successfully, but the D-21's film was dropped and lost at sea after almost being recovered shipside. Another flight took place around two weeks afterwards, being tracked inside China for 1,900 miles and then lost. The Department of Defense informed Johnson that the program was canceled in 1971; they also informed him that all tooling for the project had to be destroyed. This was a frustrating end to the program; it was unfortunate that the bugs were not worked out, as the D-21 could have been a formidable tool when used in conjunction with the B-52.

South Bay

This upgrade was intended to increase the conventional-warfare ability of the B-52Fs. This would allow the B-52Fs to carry twenty-four 750-lb Mk 17 bombs externally or on modified wing ranks. The Air Staff approval for this program came in June 1964, and twenty-eight aircraft were adapted by October. Several months later, these were the first B-52s to see combat in Vietnam.

Sun Bath

This program involved forty-six B-52Fs between June and July 1965. The modifications were identical to those made to the South Bay bombers, but a shortage of equipment forced the Oklahoma City AMA to go to their war reserve and Tactical Air Command (TAC) supply to satisfy the deadline set by Robert McNamara, who commenced the program. Like the South Bay B-52s, the Sun Bath aircraft were sent to Vietnam a few months later.

Strategic Radar Modifications

In 1985, the ASQ-17 units on B-52 'H' and 'G' models were replaced by the AN/APQ-156 strategic radar (STRAT-RADAR). This modification was more complex than simply taking off one antenna and putting on a new one; it would eventually cost $700 million.

Sunflower

This program was carried out by the Wichita plant from late 1956 to late 1957. A total of seven B-52Bs were brought to a design that was close to the B-52Cs; this process necessitated the installation of around 150 kits. The aircraft involved were all production models that were used for various aspects of developmental flight testing; revamped, they were assigned to SAC upon the completion of the test program.

The Salt II Treaty

In May 1982, President Ronald Reagan stated that he would do nothing to undercut the new Salt II agreement that the US had signed with the Soviet

Union—provided that the Soviets showed equal restraint. By 1984 Reagan declared that the Soviet Union had already violated their commitment to the treaty, but he decided that the interim framework of mutual restraint enshrined by the treaty was still of benefit to the United States. In June 1985 he declared that the United States would continue to refrain from undercutting existing strategic arms agreements to the extent that the Soviets already had, as long as from that point the USSR actively pursued the arms-reduction agreement.

On 26 May 1986 President Reagan stated that he had again reviewed the status of the US interim restraint policy, and that he had given three detailed reports to Congress. In these reports, he stated that the USSR had not complied with its political commitment to observe the SALT agreement (including Salt II), and that they had not shown willingness to join the US in the framework of mutual restraint. Reagan stated:

> Given this situation ... in the future the US must base decisions regarding its strategic force structure on the nature and magnitude of the threats posed by Soviet strategic forces and not on standards contained in the SALT structure ... The United States would not display more strategic nuclear delivery vehicles or strategic ballistic missile warheads than the Soviets.

The USSR was failing to live up to its end of the bargain, forcing SAC to maintain their constant-alert status while not surpassing the parameters set by the SALT treaty. This was no easy task. The stipulations of the not-yet-ratified Salt II agreement were only partially followed by the US within this context, as shown by the deployment of 130 ALCM-laden bombers. On 28 November 1986, the 131st ALCM was delivered to B-52H #60-0055—aptly named *Salt Shaker*. This addition put the United States over the agreed threshold of 1,320 strategic nuclear-delivery systems. The ALCM integrations continued until the United States was able to count 194 B-52s loaded with ALCMs, which were adopted as weapons for regular use. These systems would later be used in the opening days of Operation Desert Storm.

6
Vietnam and the B-52

The Vietnam War was one of the United States' most protracted, dirtiest political nightmares the twentieth century. Far from developing overnight, the mess was the product of many years of foreign-power involvement and neo-colonialism in Asia, stretching back far into history. The Vietnam War actually began back in 1954, when it was known as the Second Indochina War (1954–73). Under the Eisenhower administration, the United States was struggling with issues relating to the Korean War truce; meanwhile, towards the end of the year, the Chinese were threatening to invade Formosa (now Taiwan). President Eisenhower and his Secretary of State, Allan Dulles, were being hammered over their policy of 'deterrence.' In a press conference on 7 April 1954, Eisenhower attempted to explain the strategic importance of Indochina and its position in Southeast Asia. He referred to the 'Falling Domino Effect', where Indochina would be the first in a row of countries to succumb to communist rule—followed by Burma, Thailand, Malaysia, and Indonesia. Left unchecked, Eisenhower argued, this trend would leave India surrounded by communism on all sides, with Australia, New Zealand, the Philippines, Formosa, and Japan also in precarious states. Henry Navarre, the French commander in Indochina, asked the United States for a $400-million contribution to the French defense fund for Indochina, a country in which they had a major stake.

Eisenhower gave the French $785 million instead, effectively enabling the French to expand their military operations in Indochina. He did this for two reasons—firstly to help the situation in Southeast Asia, and secondly to encourage the formation of the European Defense Community Treaty. However, the French needed more than money; the government turned to the United States' military might, requesting help to slap down the Viet Minh at Dien Bien Phu. The French asked for the launch of air strikes from US aircraft carriers in the area, and the Chairman of the Joint Chiefs of Staff,

Admiral Redford, and the USAF Chief of Staff, General Nathan Twining, were happy to agree to this request; Eisenhower, meanwhile, was totally against it.

The President had just avoided a war with communist China in Korea, and he was not ready to go to Congress to ask permission to begin another 'small war.' He had already had problems trying to get Congress to approve the sending of technical aid to Indochina via small groups of Air Force technicians, with no combat involved. Eisenhower said bluntly, 'If we ever have to go back to that, there will be a tremendous explosion in the world.'

John F. Kennedy—A New President, and a New War

The Eisenhower administration vacated the White House to a new, young, vibrant president. John Fitzgerald Kennedy was sworn into office on 20 January 1961 as the thirty-fifth President of the United States. It was felt that it was the beginning of a new era, but the optimism would not last forever; USSR leader Nikita Khrushchev was already pledging Soviet support to the communists in North Vietnam. He called for them to 'escalate' their efforts to bring communism to Southeast Asia.

In May, Vice President Lyndon Johnson visited President Diem in South Vietnam, bolstering his support by calling the leader the 'Winston Churchill of Asia.' Kennedy backed up the trip by sending some 400 Green Beret 'Special Advisors' to the country, where they would train South Vietnamese soldiers to fight against the Viet Cong guerillas. The Green Berets began to establish 'Civilian Irregular Defense Groups', which were made up of tough fighters known as *Montagnards* (Christian fighters from Cambodia). They set up stronghold camps in the hills to counter the communist uprising in the northern country. However, by the fall of 1961 some 26,000 Viet Cong launched successful raids on South Vietnamese troops. President Diem asked Kennedy for more help, and in October Maxwell Taylor and Walt Rostow, Kennedy's aides, traveled to Vietnam to get a first-hand look at what was really going on. Both men advised the President to expand the number of US Military advisors in the country, and to send an additional 8,000 combat soldiers.

Kennedy turned to Robert McNamara, his Secretary of Defense; McNamara and the Joint Chiefs agreed that a substantial show of force was the best option, including the deployment of 20,000 US troops to Vietnam. Kennedy didn't agree, instead sending more advisors along with military equipment such as US helicopter units, which were used to transport the South Vietnamese soldiers to battle. This meant that US soldiers were still involved in combat operations. The President tried to justify the new US role in the conflict as 'a means to prevent a communist takeover of Vietnam, which is in accordance with a policy our government has followed since 1954.' Despite this renewed effort, the Viet Cong still controlled most of the South Vietnamese countryside. The JFK administration adopted the 'flexible response' strategy, which meant stressing conventional warfare over other methods; as part of this, SAC took a look at the tactical potential of its strategic bombers in the conflict. The B-52 was chosen for operations in the country because it was better-suited for heavier activity than tactical fighter-bombers (such as the B-47 or the B-58 Hustler).

John F. Kennedy was assassinated in Dallas, Texas, on 22 November 1963. He was succeeded by Lyndon B. Johnson, who inherited a situation in Vietnam that was quickly becoming a quagmire. On 24 November 1963, Johnson declared that he would 'not lose Vietnam.' However, by the end of the year there were over 16,000 US Military advisors in South Vietnam, sucking over $500 million in US aid over the course of 1963 alone. Things were not improving at any rate. In March 1964 the US conducted secret bombing raids against the Ho Chi Minh trail to cut off North Vietnamese supplies.

On 3 August 1964 the US Navy destroyers *Maddox* and *C. Turner Joy* were working in a zig-zag pattern across the Gulf of Tonkin, coming within 8 miles of the North Vietnamese coast. At the same time, South Vietnamese commandos in speed boats attempted to light up the North Vietnamese radar. Later that night, the weather turned bad, with severe thunderstorms. This led the *Maddox* to believe she was under attack by North Vietnamese patrol boats; both US destroyers opened fire on various targets without visually identifying them. The press in the United States reacted strongly to the incident, and LBJ decided to retaliate for the 'attack.' Sixty-four US Navy fighters bombed North Vietnam for the first time, with Johnson giving a televised speech at midnight, an hour after the assault: 'We Americans know, although others appear to forget, the risk of spreading conflict. We still see no wider war.' Two Navy jets were shot down in the attack, and the first American prisoner of war was taken—Lt Everett Alvarez, from San Jose, California. He was taken to the infamous 'Hanoi Hilton', which would hold over 600 US PoWs over the course of the conflict. It was a cursed and vile place.

From this point onwards the situation escalated rapidly, with more ground troops being sent over. Some of the higher SAC commanders started to push for the organization to get more involved in the war, but they needed a specific mission; it was unclear how a nuclear-armed strategic bomber would fit into this specific conflict. The solution was found in upgrades. In the summer of 1964, Robert McNamara asked SAC to improve their capabilities for limited warfare. The organization carried out B-52 tests with conventional 'iron bombs' to assess their abilities, which loads were acceptable, and how long their release intervals should be to get the impact patterns they needed. They used multiple ejector racks for twelve bombs, attached to the two underwing pylons that were otherwise used to carry the Hound Dog missiles. The 320th Bomb Wing and the 2nd Bomb Wing were chosen to have their bombers upgraded for carrying these conventional, unsophisticated 'iron' bombs. Another B-52 'upgrade' for this conflict enabled the bomber to hold eighty-four 500-lb bombs internally, carrying twenty-four 750-lb on the underwing racks. The 320th and 2nd Bomb Wings were sent to Guam and Andersen AFBs as the 133rd Provisional Wing. In time, more wings would be deployed to both Thailand and Okinawa to cut the flight time to Vietnam and allow for a faster warning time for the bombers.

The first B-52 attacks on guerillas in South Vietnam occurred on 18 June 1965. A Viet Cong holdout in the jungle was chosen as the first target; it was not a good choice. Two B-52s ended up colliding in mid-flight to the target, with both crashing into the Pacific Ocean. There was no way to assess the bomb damage of the area hit, as it was still controlled by the Viet Cong. The news of the accident didn't take long to reach the US, with the press blasting the military for using a heavy bomber like the B-52 in a conflict like the Vietnam War; however, the strength of the B-52 and her bombers allowed them to swallow the criticism soon enough.

The best use of the B-52 in Vietnam turned out to be the support of ground troops. The B-52s were called in to destroy the enemy from above, and the aircraft destroyed opposing troops or supply depots with devastating quickness. B-52s were deployed against North Vietnam, Cambodia, and Laos. From June 1965 to August 1973, the B-52 flew 124,532 missions in this conflict; thirty-one B-52s were lost, with eighteen shot down by enemy gunfire and thirteen lost to in-flight technical problems.

Operation Arc Light Searches for the Enemy

Operation Arc Light involved the deployment of B-52s to Andersen AFB, Guam. On 18 June 1965, thirty B-52Fs were loaded with conventional bombs and took off from Andersen AFB, heading west. Their mission spanned some 3,000 miles from Guam to Vietnam, crossing the western Pacific to the Philippines, and then heading towards the South China Sea. This represented five and a half hours of outbound flying time, one hour over the country to carry out the mission, and another five and a half hours back to base. On the outbound leg, the aircraft refueled on the northern coast of Luzon, in the Philippines, with another KC-135 stationed near Kadena AFB, Okinawa. Arc Light represented the first hard strike against the North Vietnamese.

Big Belly

As the Vietnam War had begun to increase in intensity, the Joint Chiefs of Staff had deployed B-52Fs to Andersen AFB, Guam. In February 1965, Lt Gen. William Westmoreland was the new Commander of the Military in Vietnam. He wanted to use the idle B-52s stationed on Guam to support the ground troops (as a joint operation with the US and South Vietnamese tactical aircraft), but he had no support for this proposal. However, on 15 April, near the Black Virgin Mountains in the Tây Ninh Province, things changed—a highly ineffectual bombing campaign (despite the large number of fighters and bombers involved) led Westmoreland to push harder for the deployments of the B-52s. In Honolulu on 19 April, Secretary of Defense Robert McNamara informed Westmoreland that the B-52 was authorized for use in tactical operations in South Vietnam.

There was another modification to the B-52 aircraft; it was codenamed 'Big Belly.' The modification began in December 1965, and the basic concept was to enlarge the internal bomb-carrying capacity from twenty-four to eighty-four 500-lb Mk 82 bombs and forty-two 750-lbs Mk 17 bombs. These were conventional weapons known as 'iron bombs.' The modifications also allowed for twenty-four more bombs to be carried on altered wing racks, and the sum of the changes gave the modified B-52 a payload of 60,000 lbs. All surviving B-52Ds were given this upgrade (totaling 150 aircraft), and others were adapted to carry aerial mines later, in 1969–71.

Big Belly B-52Ds were given new paint schemes after tests were carried out to find the best upper-fuselage camouflage to avoid visual detection of the low-flying aircraft. SAC picked a mottled pattern of tan mixed with two shades of green; this was chosen alongside a black underbelly and tail fin, designed to nullify the threat of North Vietnam's optically guided anti-aircraft guns (which were a major defense factor). Meanwhile, the B-52Fs based in Guam received a temporary coat of black paint over their white, nuclear-blast-reflective belly paint. The black camouflage paint was only received by the B-52Ds.

When the B-52s entered the war, things were escalating quickly. As the aircraft were being delivered to various wings and squadrons, the North Vietnamese (with the help of communist China) were attempting to take over the entirety of Vietnam. The B-52 lined up to do the dirty work for the US was the B-52D. Andersen AFB operated two squadrons of B-52Fs until mid-1966, when the newly modified 'Big Belly' B-52Ds were rolled into the AFB's inventory. Even at an early date, it was clear that these bigger-capacity B-52s were needed; Andersen AFB's original 'F' models flew just 1 percent of the flights for Arc Light.

Operation Arc Light was implemented by SAC for seven and a half years; the arrival of the 'D' models helped it to mature as an operation, and, almost overnight, the B-52 became the dominant aircraft in the conflict.

The B-52s were deployed in a three-ship formation known as a 'cell.' The B-52F would strike out in front, with a B-52D positioned staggered to the right, 1 nm behind the leader. The third bomber would be positioned 2 nm back, to the left of the B-52D. The combined weapons loads of the aircraft were 250 500-lb and seventy-two 750-lb bombs, which could decimate all in their path when delivered to the 'kill box'—the area targeted for bombing. Arc Light conventional weapons were delivered in two ways: via the radar-synchronous bomb run, or via the ground-directed Operation Combat Skyspot, which was introduced in 1966.

Combat Skyspot

On 1 July 1966, the 3rd Air Division got the chance to put six B-52s on a ten-hour alert as a 'Quick Reaction Force', which would respond to a strike request from the field commanders. This was much better than the twenty-four-hour alert available previously. Skyspot also allowed mission control to divert the aircraft to targets that appeared while the bombers were in the air.

The heart of the Skyspot bombing system was the MSQ-77. This new system was made available to Tactical Air Command (TAC) for use in both fighter and bomber attacks. In early 1968, the US Military Assistance Command in Vietnam (also known as MACV) utilized Arc Light to give it flexibility in dealing with fast-moving combat situations. Combat Skyspot was refined to become 'Bugle Note'; this involved B-52 cells arriving at a pre-briefed initial point, as before, but then being diverted by the MSQ controller to a target of opportunity.

Another advantage to Skyspot was bomb-damage-assessment (BDA) comparisons between radar, synchronous radar, and MSA or Bugle Note, showing the accuracy of the strikes. By early 1967, Skyspot and the B-52D were veteran components of the Vietnam War.

The Pratt and Whitney J-57 engines were crucial to the B-52's success in the war. The water-injection capability gave the aircraft the ability to take off easily while at its maximum gross weight. The sweltering heat of the tropical environment in Guam and the Pacific made it very difficult to get a 450,000-lb aircraft off a runway. Water injection was one method, but this was used in conjunction with cartridge starters and other means discussed earlier.

A B-52 crew's first mission was flown 'tail-end Charlie', the last position in a standard six-ship formation. The B-52's take-off was stunning, with eight Pratt and Whitney J-57s howling, the water-injected engines throwing clouds of thick black smoke out behind them; while this was amazing to witness, the pilot behind the bomber had difficulty seeing due to the smoke. If the method was used today, the Environmental Protection Agency would not be in love with it.

Arc Light I Goes Live

The first Arc Light B-52 mission was flown on 18 June 1965, with the last being flown on 15 August 1973; the operation spanned eight years, 125,000 sorties, and 10,000,000 bombs. The B-52 targets comprised South Vietnam (55 percent), Laos (27 percent), Cambodia (12 percent), and North Vietnam (6 percent). At Andersen AFB, Guam, 5,000 missions were carried out in Operation Arc Light in 1966. In the first full year of the operation, the rate doubled to 10,000 missions.

For Operation Arc Light's first mission, the 9th Bomb Squadron and the 7th Bomb Wing (alongside the 441st Bomb Squadron and the 20th Bomb Wing) were the headliners. Preparations were made at Andersen AFB, with weapon bays and racks reloaded and ammunition placed for the tail gunner. The air crews were busy getting updated. At Kadena AFB, Okinawa, twenty-four KC-135 tankers were ready to refuel the bombers on the outbound part of the mission. They all left on schedule, with the bombers and the tankers leaving within thirty minutes of each other. They flew at a high altitude for the six-hour flight to Vietnam.

All was going well until it was time for the bombers to meet up with their tankers. This part of the operation was called 'Parcel Post', and occurred over the Atlantic Ocean, west of the Philippines. The bombers arrived slightly early thanks to a heavy tailwind, and they began to work out the rendezvous with the tankers. There were ten cells of three aircraft, and one containing B-52Fs ('Green Cell') began to make a 360-degree turn to prepare for refueling. However, this maneuver threw one of the B-52Fs off-track and into the path of 'Blue Cell', causing them to run into 'Yellow Cell.' By this point, all the bombers were 40 miles off course; it was a nightmare. Two of the bombers collided, crashing into the sea, and causing the death of eight of the twelve-man crew. After this horrendous accident, SAC would change the refueling procedure.

The surviving B-52Fs were still over the Atlantic, but one suffered a failure in its hydraulic pump; it could not refuel, instead returning to Kadena. These losses meant a total of twenty-seven aircraft was left to go to the target. Crossing into the target area at approximately 6.30 p.m., the first of the bombers began unloading everything they had from an altitude of 22,000 feet. After they were finished, the group headed to Guam. Another bomber had to divert towards Clark AFB, in the Philippines, due to electrical problems.

The last of the pack of twenty-six B-52Fs landed back at Andersen AFB thirteen hours after their initial take-off. The first mission of Arc Light was over. The first raids were a qualified success, with up to thirty aircraft simultaneously dropping bombs on the target, but there were clear concerns with regards to the fatal refueling accident. Changes to the process were made by August—this included carrying out more frequent raids with fewer numbers of bombers, reducing the chance of a collision. Two new targets were chosen north of Saigon, with two others in the south and a fifth south-east of Da Nang. With the newly designated 'bomb-free zones', the B-52s could deal with local commanders much more easily.

Until this point, the only individual who could authorize Arc Light strikes was the US President, relaying the orders to the Joint Chiefs of Staff who would then, in turn, pass them to the commanders. This system took an inordinate amount of time and was the source of much aggravation. The local commanders and SAC were unhappy about being kept out of the loop when it came to the decision-making process. On 26 August 1965 the President finally relinquished the command, giving the final word on strikes to the Joint Chiefs instead. From this point onwards, the strike-packages authorization changed, and the amount of missions carried out rose from 162 in August to 322 in September. For the remainder of the B-52F's operations in Vietnam, the bombers went on over 300 missions per month. In March 1966 the number of operations increased again with the addition of the Big Belly B-52s; this brought more bombing runs and heavier payloads.

U-Tapao Royal Thai Naval Air Base (located in the Gulf of Siam, 80 miles south of Bangkok) was opened to the B-52s, increasing SAC's ability to hit the growing lists of targets that were coming out of the Saigon-based MACV. In February 1968, after the capture of the USS *Pueblo* by the North Koreans, Kadena AFB in Okinawa was added to the active bases for the operation. This was the third and final of the Southeast Asian B-52 bases.

The Arc Light flying routine had been built around a format of special, regularly scheduled daily launches for missions. These were made up of two to three-ship cells that set off ten minutes apart, with a total of six aircraft in a wave; this was the optimum number of B-52s for a ground-support strike. A typical day at Andersen saw four launches, spaced six hours apart. They were officially called 'Red' and 'Blue' (for morning and evening raids respectively), but to the B-52 crews that were carrying out the missions, the ones in the morning were known as 'Breakfast Club', as they took place at 7 a.m. The ones at night (at 'zero dark thirty') were known as the 'Graveyard Shift.'

Arc Light and Air Bases

The majority of aircraft that went into Vietnam and Arclight came from Barksdale AFB, Louisiana, and Mather AFB, California. The aircraft of choice at the beginning of the war was the B-52F, and these aircraft came from the 20th Bomb Squadron (2nd Bomb Wing, Barksdale AFB) and the 441st Bomb

Squad (320th Bomb Wing, Mather AFB). All the B-52Fs were dispatched to Andersen AFB, Guam, as of 6 February 1963, having been subjected to South Bay modifications just a few months before their deployment. By June 1965, Robert McNamara requested forty-six more B-52Fs to be brought up to a similar configuration; the request was approved, but McNamara gave SAC a deadline that was only one month away. The Sun Bath upgrades were completed on time thanks to the Oklahoma City Air Materiel Center, and the first of the newly modified aircraft were operating out of Andersen just a few weeks after the orders had been given.

Once the B-52Fs reached Andersen, they had little to do other than wait for the politicians and military commanders to decide how they wanted to use the bombers. This took four months. One early proposal from the Joint Chiefs of Staff came after the loss of a US aircraft and crew to an enemy strike, and it involved using the bombers to hit all the relevant targets in the north of the country. The politicians disagreed with this suggestion, and this is an example of their poor handling of the war in Vietnam; if they had decided to use the B-52 and her crews to their full capacity and as soon as possible, things could have turned out very differently. Instead, the US found itself more deeply entrenched in a war the country did not fully understand.

For four months in 1965, Operation Arc Light was the only thing that the 7th Bomb Wing thought about. From December that year, two squadrons went home to Barksdale, with their places being filled by the 736th Bomb Squadron and the 454th Bomb Wing (Columbus AFB, Mississippi). With the arrival of these two units, Arc Light waves were identified by their cell call signs, which were always a color—'Red', 'Blue', 'Purple', 'Grape', 'Copper', or 'Gold.' These labels were permanent and so fixed in the crews' minds that the men only had to hear their color to know the details of what was to come. The missions from Andersen were stressful and tiring; they always involved a refueling stop, and took between twelve and thirteen hours for the round trip. Meanwhile crews operating out of Kadena AFB, Okinawa, did not need a tanker crew or a refueling stop, and their flights were 'only' eight to nine hours. U-Tapao Thai Naval Air Base averaged a five-hour flight, but this had a drawback—crews were scheduled to fly every day. During a six-month tour of duty, the airmen could be sent to all three bases at least three to four times. The crews lived out of their duffle bags.

Andersen AFB—known among the aircrews and ground staff as 'The Rock'—was the least desirable base to be deployed to. The missions from there were long, and there was nothing much to do in the off hours. There was no privacy in the bunks, and meals were usually taken at an outside cafeteria known as 'The Rice Palace' or 'The Officer's Club.' The gunners and enlisted men were sometimes driven by bus to a place for a post-flight beer and a hot dog; at least there were sessions at 'Gilligan's Island', the separate quarters for non-commissioned officers (NCOs), where they all roomed and ate together.

The ranking of Kadena AFB versus U-Tapao depended on individual tastes. Missions were longer at Kadena, but the climate was better—as were the food and quarters. There were just two men per room, which was a lot easier on the nerves. There was also more opportunity for shopping and sightseeing in Okinawa.

U-Tapao was a forward operating station, and it was the least military-like base of the three. It was more relaxed than usual SAC surroundings, with the crews housed in temporary trailers of four men, with two pairs sharing a bathroom in the middle of the trailer. Anything went at U-Tapao as long as no one got hurt and everyone was sober and ready for the next day's mission.

The combination of the three Arc Light basses allowed the B-52 iron-bomb sorties to peak in 1968 and 1969, with a total of 20,000 missions taking place in each of these years. By 1970 the war decreased in intensity due to domestic unrest in the US and a loss of political support. The B-52 sorties accordingly decreased, with a spike not seen until the Linebacker program started in 1972.

By September 1970, strike requests from the Army and the Marines dropped heavily at both Andersen and Kadena; Arc Light could have been shut down due to lack of work. The entire operation was consolidated at U-Tapao, which had always been a more efficient facility than the other two anyway—besides, the flight time to any potential Southeast Asian target was just two and a half hours. The bomber force could also be called back quickly, without adversely affecting their productivity. The political problems associated with Kadena were eased with the cessation of the base's involvement, and Andersen AFB no longer had to deal with the air-refueling requirement. A relatively compact force of forty-five to fifty U-Tapao-based B-52Ds were able effectively able to handle all of the MACV's air-support requests in 1971. Arc Light missions continued to be operated solely out of Thailand until early 1972, when North Vietnam launched another massive invasion of South Vietnam; at this point, Andersen AFB had to be reopened.

The B-52s found themselves in a large battle for the first time in October 1965. They gave direct support to the cavalry division at La Drang; the mission also involved the use of the Huey helicopter. In December, Arc Light lent a hand to the 3rd Marine Division during Operation Harvest Moon in the Que Son Valley. This was a saturation-bombing run—a wide-area, blunt-instrument attack. It was felt that by dropping large amounts of bombs or 'aerial artillery', the B-52s would terrorize the Viet Cong and drive them back into their jungle lairs, hopefully cowered into a complete surrender. However, the Viet Cong had no plans to give up that easily.

The North Vietnamese were becoming increasingly determined to attain enough material to fight on indefinitely. This meant much of the B-52 force had to be shifted to cover the ever-increasing enemy infiltration routes, which ran north and south along the infamous Ho Chi Minh Trail. The trail began in the western mountain range of North Vietnam—just south of Vinh—and worked its way down along the border separating Laos, Cambodia, and Vietnam. It ended up in the notorious 'Parrot's Beak', just above Saigon. This trail remained the backbone of North Vietnam's logistical framework throughout the entirety of Southeast Asia

In the summer of 1965, the Plain of Jars incident occurred. According to the peace accords signed by the US and her allies, Laos began an intelligence war that meant all foreign fighters had to leave the country. President Lyndon Johnson sent thousands of ground troops to Vietnam; meanwhile, the war in Laos was being run by thirty CIA officers backed up by military supplies that were being flown in by Air America—civilian pilots working for the CIA. CIA officers armed the local tribes, turning them into guerilla fighters and putting them on the edge of the Ho Chi Minh trail. The USAF also began turning the jungles of Laos into a wasteland, thanks to the B-52s that went to North Vietnam and destroyed targets in the area. It is alleged that the bombing destroyed civilian targets, but there will always be collateral damage in war. The villages and civilians that were hit were under fire because the Viet Cong had chosen to hide there, or they were being hid there by the villagers themselves; these were not the vicious attacks that the press made them out to be. The crews of the B-52s did not intentionally destroy villages and people for no reason; regardless, the US press gave them a hard time.

1967 saw more Viet Cong activity across the entire area. Arc Light began mounting increasing numbers of sorties as the days went on; they were particularly focused on a hot spot named the 'Iron Triangle.' This was in the general area of 'Parrot's Beak', and it would form the center of an intensive new campaign called Operation Cedar Falls. Here, the B-52s' job was to emphatically destroy any enemy asset they could find. The bombers were simultaneously carrying out raids on the Ho Chi Minh Trail. The Mugia Pass—on the border of Laos and North Vietnam—was a funnel point that left the enemy exposed to attack, and the Q-48BNS radar always honed in on this area. By the end of 1967, the Arc Light trips to the north—Mugia Ban, the Karai Pass, Ban Laboy Ford, and other mountain locations—were becoming routine, as air refueling above the Philippines continued.

Operation Arc Light finished in August 1973. Over the course of the operation, the B-52 crews flew 125,000 sorties, dropping 3.5 million tons of bombs and leveling the playing field for the Army ground troops. One half of the Arc Light missions were flown over South Vietnam, with the rest of the raids located in Cambodia, Laos, and North Vietnam.

Operation Barrel Roll and Steel Tiger

Operation Barrel Roll and Steel Tiger took place between 1964 and 1973, and was undertaken in support of the Royal Lao Government. The United States wanted to keep the operation top secret because Laos was the slim corridor between North and South Vietnam; the idea was to stop the flow of supplies into North Vietnam, with the strikes concentrating around the Ho Chi Minh Trail. Barrel Roll was also carried out clandestinely because the United States did not want to violate the 1962 Geneva Convention, which recognized Laos as a neutral state.

South Vietnam remained the main part of the US plan in Southeast Asia. The US government was fearful that if the news of their involvement in Laos was leaked, the public relations consequences at home could be disastrous; the American public's attitude towards the war was already deteriorating.

The US carried out two sorties per week in Laos, actually failing to do anything to stop the NVA's progression through the country. The operation was halted in 1973.

The Tet Offensive

January 1968 saw a turning point in the war; this became known as the Tet Offensive. The Viet Cong and the North Vietnamese Army decided to undertake a surprise attack against all the main cities in South Vietnam, from Saigon, in the south, to Hue, in the north. The NVA had certain prime objectives in mind during this offensive: firstly, Hanoi wanted to encourage a popular uprising in South Vietnam; secondly, they wanted to press for the collapse of the South Vietnamese Army; and thirdly, Hanoi and the NVA wanted to dramatically decrease support for the war in the United States.

The first two goals failed. North Vietnam got hit hard, although the three months of hard, bitter fighting cost the allied armies. Five thousand US and South Vietnamese troops were killed, with 16,000 wounded, but the enemy forces were forced to withdraw from South Vietnam, with 16,000 of their own men killed or captured.

Hanoi's third goal, however, was partially achieved. The combination of long casualty lists, occasionally ill-informed and misleading newspaper reports, and live colour-television footage of the conflict gave those in the United States the impression that the battle had already been lost. These factors cost the US the necessary morale and will to continue the fight. There was intense domestic anger on 31 March 1968. President Lyndon Johnson made two major announcements; firstly, he extended an olive branch to North Vietnam by ordering a halt to bombing along the twentieth parallel in and around Hanoi, Haiphong Harbor, and Red Valley. He then revealed that he had himself become a casualty of the war, announcing that he would not run for another term in office: 'I shall not seek and I will not accept the nomination of my party for another term as President.' He had reached the conclusion that the war in Vietnam could no longer be conducted in a conventional manner, nor was it possible to decide the outcome solely through the use of arms.

Arc Light veterans were worried about the close-air-support bombing sorties (known as 'Golf Missions') by the 8th Air Force. These would involve bombers flying in to help the Marines at Fire Base Khe Sanh. The B-52 raids at Khe Sanh were carried out at high altitude, unloading unpredictable weapons within a mile or so of the US troops. To a B-52 navigator and bombardier, 1,000 meters (3,200 feet) was almost a distortion on a radar screen. Regardless, after a few days of Golf Missions it was a relief for the beleaguered Marines to know that the B-52s were okay and inflicting high casualties on the enemy. This also gave them some room to receive supply drops. However, the enemy came back in a unique way—they tried to get as close to the Marines as possible, trying to use them as a makeshift human shield against the B-52 bomb drops.

During the Khe Sanh Siege, the B-52s flew over 2,500 sorties in support, dropping over 60,000 tons of bombs against the North Vietnamese. The crews reported over 1,400 secondary explosions, which meant that they were blowing up the North Vietnamese munitions with their bombs.

Propaganda

After the Tet Offensive, the North Vietnamese and the Viet Cong were content with their large propaganda victory and settled back into a 'static' war. By 1969 the war was almost stagnant. However, there was something big happening at all three of the Arc Light bases by 28 February; sixty B-52Ds with varying bomb loads were launched against freshly grouped enemy formations. Over a four-hour period on the night of 28 February to 1 March, the B-52s smashed a 10-mile target box with an extreme northern edge very close to Cambodia. Heading back to Guam in the dark early morning hours, the crews could see the secondary explosions and fires burning beneath them.

On 17 March 1969, just before briefings were to resume on Operation Arc Light, the theater was cleared of everyone apart from the commanding officers, two or three of the key staffers, and basic crews. Everyone else—wing staff, weathermen, intelligence officers, maintenance officers, chaplains, and extra crew—were ordered outside, after which the room was sealed by guards. The commanders took to the podium and announced that a total of sixty bombers would strike the 'Fish Hook' area, but that this time they would be dropping bombs inside Cambodia on a target called 'Base Area 3.' This was the combined NVA and Viet Cong nerve centre, known as the enemy's COSVIN Headquarter for South Vietnam. The navigators were not to chart any position that might show the B-52s on the wrong side of the Vietnam-Cambodia border, and bombardiers were to ensure that their BDA paperwork indicated that the weapons were dropped on the Vietnamese side. The justification was that although Cambodia was nominally a neutral nation, it was clear that the NVA ran the part of Cambodia bordering the 'Parrot's Beak' and 'Fish Hook' areas. Despite this justification, the decision to bomb inside Cambodia could be seen as an illegal act of war.

The B-52s hit the strip hard, reporting extensive damage to an enemy ammunition dump. Seventy B-52s were involved in the raid, and they were the only aircraft suitable for this mission. More heavy strikes followed in April, after which the 'clandestine' Cambodia strikes settled into a still-secret but now routine campaign. In April 1970, the US and ARVN (the Army of the Republic of Vietnam) carried out a ground operation that went into Cambodia to clean up the infested border area. At this point, air strikes on Cambodia were acknowledged openly. In 1970, the new US President, Richard Milhous Nixon, ordered a highly controversial surface 'sortie' at around the same time as withdrawing some 150,00 troops. The idea was to invade Cambodia while the withdrawal of troops from South Vietnam was underway, seeking to protect the flank of the US forces. US citizens were not too happy about the plan, and there was still significant discontent about the results of the Vietnam War so far. For the public, anything Nixon did (short of completely pulling out and bringing everyone home) would not be enough.

In the early 1970s North Vietnam brought in fresh manpower through northern Laos. The USAF decided that it was time to bring in the big guns again—the B-52s. On 17 February the bombers were used to hit targets in northern Laos; meanwhile the Laotian troops stopped the advance of the North Vietnamese, but a stalemate ensued and lasted for the rest of the year.

The USS *Pueblo*

The USS *Pueblo*, an Ager-2 intelligence ship in international waters, was seized by the North Koreans on 23 January 1968. SAC decided that it was necessary to build up an aircraft force until the North Korean motives became clear. On 25 January 1968, with the help of the CIA and the CIA black project known as 'Oxcart', CIA pilot Jack Weeks made a clandestine flight over North Korea in the A-12 Blackbird. He found the USS *Pueblo* frozen over in Wonson harbor.

The ship's crew was taken into custody by the North Koreans and subjected to eighteen months of hellish torture.

Weeks determined that the North Koreans were not building up troops or moving towards any kind of aggressive movement against South Korea, but SAC still felt that their bomber load should be increased. As such, Operation Port Bow was put into effect. This meant that twenty-six B-52Ds and ten KC-135A tankers were loaded into the mission. Eleven of the bombers were added to Andersen AFB in Guam, while the rest were sent to Kadena AFB in Okinawa, attached to the 4252nd Strategic Wing. Operation Port Bow took place from 3–7 February 1968, bringing the number of B-52Ds in the Pacific up to 105—way more than the seventy-nine that were initially called for. Despite this operation, there was little that could be done to help the crew of the USS *Pueblo*; it was some eighteen months before they were released. In the meantime, General Westmoreland decided that the extra bombers should be used in Operation Arc Light. Washington agreed, and on 11 February the extra B-52s were approved for this use, bringing the number of B-52 missions in Vietnam up to 1,800 per month from 18 February onwards.

Linebacker

In early 1971, the allied forces attacked the North Vietnamese troops inside Laos in an attempt to retake the ground from the enemy and validate Nixon's policy. This extensive action was designated 'Operation Lam Son 719.' The objective was to put a chokehold on the Ho Chi Minh Trail and therefore stop the line of supply to the NVA. The Arc Light force was quickly reorganized to help with the assault. The reinforced program was called 'Bullet Shot', and included the reopening of Andersen AFB in Guam and sending every available B-52D back to Asia. Several squads of B-52Gs were also sent; these were the first non-'D' models used since 1966. By the late spring of 1972, over 200 B-52Ds and B-52Gs were working out of Andersen and U-Tapao. SAC gave the movement the name 'Operation Linebacker.'

Nixon suspended peace talks on 8 May and ordered the start of the new US campaign. Operation Linebacker meant a renewed bombing effort against North Vietnam, alongside the aerial mining of harbors and local rivers. After suffering the assault, North Vietnam was ready to resume peace talks in October; Nixon called off the campaign once again, but the North Vietnamese baulked at the ceasefire proviso. Nixon pushed forward again, ordering strikes against Hanoi and Haiphong. This would lead to Operation Linebacker II, which represented the heaviest bombing of the entire Vietnam War.

Linebacker II

This operation began on 18 December 1972, and the main objective was to force the North Vietnamese back to the negotiating table to agree a ceasefire. Both Air Force and Navy tactical aircraft were part of this twenty-four-hour-a-day bombardment of the prime targets in North Vietnam. The B-52s did their magic under the cover of night, rocking Hanoi and Haiphong with their considerable bomb loads. The F-111s and Navy aircraft aided the B-52s' efforts by carrying out suppression strikes on enemy airfields and surface-to-air missile sites. Daylight operations were carried out by Navy A-7 Corsairs and F-4 Phantoms, who bombed visually or by using long-range navigation systems (LORAN). There was also plenty of escort aircraft like the USAF's EB-66s and the Navy's EA-6s, which threw out jamming signals to interrupt the North Vietnamese radar control defense. SAC also used the KC-135 tankers to support in-flight refueling of their aircraft.

The Linebacker II B-52 missions are the best-known of the Vietnam War. While the North Vietnamese stalled the peace talks, the ninety-nine B-52Gs and fifty-three B-52Ds at Guam and the fifty-four B-52Ds at U-Tapao started to form a very dark cloud over Hanoi and Haiphong. Linebacker II ran from 18–29 December 1972.

The B-52s used the three-ship 'cell' formation through the narrow slip into North Vietnam. This formation had to be used to prevent the aircraft from colliding in midair, with the raids occurring in the middle of the pitch-black night. The famous Wild Weasels—which consisted of F-105G Thunderchiefs from the 561 TAC Fighter Squadron and the F-4C—were indispensable to the operation's success, getting rid of 200 SA-2 SAM-launcher sites that had been set up by the North Vietnamese. The F-4 Phantoms were dropping chaff to disrupt radar and help the B-52's on-board radar-jamming units. This allowed the bombers to make sharp turns away from the target after blasting them with bombs. However, this plan wasn't flawless; the winds sometimes ended up blowing the chaff away, forcing the B-52 jamming units to point the wrong way. Besides, since the B-52s flew the same routes every mission, the surprise factor was short-lived.

The 17th Air Division Commander, Brigadier General Glenn Sullivan, called his bosses in Washington to request a change of tactics and help the bombers regain their surprise element. Aside from the loss of four more B-52s, the damage to the bombers almost stopped. Fifteen thousand tons of bombs were dumped on many urgent targets, forcing the North Vietnamese back to the negotiating table. It had been a complicated operation, requiring much in the way of manpower and machines. It was eleven days of losses, near misses, and exhausting work for all involved; in the end, however, it was worth every drop of sweat.

Linebacker II Day One: 18 December 1972

The pilots learned cell-coordination communication procedures that would be followed if one aircraft in the cell got shot down or damaged. The radar operator or navigator and bombardier were busy with radar predictions, aiming points for targets, and taking vertical photos of the targeted area. If they were not 100 percent sure of the aiming point, the radar operators were told not to drop the bomb, but to bring it back instead.

On the first day, the electric warfare officers (EWOs) and the rest of the crews filled up the briefing room, waiting until it was quiet and General James McCarthy could begin speaking to Wave I. He informed them that the target for that night was to be Hanoi, and he was met by dead silence. Once this was over, the crews broke up for their own special briefings. EWO officers were given update information about the position of SAM sites, early warning radar, ground-control intercept radars, and heat-seeking missiles and other enemy tricks. The tail gunners were preparing for their duty, which was to deal with the threats from enemy fighters. In the B-52Ds, the gunner compartment was a tiny area to the rear of the aircraft. The gunner had optical radar and a radar sight for his .50-caliber guns. In the B-52Gs, however, the tail gunner was in the forward crew compartment, next to the EWOs; he had a radar gun sight, but no optics. The B-52Gs originally had a remote-controlled camera, but these had been removed by the time the aircraft arrived at Guam. Nevertheless, even if these had been included they would be no substitute for the eyes of a tail gunner.

The B-52D gunners could monitor other aircraft or missiles (such as SAMs) flying along the flight paths to the rear of the aircraft, and this was an advantage to the crew. The fear of SAMs and MiGs was ubiquitous amongst the crews, but some held the threat of the SAMs higher than the MiGs and *vice versa*. The best response to both threats was to ensure the B-52 formation remained tight; there was safety in numbers. To help with navigation, the leading aircraft in a cell would have a red light on top of the airframe that would flash, enabling the rest of the cell to home in on it. If MiGs were in the area, the light would be turned off.

The first B-52D, *Rose I*, was painted with a black belly. As the aircraft rolled to the runway, the pilot lined up with the white center line and throttled the eight engines to rev the big girl up for her take-off roll. As the water-injection system kicked in, huge billows of black smoke started to rise from the engines. Starting slowly, the B-52D soon began to pick up some speed. On these runs, the weight of the aircraft reached 450,000 lbs. Complicating matters, Andersen AFB had a 150-foot dip and rise that the aircraft had to overcome on take-off. As the lumbering *Rose I* began to pick up speed in earnest, she reached the point of no return—when the pilot would either pick the nose up or push down the throttles. All the crew could do was pray that the aircraft would be able to smell the skies. The flight commander pulled on the yoke, and *Rose I* slowly rotated off the runway and into the air. In total, twenty-six B-52Ds and B-52Gs followed *Rose I* in the first wave.

The rest of Wave I began their take-off rolls from U-Tapao Royal Thai Air Base as the rest of the bases were preparing their own sorties. Meanwhile, the USS *Chicago* (call sign 'Red Crown') waited out at sea, ready to help anyone who got into trouble off the coast of Haiphong.

Wave II were receiving their briefing, ready to get underway. However, news came that Wave I were reporting that one of their aircraft had received just 196,000 lbs of fuel during a refueling when they should have received 216,000 lbs. This B-52 was 20,000 lbs short of fuel, and this would only just get it to Guam if it was lucky. At this point, the mission should technically have been terminated. The KC-135 tankers already had appointments covering the other TAC aircraft such as F-4s, EB-66s, and F-105s, and the only other tankers were those at Kadena AFB, Okinawa. This meant that refuels would now have to take place close to Kadena, and that meant a fourteen-hour bomber mission would now become an eighteen-hour mission. Despite this, the commanders gave the order to go ahead.

The flight plan showed much heavier winds than were initially anticipated; this would not affect the B-52Gs so much because they could carry more fuel and had better engines than the B-52Ds. The 376th Air Refueling Wing at Kadena was told by the command of the 8th Air Force to modify their schedules in order to make sure that there were enough tankers in the area for post-strike refueling if needed. This was a big change to the 376th Wing's mission; nevertheless, their commander, Colonel Dudley G. Kavanagh, ensured that they reached all the goals that were set for them. Throughout the eleven days of Linebacker II, not one mission was lost due to a lack of refueling. Tanker crews suffered poor weather, last-minute changes, and mechanical issues, but they hung tough and completed their work.

Things improved as the waves rolled out. The Wave III presentation was very professional. Lt Col. George Allison, flew a twelve-hour mission near Quang Tri, South Vietnam, on day one. He recalled:

> We all knew something was up, there was no way to hide it. The previous stand down, during which only a few of us flew, and then the abrupt gearing up for action could only mean one thing. A list of flyers for the day as long as your arm, cell color designators many had never heard of before, a parking lot so full of crew buses that it looked like a staging area, hundreds of your contemporaries threading their way through the main door of the Arc Light center, plus a day of rumors made it all to clear. The whole force was set in

motion to do something big, and it didn't take a very shrewd person to figure out what.

By midnight, all the aircraft had taken off. The silence on the base was a stark contrast to all the B-52 engines spooling up. Many of the crews left behind were thinking about how many of their friends and fellow crewmembers would be coming back. Lt Col. Conner flew *Peach-2*, a B-52G. He recalled:

> Each squadron was given responsibility for one wave of each raid. The staff and I worked almost around the clock getting things ready for the first raid. The schedule was prepared, crews were notified, transportation ordered, flying equipment prepared, meals ordered and all this myriad of things that must be done to provide thirty-three crews and airplanes for a combat mission.

For each of the missions there was a senior officer and a mission commander, better known as the 'Airborne Mission Commander' or 'ABC.' There was a lead ABC and then a deputy ABC in the second wave. The ABC would not fly in a crew position, but would rather travel in the instructor pilot's seat as the seventh man in the crew. His responsibility was to concentrate on the mission's progress and scout any problems that might affect the wave.

Wave II was planned to leave at 7 p.m.—all the Linebacker II missions were flown at night. When the launch began, a fully loaded B-52 would launch around every ninety seconds. After take-off, as the aircraft started to level off, some of the crew tried to sleep while on the way to their target. However, there was little time for this before in-flight refueling. Once this was over, the crew knew they would be able to hear how the first wave was doing. It had been a tough time for Wave I; a SAM missile had taken out one of the B-52s, and two others were unaccounted for. One aircraft had also suffered serious damage. The North Vietnamese had launched some 200 SAMS at the wave, but at least there were no reports of MiGs in the air. The anti-aircraft guns continued to blaze away, below the B-52's flight level. The worst part for the crews was knowing that the NVA was waiting for them.

The air was peppered with SAMs when the second wave reached the target area, leaving white streaks across the night sky. Just before the bomb run was about to start, the crew went through a check of all the emergency gear, just in case they got hit. The next part was the toughest part of their flight—keeping the B-52 level, in their most exposed position, while dropping bombs. There was no chance of any evasive maneuvers.

The targets were solely military targets. Precision bombing was the center of the mission, and this is how the crews were instructed. Around halfway through the bombing run, the EWO started to call on the aircraft's interphone that SAMs were incoming. This was ignored, with the pilot keeping the plane in straight and level flight until the bombardier called 'Bombs away!' Only then could a turn be made, with the aircraft soaring out of the target area. For the crews, it must have felt like a trip to hell and back. The noise emanating from below was deafening as their bombs and other munitions exploded. The crews later said that they could smell the ozone in the air.

The first of the B-52s to go down was *Charcoal I*. Lt Col. Donald Rissi and his crew hailed from Blytheville AFB in Arkansas; they were supposed have to rotated out on 4 December, but their replacements had got snowed in at Loring AFB, Maine. No crew was allowed to leave rotation until their back-up crew was on the ground at their home base. By the time the crew from Loring finally got there, their predecessors were short two members. These teams were well-honed and used to each other, and it was hard to break in new guys. Sadly, Lt Col. Rissi lost his life on the first day of Linebacker II; his B-52 was hit by an SAM while over the Yen Vien railroad yards. The tail gunner, Sgt Walt Ferguson, also died, while 1st Lt Bob Thomas was missing in action. The radar navigator, Maj. Dick Johnson, made international headlines when he was pictured being paraded around in his underwear by the Viet Cong, on his way to the infamous 'Hanoi Hilton' prison camp. Johnson was not alone, as Capt. Bob Certain and EWO Capt. Dick Simpson were also taken to the facility.

Despite the tragic loss, the day also saw the first claim of an enemy MiG. Staff Sgt Sam Brown became the first tail gunner to have that distinction.

Linebacker II Day Two

The early results of the operation were encouraging. Day two followed much of the same procedure as day one, with the last of the cells from the previous day landing as the new ones were on their way out. With no more than four missions carried out, pilots were already effectively rocking downtown Hanoi.

Some changes did need to be made; the routes in and out of the country needed to be altered to prevent them becoming predictable to the enemy. After receiving the debrief comments from Waves I and II, Colonel McCarthy was convinced that increased ECM protection would be the best way to reduce losses. McCarthy gave the 43rd Strategic Wing crews an order that was not well-received—he threatened to court-martial any commander who 'knowingly disrupted cell integrity to evade SAMs.' Many of the crews disliked this because they felt they had the ability to evade these missiles without compromising the mission. The previous day's pilots briefed the ABC and the aircraft commanders. Since the MiGs were not an issue and the weather was cloudy again, the red beacons on the cell leader could be seen, and this would help keep everyone in formation.

The target for the first wave of day two was the Kinh Ng railroad and the storage areas on the outside of Hanoi. The strike force consisted of twelve B-52Ds and nine B-52Gs from Andersen AFB. The B-52Ds were loaded with forty-two 750-lb Mk 117 bombs internally and twenty-four 500-lb Mk 82 bombs on pylons under the wings. The B-52Gs carried a smaller internal load of twenty-seven Mk 117s. Because the B-52Gs were unmodified, the crews only carried that much in the way of armament when the mission did not involve penetration. The aircraft also suffered from release-system malfunctions, meaning that there were several occasions where a B-52G was unable to release a bomb.

The launch of the first wave went well, with only a couple of burps in the strike force's aircraft. Even with the poor visibility, in-air refueling went off as planned. To ensure that there was a safe amount of distance between the cells when refueling, the aircraft used a series of timing triangles. This gave the best chance of getting the maximum amount of bombs dropped on the target over the minimum amount of time. Straight after the maneuver, the second aircraft in the lead cell reported the loss of an engine, and the crew stated that they were having trouble holding speed and altitude due to the heaviness of the aircraft; despite this, the orders were given to 'press on.' Even the loss of an engine was not a good enough reason to abort a mission. It was thought that by the time the pilot had burned enough fuel (lightening his load), he would be able to catch up with the rest of the cell; however, in the meantime, the cell's ECM support would drop by one third. The only other option would be to increase the aircraft's power beyond Wave I settings, which would have caused the aircraft to burn excess fuel, depleting its reserves and forcing it to recover at U-Tapao or receive post-strike refueling.

On reaching the target area, the EWO reported a SAM lock-on. They were southwest of Hanoi. The tail gunner reported that two SAMs had been launched against the aircraft; a Shrike anti-radiation missile was deployed by the friendly TAC air support to counter against the incoming hostile missiles.

The USS *Chicago* also reported SAM launches and anti-aircraft fire. Three SAMs exploded at the same altitude as the bombers, but they detonated too far away to make a difference. Two others passed the aircraft, exploding above them. One hundred and twenty seconds after releasing the bombs, the SAMs were backed up by heavy AA fire that narrowly missed the bombers. The attack focused on the 'White' cell.

A cell further back in the wave reported MiGs, requesting support from TAC. One minute before dropping their bombs, the EWO's radar screen was peppered with SAM lock-ons. Ten seconds before bombs away, the EWO also noticed Shrike missiles being fired low and forward of the B-52's nose. Five seconds later, the SAMs were no longer being fired. The bomb bay doors were already open, and bombs began to fall like lead snowflakes, and soon afterwards they impacted at the SAM sites.

The release of 22 tons of ordnance made the B-52s shake slightly. The aircraft wanted to head up after the loss of weight, and it took a lot for the pilots to keep them under control. The bomb doors closed and the aircraft went into a steep right turn. A SAM exploded nearby. Only small maneuvers were permitted as the aircraft turned one-by-one. Soon SAMs were again being launched, seeking their prey. Another Shrike missile was launched, and the threat disappeared; the Shrikes had come from F-105 Wild Weasels from the 388th TAC, who were really earning their pay that night. Colonel McCarthy made a note to thank Colonel Mele Vojvodich for the services rendered. Both colonels served together in Korat, Thailand; Vojvodich later went on to become a pilot for the CIA's Oxcart program.

Linebacker II Day Three

The last B-52G cell, 'Cinnamon', returned to Andersen AFB early in the afternoon on 20 December. The 'Quilt' cell was just getting ready to leave. The Cinnamon crews were exhausted, but they stopped to watch as Quilt started its roll. They did not know if any of the crewmembers would come back or if they would become a resident of the 'Hanoi Hilton', but they still waited to see them off.

Things were running late. The Order of Battle for the Viet Cong (the enemy's unit formation) had changed, and this necessitated changes in targets. There was much discussion among crews about how they were handling the post-target turn (PTT), which was undertaken after they had dropped their bomb loads. There was significant concern, but this had to go through the usual bureaucracy before anything could be approved—first to SAC HQ in Nebraska, then to the 8th Air Force, and then to Lt Gen. Glenn Martin, who was the Vice Commander of SAC. In his own words:

> We in SAC perceived early in November that the mini-changes in timing and in aircraft course, speed, and altitude could make the difference between a hit and a miss in the daily battle between the B-52s and the Communist SAMs. The same considerations applied to the joint operations, which included not only coordinated strike operations by the 7th Air Force and the 7th Fleet, but diversionary, ECM electronic and chaff dropping, and MIGCAP operations as well. As a consequence, the operational planning and tactical analysis were

incitingly complex, with little time available in the twenty-four-hour kaleidoscope to take advantage of all cross feed and potential improvements … Nor was that all. We also learned early that the B-52 ECM system needed immediate adjustment for better protection against the enemy SAM guidance radar.

This testing had the result of holding the mission back. The new maneuvers were pre-target evasive tactics, adding to the EWO's workload as they had to change their procedures for jamming SAM SA-2 systems. Despite this, day three's results were better than day two's.

The biggest problem for the supervisors was that they could not get the incoming crews to rest; they refused because they knew the operation was historic, and they wanted to be a part of it.

The word came down that Linebacker II was to be allocated 'indefinite status.' This meant that the push was on, and there was no relief in sight for anyone. This did not bother the crews at all, as they were ready for anything that was thrown at them. Day three saw the biggest push so far from the North Vietnamese defences against the B-52. It would be the worst day of Linebacker II, with the highest level of losses occurring over one day. Many of the cells had MiGs to contend with, while others had MiGs flying close by, attempting to force the B-52s to decrease their altitude and speed and make them a better target for the NVA SAM sites on the ground. Anti-aircraft fire and flak was brutal for the B-52 cells. Due to the strikes the night before, the SAM sites were running low on missiles, and this meant only around 220 were fired at the B-52s.

The NVA would let one cell of B-52s go by just to judge their progress; when the next cell came over, they would unleash miserable hell on them, especially when they were in straight and level flight, preparing to drop their bombs, and when they were undertaking their post-flight turn. The hectic nature of the day-three runs were no surprise. The Hanoi attacks were coming in from the northwest, and things were tighter than in the previous two days. The NVA was catching on.

Of the eleven cells flying in Wave I, nine aircraft went to the Yen Vien railyards, which were adjacent to the Ai Mo warehouse. The 'Quilt' cell had two ECM-degraded aircraft leading their attack, with *Quilt 3* being hit in its post-target turn. The aircraft suffered major damage, but it managed to make it back to Thailand before its crew (who hailed from Loring AFB, Maine) had to bail out. The B-52Ds—the 'Snow' and 'Grape' cells—made it through. They were followed the 'Orange' cell, in which *Orange 3* was hit by SAMs just seconds before releasing its bombs. The aircraft exploded, with four of its crewmembers (hailing from Westover AFB) being MIA. There were more casualties; two B-52Gs and one B-52D went down, and three of the nine cells suffered losses. The optimism present at the start of the day had been crushed, and the bad news traveled fast. At SAC headquarters in Nebraska, the Deputy Chief of Staff for Intelligence, Brigadier Gen. Harley N. Cordes, saw it all. He stated: 'The SAC staff virtually lived together throughout Linebacker II. No one slept much. Days and nights were spent together, selecting targets, developing tactics, explaining results.'

The darkest hours of the conflict were therefore felt just as much at SAC headquarters as they were in Guam and U-Tapao. In addition to the personal concerns of the SAC staff as to where the operation was heading, there was also much external pressure. General Meyer, the Commander in Chief of SAC, felt that many were worried that the USAF would fail to bring Hanoi to its knees. Many senior Air Force officers were concerned about unacceptable losses if the bombing continued, and that would undermine the air power doctrine. The Chairman of the Joint Chiefs of Staff, Admiral Moore, shared the concern, but he left the ultimate decision on how to move forward to General Meyer.

Halfway through day three more reports of losses came in, just as the next wave was setting up. General Meyer wanted a breakdown of everything going on, and a reassurance that the Air Force doctrine was being upheld. He knew what it was like to be alone at the top of the food chain. In his own words, Meyer wanted everybody to 'press on.' The losses, damages, and near misses with the B-52Gs were partially due to the fact that half of them were modified and given a more extensive ECM package than the other half. The unmodified B-52Gs were not protecting their cells or themselves very well; they were carrying the load of the SAM hits from Hanoi.

Six aircraft were recalled from Wave II, which came four hours after Wave II. Their loads would not affect the targets, so the rest of the wave went on without them. The wave was due to hit the Thai Nguyen thermal power plant for the second day in a row, with two cells bombing the Bac Giang transshipment point. There were no losses or damage to report.

Three of the four third-wave targets were in or around Hanoi. The wave consisted of modified and unmodified B-52Gs, and twelve were set to attack the Kinh No complex, which contained four internal targets. Minutes ahead of the B-52Gs, nine B-52Ds were hitting the Hanoi railroad repair shop at Gia Lam. *Straw 2*, the fifth aircraft to reach the target, was hit by a SAM during its post-target turn; the aircraft made it to Laos. All the crewmembers (except for the radar navigator) were picked up by the HH-53 Jolly Green Giant combat search-and-rescue helicopters of the 40th Aerospace Rescue and Recovery Squad. This was the first B-52D from Andersen to be lost.

Only eight minutes after the 'Straw' cell's attack, *Olive 1*, an unmodified B-52G, led a raid on a target at Kin No. She took a hit after releasing her bombs. Two cells back from the 'Olive' cell, *Tan-3*, another unmodified B-52G, lost her bombing and navigation radar. The tail gunner in the B-52G in front fixed the problem by using his own radar to send precise radar information to the aircraft in trouble. However, just after *Tan-1* and *Tan-2* reached their release point, a SAM exploded under *Tan-3*, and then the aircraft suffered a direct hit. It entered a steep dive, and the crew bailed out. Only one crewmember escaped, and he was taken as a prisoner of war.

Linebacker II Day Four

On 21 December, two tactical wing commanders and their executive officers and chaplains spent the morning meeting with the families of the missing crew members from Guam. It was not a good morning. Day three marked the end of the first bombing phase, and the plans for day four were in flux. The increase in losses—especially of the B-52Gs—was painful.

Andersen AFB enjoyed a reduction in missions on day four; they would also rest on the fifth and seventh days. The sortie rate was dropped to thirty per day, which U-Tapao could manage alone; this was possible because of U-Tapao's four-hour flight time from the targets. Even last-minute changes of plan were managed easily from there, and the decreased fuel weight allowed for a bigger bomb load.

Andersen AFB used thirty aircraft to support the war in South Vietnam. The new crews had a chance to get checked out on cell procedure, something the men had not worked with before. They would also go on a couple of practice missions before going to downtown Hanoi. Meanwhile, at U-Tapao, the seasoned crews had three new targets—Hanoi Storage (Bac Mai), Van Dien Storage Depot, and Quang Te Airport. It would be a hard night for two of the flights sent to Hanoi Storage.

The Guam teams were going back to cycling operations. Lieutenant General Johnson told the staff that the raids would continue indefinitely, and that all work schedules would ensure support for the new plans. This meant that the crews on Andersen would be fighting on two fronts. General Johnson remembered:

> … what bothers maintenance is change. If you're in a cyclic operation—meaning that a given commitment is spread over a 24 hour period—you can sustain this, and that's really the thing our maintenance manning is best suited for. However, if you go into a compression, meaning that you can launch and recover more or less at the same time every day, then you can stay in that compression. What causes maintenance problems is being in a cyclic operation and having to go into a compression then come out of a compression and into a cyclic and then back

to a compression. That's where you lose sorties; but if you can stay in one or the other, then you can continue it. The thing that helps maintenance [is] more or less to do the same thing every 24 hours whether it is cyclic or compressed.

During the afternoon the staff asked crews for ideas on how to improve tactics when (and if) the bombing in the north resumed from Guam. One crew had been shot down, and they were heading back to the US for rest and recuperation. A short layover at Andersen AFB provided a chance to debrief them. New tactics were developed from all the cross talk, and these were sent to the 8th Air Force and SAC headquarters for evaluation. SAC sent the information to the various bomber wings, and it was used at the Eglin Test Range in Florida to simulate attacks on SAM sites.

This analysis was crucial to the next step in Linebacker II. There was a critical need to change tactics and routes so that the enemy could not learn the pattern of attack. One of the new ideas concerned the use of the taillights on B-52s (which were used to hold the formations together); a new procedure was developed by the 307th Wing at U-Tapao, involving a B-52D gunner shining an Aldis lamp in the direction of the aircraft behind him. This gave the back-end pilot a way to stay in formation.

There was also the issue of identifying the color for each cell. To ensure that no two sounded the same, it was ensured that no two cell designations were phonetically similar. On 20 December, the deployment of the 'Green' and 'Cream' cells in the same wave had caused confusion.

General James R. Allen, who was the Assistant Deputy Chief of Staff for Operations in SAC, remembers formulating new ways to deal with the SAM threat:

> One aspect of the eleven-day effort which I thought had considerable significance involved the SAM storage sites ... It was on Day 3 that we realized that although the individual SAM sites seemed to have an inexhaustible supply of SAM missiles, current photography indicated no spare missiles at the firing sites. This implied centralized storage and distribution points, and based on the available road and bridge systems in the Hanoi-Haiphong area, one could almost predict the location of stager facilities.

Andersen AFB had been a hive of activity up to his point, but a certain amount of calm descended as the base began to return to its traditional Arc Light role—the support of South Vietnam. However, with the slowdown came an increased awareness of how the war was being reported back home. The press was having a field day reporting on the war, but they were getting it wrong. For the B-52 crews, the losses were tough enough to bear, but the press coverage and the anti-war sentiment on the college campuses of the United States were almost too much. These men were risking their lives over enemy territory every single night; they were heroes in the truest sense of the word, yet they were being demonized in their own hometowns.

A total of eleven B-52s were lost on day four; eight were brought down over Hanoi, while three made it to safety. A total of sixteen B-52s were involved, with six B-52Gs and one B-52D from Andersen, and four B-52Ds from U-Tapao. The B-52D from Andersen returned safely.

Linebacker II Day Five

Friday 22 December was a busy day for the crews. At Andersen AFB there was more brainstorming, but the suggestions coming in were often too much for the B-52s to handle. The crews were building their spirits back up in spite of the opposition in the US college campuses.

Twenty-eight sorties were flown out of Andersen, involving twenty-two B-52Gs and six B-52Ds. The B-52s were spread out over 5 miles of unlit ramps at the air base. The maintenance crews were thanked profusely for their unending support for the missions and their proficiency in keeping the massive B-52s up to speed.

Linebacker II Day Six

Christmas was closing in, and the holiday feeling was in the air despite the hot and humid conditions. This had the effect of bringing some brightness to the constant missions and waves.

On the night of the 23rd, twelve of Andersen's B-52Ds joined up with eighteen B-52s from U-Tapao. They were airborne four hours before the Christmas dinner dance at the base would start. The plan for the night was to hit the Land Dang railyards, some 45 miles north of Haiphong. Another of Andersen's six birds would be hitting SAM sites 30 miles north of the city; these targets were welcomed by the B-52 crews because the Viet Cong who manned the sites were renowned for their rather poor shooting skills. It would be a pleasure to take them out. The night's targets were interesting because they were close to the Chinese buffer zone, and the SAM sites were just north of Haiphong. The area was very narrow when approaching from the Gulf of Tonkin.

There was an issue with support forces; they would not be able to reach the rendezvous with the bombers in time to be in position for the agreed SAM suppression and MIGCAP. As this emerged, the bombers were reaching the final point from which they could be recalled. The support forces had heavily counted on keeping the SAM sites busy until late in the bomb drops, and the odds of success were much lower if the bombers went in alone. Nevertheless, the officers agreed that the mission should go on as planned. As it turned out, none of the thirty-six B-52Gs or the B-52D cell were lost. Due to the heavy strain on U-Tapao, the 43rd Strategic Wing sent in twenty-two B-52Ds to U-Tapao. This helped to replace the crews lost there.

Linebacker II Day Seven: 24 December

Christmas Eve had arrived. There would be no Linebacker II flights on this day or the 25th, although thirty Arc Light missions took place in the south. However, this did not mean the planning stopped; the commanders turned their attention to the raids on the 26th.

Linebacker II Day Eight: 26 December

It was back to business. All the crews at Andersen AFB would launch in one big block; they were briefed at the same time, but since no briefing room was large enough to hold everyone, the commanders split the force into units of B-52Ds and B-52Gs. Within two hours and twenty minutes, the last aircraft, *Opal 1*, took off from the base. The North Vietnamese had enjoyed a Christmas break of their own, with time to refill their SAM sites, tune up their radar, and have their SAM operators prepare for the next wave of B-52s.

Almost 1,400 miles from Guam, an incident occurred that could have meant the cancellation of the day's missions. At Kadena AFB, Okinawa, the KC-135 tankers were getting ready to take off and meet their bombers. However, a C-141 was inbound to Kadena for an emergency landing, and it could not be refused. The emergency kept the Kadena runway busy for twenty minutes, delaying the KC-135s' take-off. Waves I and III (B-52Ds) were in the middle of refueling when word was passed on that some of the tankers would be fifteen minutes late for the next wave. According to the book of Air Force Doctrine, the missions should have been ended right there. However, all the aircraft were needed, and they didn't have fifteen minutes to spare. Wave III would not be able to catch up. The commanders started looking for alternatives; if they canceled, all the time, money, and effort spent over the raid would have been for nothing.

The commanders decided to go for it, moving the refueling point closer and hoping that some time could be made up. If Wave III could not get into position by the time Wave I was crossing the seventeenth parallel and heading north, the mission would be aborted. The pressure was one. TAC fighters and other support forces would take off from Thailand with the tankers; it was a huge effort, with the Navy also represented. Against all the odds, the crews made it, and all their bombs were dispatched.

The problems were not over—at least not yet. There was a flock of strike and support aircraft that was supposed to be homing in on a 'mass effort' objective, with all the B-52s scheduled to be over the targets just short of their fifteen-minute window. The whole show was running fifteen minutes behind, but all the crews were focused. The waves coming from the south crossed into South Vietnam and started a very complex maneuver to get the bombers compressed to their cell formation. Fortunately, the weather held up and the aircraft got where they needed to be. The compression maneuver held—it worked! General McCarthy later recalled:

> As we headed north over the Gulf of Tonkin, I heard Tom LeBar call in that his wave was at the join up point on time and that the wave was compressed. They had done a hell of a fine job!

As the mission continued, however, a B-52D, *Ebony-2*, was hit. It exploded in midair. Four of the crews escaped and became POWs. Soon afterwards, *Ash 1* had been hit, and she was diving into the water. The pilot stated he was losing altitude and couldn't control the aircraft. The faithful US Navy USS *Chicago* was in the South China Sea, vectoring F-4 Phantoms to stay with the bomber until she was safe. SAMs flew around the bombers in the dark skies, and MiGs started to close in. Calls for fighter support went out. The USS *Chicago* was busy trying to get the F-4s to *Ash 1*, but another B-52 was under attack. When the F-4s turned up the MiGs broke away in fear; the MiGs had most likely been pacing the B-52s and relaying information to the SAM sites below. The last aircraft finally left the danger zone, and the calls came in that the cells were safe; *Cream 1* and *Cream 2* had both suffered radar damage from a SAM detonation, but both were going home to Andersen.

The crews of *Ash 1* and the USS *Chicago* were looking for friendly ships to pick up the crew of the stricken B-52. The aircraft was still in the air, however, and they decided to try and get to U-Tapao. Sadly, *Ash 1* crashed just beyond the runway after attempting to land at the base. The gunner and the co-pilot were the sole survivors, despite the pilot's valiant attempts to get home.

It had been one of the most successful days of Linebacker II. The day had seen 133 support sorties flown over North Vietnam and the Gulf of Tonkin, with the KC-135s having a glorious day with round-the-clock refueling. Ninety-five sorties were provided from Kadena, with 156 refuelings undertaken—a record. The SAC tankers from U-Tapao, Takhli, Clark AFB, and the Philippine Islands saw 607 refueling sorties for TAC air support. There were 194 KC-135 tankers in the theater—a huge effort to support these extensive operations. Maintenance crews delivered the KC-135s, and the KC-135 crews delivered the fuel; the exhausted B-52 crews thanked them both.

Day eight also brought a gift to those in the prisoner of war camps—especially the infamous 'Hanoi Hilton.' These men listened for the sounds of the B-52, taking joy in the knowledge that these big, beautiful birds terrified the Viet Cong, and that they were blowing the hell out of SAM sites and NVA targets.

Linebacker II Day Nine

The loss of *Ash 1* and *Ebony-2* showed that if one aircraft went out of the cell formation *en route* to the target, then the remaining two aircraft would have to move in with the cell ahead or behind to create a five-aircraft cell. The taillight signal used to keep the cells in position were perfected; both the post-target turn and the expanded-altitude separation between the waves and the cells within the waves were proving to be very effective tactics. The use of chaff was great, as many of the B-52 crews saw the SAM detonations when the missiles went into the chaff clouds. These new procedures were the result of suggestions from crews who had flown earlier missions.

Day nine's action was much the same as the previous day, except the raids were smaller and Haiphong was off the target list. The commanders were looking for new targets, with the crews getting superior results by hitting their targets head-on. The NVA could not keep up with the bomb damage inflicted by the B-52s.

On this night's route, sixty bombers (twenty-one B-52Gs and thirty-nine B-52Ds, including thirty from U-Tapao and Andersen) flew an additional thirty sorties. This amounted to six in South Vietnam and twenty-four in various parts of North Vietnam. The strike team for the north flew in six waves, hitting seven targets by using simultaneous times over target (TOT). The entire force dropped their loads in ten minutes instead of fifteen—the usual allotted time. The wave was split into three smaller streams, attacking separate targets and then reforming before the post-target turn; this was a new tactic. The aircraft going to the southeast followed an identical pattern except that they split into two teams from the initial point inbound.

One of the golden rules of employing strategic air power is to destroy enemy defenses first. The military and industrial targets can be focused on with little threat of loss to the attackers. On this night, however, one particular site proved to be difficult. It was just southwest of Hanoi, and it was called 'Killer Site VN-549.' It survived the assault, taking *Ash 2* out in the process. According to the crews from the 'Paint' cell, who were just behind, the 'Ash' cell's bombs had destroyed a SAM that had just been launched, and others were following peculiar trajectories. When leaving the area they had to pass Killer VN-549's shooters, who were very troublesome. One missile exploded near *Ash 2*, and every man inside was injured. Despite being hurt, the pilot flew the B-52 for forty more minutes, reaching Laos, before the crew bailed out. Thankfully, they were recovered safely. After *Ash 2* was hit, *Cobalt 1* was also struck by a SAM from another site; the aircraft was only seconds away from releasing its bombs over the Trung Quang railyards. There was only just enough time for the EWO to call out that they had been hit; the aircraft was in trouble, with damage to the forward wheel well and the right wing root. The crew bailed out. One became MIA, while another found his way to the 'Hanoi Hilton.' Meanwhile, 'Green' cell counted thirty-one SAMs fired against them. *Cobalt 2* was flying with the cell since *Cobalt 1* had been hit and was seen going down.

Andersen's crews undertook two sorties each, with some of them stretching to three; however, the rate at U-Tapao was five to six sorties per crew. This was just about the limit, considering it was usual in Guam to only have three Linebacker II operations over eight days. For their efforts, the 303 CAMW won the 1072 Dandelion Systems Weapons Systems Maintenance Award, the USAF's prestigious maintenance award. The wing was cited for providing superior performance by supplying safe and highly reliable aircraft in support of the mission in Southeast Asia.

Day nine had been smooth. The good weather had aided efforts in the refueling area, and the support aircraft were taking care of Vietnamese defenses and escorting the B-52s. The North Vietnamese had spent the Christmas period getting ready for the post-holiday attacks, but it was clear that the NVA was getting worse at aiming SAMs. They were making one last desperate attempt to defend Hanoi.

Linebacker II Day Ten

The plans for day ten called for sixty B-52s, including fifteen B-52Gs and B-52Ds from Andersen and thirty B-52Ds from U-Tapao to go out on a run. There were six waves for five targets. Four waves were sent to four targets in the Hanoi area, while two others headed to the Lang Dong railyards. These railyards were the main point on the supply routes from China, and they received a lot of attention during the last two days of Linebacker II. There were four targets around Hanoi, with three of them being SAM sites; the B-52s had to go after them because they were still active. Heavy chaff was thrown over Hanoi, but none was put over the Lang Dang railyards.

Another new tactic was tried out; one wave attacked Lang Dang while another was inbound. In this way, the last aircraft of the first wave would release its bombs ten minutes before the first aircraft of the following wave. General McCarthy recalled:

> Although many of the proposed tactics looked relatively simple on paper, they were in actuality very complex when you remember that the pilots were manhandling a 400,000-lb airplane around the sky. Unlike a performance fighter or the new B-52G and 'H' models, the B-52D does not have powered controls. It takes a lot of old-fashioned muscle power to fly precision formation or maneuvers with that 'D' model. Some of the 'D' crews at the time were 'G' and 'H' model crews who had only experience gained by the two-week 'D' difference course. Performance characteristics were so pronounced that some 'H' model pilots might take as much as two months of flying the 'D' before they felt comfortable in the aircraft. Flying the B-52D has been compared to driving an eighteen-wheeler truck without power steering, air brakes, or automatic transmission in downtown Washington at rush hour.

Andersen AFB brought the day-ten efforts up by sending twenty-eight aircraft to hit targets in southern North Vietnam, northern South Vietnam, Laos, and Cambodia. There were three major points being made here. Firstly, North Vietnam was not experiencing anywhere near the beating it might have. Secondly, the target damage levels had been met so effectively that strategic targets were now scarce. Thirdly, the US was attempting to give clear proof that bomber forces could meet a dual commitment of theater-support interdiction bombing and northern strategic bombardment—and for an indefinite period. The latter point turned out to be false.

Linebacker II Day Eleven

Over the course of the offensive, the B-52s dropped some 58,000 tons of bombs, equaling out to 18,000 tons of destruction. Over 15,000 tons hit the North Vietnamese heartland, while the rest were theater targets. On the final day of the operation, *Wine-3* suffered from an inoperative refueling system and went back to Andersen. The other two aircraft in the 'Wine' cell joined the 'Walnut' cell, which was just ahead of them; they hit Phuc Yen as a five-ship cell. This was a chance to perform the SAM evasive maneuver, and it went off perfectly. There were no aircraft lost or damaged, and this became the second night in a row with nothing to report. Some SAMs were fired, but they were erratic. One MiG pilot made a halfhearted attempt to start something with 'Aqua' cell, but nothing came of it.

The End of Linebacker II

Linebacker II started on 18 December 1972 and ended eleven days later, on 29 December. Those eleven days were an acrimonious hell for both sides, and the intensity of the operation was a new magnitude in the Vietnam War.

Via bomb-damage assessment (BDA), we can say that the B-52s did their job well, carrying and dropping tons of munitions. The BDA showed that 1,600 military buildings were destroyed or badly damaged, 500 railways were interrupted, 372 pieces of moving equipment were destroyed, and 3 million gallons of precious fuel were destroyed (a quarter of North Vietnam's reserve stock). Airfields and runways were turned into pockmarked, useless gopher holes. Eighty percent of the North Vietnamese electrical-power production was also destroyed. There were other specialized damages, including the disruption of open storage stockpiles and missile launchers.

There was no way to measure the collateral damage in the face of what Linebacker II accomplished. The important part was that traveling via railroad, land, or ship was so disrupted that it would take the North Vietnamese a long time to pick up the pieces. Their communications were in disarray, and this combination of circumstances forced the enemy back to the peace table in Paris, France. While Haiphong harbor was still under blockade when Linebacker II started, the bombardment increased from 16,000 tons per month to 30,000 tons per month. The North Vietnamese were seriously hurt, and they were on the run. They did, however, attempt to fight back; approximately 1,242 missiles were fired at the B-52s by various SAM sites, but only twenty-four of them made any contact. Of these twenty-four strikes, only fifteen were able to bring a B-52 down. Many asked if the risk to the B-52s and their crews was worth it, but the losses were lower than had ever been thought possible—especially when the B-52's size was so large compared to an F-4 Phantom. With fifteen B-52s lost out of 729 missions flown, the loss rate was a tiny 2 percent. In the face of a brutal war, this was an unprecedented success.

Some Go Home

The war was not over yet. The B-52 crews were still rotating out. The B-52D 'Big Belly' gained a new use—transporting the goods the crews had picked up when they were on leave. The forty-seven sections of the Big Belly 'D' model were stuffed to the hatches with teak wood bars, mahogany tables from Hong Kong, jewelry for wives and girlfriends, and everything else that they could lay their hands on. For all that these crews had been through, it was a minor celebration.

As soon as the B-52s arrived at their home air bases, wing and staff members were put under intense pressure to restore their crews and aircraft to combat-ready status. The commanders were keen for the crews to get back to work; each returning wing commander was given a quota and a deadline by SAC headquarters, and they lived under the fear of missing them.

Lights out on the Vietnam War

On 23 March 1973 the United Stated declared that their part in the Vietnam War was at an end. The wider conflict would continue for another couple of years, but the South Vietnamese would no longer have any assistance from the US. There had been some ten years of fighting in Vietnam, but also at home, as the reaction to the war continued at American college campuses; at Ohio State University, four students were killed at what was supposed to be a peaceful protest. Soldiers were not being welcomed home, but treated with derision. After all they had suffered through in Vietnam, they came home to a spit in the face. The number of casualties was huge—58,282 soldiers killed in action, with a further 303,644 wounded. There were countless examples of soldiers missing in action, and the US flew the POW/MIA flag for them. Many pilots had been shot down in jungles so dense that they would never be found.

The B-52s came home scarred, too. They were suffering the after effects of flying tortuous, long missions, of taking hits from exploding SAMs, and of trying to avoid MiGs and whatever else the North Vietnamese had out there. It cannot honestly be said that the US won the war, but this was not a reflection of the efforts of the frontline men and women who served out there every day, having hell played with them in the heat and rancid humidity, suffering indescribable fatigue.

Many of the B-52s and the tactical fighters that came back were completely burned out, and they were retired. For those who survived, they would have a brief rest before they were plunged into action once more, beginning an era of twenty-four-hour alert against the Soviets and their missiles.

7

The Life of a Crew Dog and Coming Home

The Vietnam War was winding down, and things at the home bases were returning to a normalcy of sorts. However, some things never went away—such as the Cold War, which was still ongoing. The crews of the B-52 were sent from a blazing hot war to a Cold one; it played hell with them. From the hot, humid, and stressful conditions of Vietnam, many of the B-52 crews had suffered their share of injuries, both mental and physical—but there wasn't much time to address that. If the crews were ready to work, then they were assigned to work—as were their B-52s.

SAC still had to face the USSR, and the US Congress still had to answer to a nervous population, which had been split down the middle by the Vietnam War. The politicians had no idea how much Vietnam had compromised SAC's ability to maintain the US's nuclear shield. Secretary of Defense Robert McNamara resigned on 29 November 1967. He was responsible for so much of what happened in Vietnam, and had also lost his good friend President John F. Kennedy, who was assassinated in Dallas, Texas, on 22 November 1963. Kennedy's death had a profound effect on McNamara; he had been very close with the family, who behooved him to stop the killing in Vietnam. From 1966 onwards, McNamara was not having much luck working with the Joint Chiefs of Staff or many of the other military leaders; it seemed that the coolness and surety of his persona was melting away. In fact, he displayed little communication at all. From this point on, President Johnson failed to give McNamara the attention and confidence that he had before.

When he decided to leave his post at the Pentagon, McNamara was left on the verge of a nervous breakdown—a broken man, physically and mentally. Towards the end of his life, he finally admitted that the Vietnam War had been 'terribly wrong.' He died, aged ninety-three, at his home in Washington, DC on 6 July 2009. It was truly the end of a confusing, painful, and dangerous era in US military history.

At the end of the Vietnam War, as the crews returned, many of the senior officers did not have the luxury of allowing a long rest interval. Despite this, these senior officers understood that the crews were tired by the evil and painful war, and that they needed time to recoup—it just wasn't possible. Rest leave gave them a couple of weeks to be with their families, but then they were back in the saddle, ready to defend the US against the Soviets. The B-52 crews needed to review the updated SIOP/Positive Control Procedures (PCP), and were recertified. The only good part was that they were operating from home shores instead of foreign soil.

The PAD Alert, or How to be Bored While Waiting to Nuke the Soviets

The PAD alert consisted of a group of bomber crews that sat around in a bunker, next to a nuclear-missile-loaded B-52, just waiting for that deadly alarm to sound. Within a year of 1 October 1957, when the fast-response ground-alert system was first introduced, nearly all SAC bases had implemented 'ALERT.' This meant that roughly a third of the aircrews and aircraft at each station were ready, twenty-four hours a day, to respond within fifteen minutes to a surprise attack by air or missile from the Soviet Union.

From 1958 SAC came up with another program to further improve its reaction time; it relocated a portion of its alert bombers closer to the Soviets. An operation called 'Reflex Action' was enacted, where a certain number of B-47s and B-52s were stationed on Pod Alert at bases in Europe and North Africa, in addition to the United States.

Several years later, 'REFLEX' inspired another programme—one which offered a greater dispersion and faster reaction time. Airborne operations called 'Chrome Dome' involved a number of additional B-52s continually orbiting the polar regions for twenty-four hours at a time; one route ran above Alaska, with the other over Greenland. Fully loaded with nuclear weapons, these alert bombers were capable of penetrating Soviet airspace within one to two hours after receiving the 'GO' code. The 'GO' code was a very special command that came only from the White House, through the Chiefs of Staff, to the SAC and TAC commanders and the Naval Operations Division.

In the mid-1960s the Chrome Dome operations were further expanded to include an orbiting alert route over Europe. In this case, things did not go as planned. Shortly thereafter, 'Chrome Dome' and the entire idea of an airborne nuclear alert was dumped; this was after the 1966 Palomares accident, in which a B-52 and its nuclear weapons were lost. Airborne alerts received a lot of attention in the 1960s, but it was the ground alert that took up the bulk of a stateside SAC crew's time. This basically centered on the 'alert shack', where crews lived for twenty-four hours a day over the course of a full week, followed by a three-day post-alert respite. Aircrew duties on a PAD alert included target and mission study, the review of positive control procedures, catching up on flight advisories, briefings, and more.

At the end of the week came a ten-to-twelve-day period of planning, flying practice sorties. For those assigned to a B-52D, it was back to PAD alert after that break. The alert shack (also referred to as the 'mole hole') was always close to the main entrance of the runway. Nuclear-loaded alert bombers were parked on the ramp in a staggered diagonal form, with a large taxiway between them. Many of the crew dogs remarked that it looked like a Christmas tree. The 'mole hole' and the bombers were centered in an area of top security, complete with very high fences that were topped off by razor wire; armed guards surrounded the vicinity. The alert building itself was a mass of concrete, and it accommodated eight to ten crew men and enough space to support supplementary staff. They were air-conditioned, and could be heated when required. Lodgings were located on the lower level, and on the upper level there was a library, a TV spot, and a small eating nook. Crews wore their best green flight suits—unlike in South East Asia, where the heat and humidity had made this much less common. Sometimes the crews would wear an ascot and a ball cap embroidered with the wing's colors and insignia.

Alert crews were never permitted to be too far away from their bombers. Crews had to travel together, and they usually used a blue USAF pickup truck to travel around the base—although they were never more than a few minutes away from their nuclear-loaded B-52s. The crews were always within audible range of the warning announcements for the alert, even if they were in the base movie theater. However, the crews mostly hung out at the 'mole hole', engrossing themselves in TV, music, reading, catching up on work, or playing pool or cards. It could be painfully boring at times. Fortunately, the food was dished up with style and it was always tasty and fresh—as was the coffee, with the vital coffee urn always filled. Other than this, it was a tough duty; the crews never knew if or when the alarm would go off, and they could get really anxious waiting. If the boredom didn't get them, the anxiety would.

When a new crew came to relieve the old one, the new guys had to go through a total recheck of the aircraft; this was called 're-cocking.' It involved a complete crew and aircraft preflight, followed by checks with the navigator and bombardier, a visual inspection, a check over the settings, and a check of the nuclear payload. Once this was done, the new crew loaded all their personal belongings and arranged their stations to wait for the first alert to sound—if it ever did.

The crews also went through a system called 'Secret Box.' This involved a sealed metal container with two locks; only the pilot and the navigator knew the combination. The locks were opened to give access to the highly classified strike folders that held all the statistics for the routes and SIOP (Single Integrated Operational Plan) targets. During the Vietnam era, SAC crews had three levels of security clearance—the gunners were at the lowest level, while pilots, co-pilots, navigators and EWOs were at the highest (top secret). The aircraft commander and radar operator/navigator were 'Top Secret Crypto'; this meant that both officers needed to read the plans together.

MAD (Mutually Assured Destruction) was the key paradigm of the Cold War. The strategy was created by John von Neumann, a physicist and mathematician who helped the US to develop nuclear weapons. Secretary of Defense Robert McNamara was the top advocate of this doctrine when running the military for both JFK and LBJ. The idea behind the strategy was a horrifying scenario, but it did help to keep the peace throughout the Cold War.

There were several types of alert messages that were processed before bombers would receive the final authorization to fly to a point short of the USSR; this was later known as 'H' hour command (HHCL). Once at this stage, the crews could go no further without the final 'GO' code.

It was impossible to recall a nuclear missile; according to MAD, once the 'GO' code was given, there was nothing to do except launch and let the Third World War begin. There was a terrible pressure on the crews of these B-52 bombers that were standing alert, and on the officers above them. Thankfully, a scenario like the one depicted in the 1964 movie *Fail Safe* never played out in reality, and that says something about the caliber of the men that were in control of the aircraft, bombs, and missiles.

As the Cold War drew to a close, there was a new enemy on the horizon; it would come from the Middle East. This was only the beginning in what would soon become a permanent state of affairs for the United States. Next on the list would be Operation Desert Storm.

DEFCON and Countdown to Disaster

DEFCON represented the levels of alert that the US military used to determine the level of threat against the nation. The old style of DEFCON 5 through to 1 is no longer used; the twenty-first century Department of Defense now has seven different 'Alert Cons.' These include the original five plus two more 'EMERGCONs', which represent national emergencies like a missile attack, an earthquake, or some other natural disaster. Homeland Security uses a different system of levels to quantify threats. Since 9/11 they have used a color-coded system—according to the new Homeland Security handbook:

DEFCON 5 [blue]—lowest state of readiness
DEFCON 4 [green]—increased state of readiness
DEFCON 3 [orange]—war is on the horizon
DEFCON 2 [red]—war is imminent
DEFCON 1 [white on black]—prepare for war

Attrition: Some Birds go Home to Roost—Forever

Some of the B-52s were just too tired to hang on any longer after the brutal beating they took in Vietnam. Valiant warriors returned to AMARG, better known as the 'boneyard' at Davis Monthan Air Force Base in Arizona. 'AMARG' stands for 'Aircraft Maintenance and Regeneration Center'; it represents the inventory list contained at the AFB. It has been the lifeline for many aircraft that needed parts, as they could be recycled from retired models situated here. AMARG has been the savior for many aircraft, including B-52s that needed spares or parts in an emergency.

The B-52Bs were retired in June 1966 after reaching the end of their structural life; the B-52Cs were retired on 29 September 1971. Only one 'B' model remained in service, and that was the one given to NASA for use in their lifting-body/parasite testing. The NB-52's claim to fame was carrying the X-15 to release at altitude, alongside lifting bodies like the M2-F1 series, the HL-10, the X-24A and B, and Pegasus. The NB-52 was finally retired (with honors) in 2004; there is one more 'B' model on display at the Colorado Aviation Museum. Most 'E' models were retired in 1967–68, but eighty-two of them were retired between May 1969 and March 1970. The majority of the 'F' models were retired between 1967 and 1973; however, twenty-three of them worked as trainers up until 1978. The famous 'D' models served for much longer, and these really took a beating in Vietnam. Eighty of the 'D' models were refurbished and used in 'PACER PLANK.' The 'D' series had given almost 10,000 hours of flight time during Vietnam, and it was showing.

Many of the B-52 aircraft had large structural cracks, and they were suffering from a host of other problems. In the mid-1970s, the modifications started, including scrapping some 15 tons of metal and parts from the aircraft before putting on new leading edges and stiffeners, re-skinning the wings, and reworking the wing pylons. The fuselage was re-skinned up at the wing root. Although the cost of the updates were $2.6 million per bird, it was well worth the money. There was also a bonus from re-working the 'D' models—

since the wings were detached from the aircraft, it was possible to rejoin and retest them. The wings were shown to be more aerodynamically efficient, and although the aircraft had put on some 3,400 lbs, the cruise range was 3 percent better than it had been before. The 'D' held on until late 1979, when the thirty-seven that were not upgraded were retired; the rest of the 'D' fleet went to Davis-Monthan between 1982 and 1983.

The 'G' and 'H' aircraft were already standing on alert as part of the 'nuclear triad', which included the Navy and their missiles, manned bombers, and other tactical fighters and bombers. Then the Cold War ended, and 325 B-52Gs were destroyed in the most heinous way; they were chopped up with a 13,000-lb guillotine and left out for some 120 days so that the Russian satellites could see them. This massacre was part of the Salt II treaty; it was loss of materials that amounted to a travesty, with the Soviets reluctant to agree on many parts of the treaty. Despite this destruction of aircraft, Salt II was never ratified by either the USA or the Soviets. The only good thing about the loss of the aircraft (if there was anything) was that they were stripped for parts that kept their sisters going for many years; this is one of the blessings of having a place like AMARG.

A Day in the Life

The B-52 crews were now home and getting back into a regular way of life on the airbase. At least some of their aircraft were on their way to storage or their new bases. Over at Fairchild Air Force Base, Washington, the system was being restored to normality.

A machinist in the USAF, Technical Sergeant Dan Freeman, talked to the author about his time with the B-52s. Dan was lucky in the sense that he not only served as a machinist with the B-52, but also later transferred to the SR-71 Blackbird. Not too many airmen had this honor, though many wished for it. Dan talked about his time at Fairchild AFB; he had spent time there as a machinist with the 92nd Bomb Wing (heavy) from 1976 to 1981. When he arrived there, the wing was still changing over from 'D' models to 'H' models.

Things got a little hot and heavy around Fairchild at 5.30 p.m. on 18 May 1980, when Mt St Helen's erupted; this was an active volcano in the Cascade Mountain Range, which had been warming up to blow since earlier that year. There had even been a couple of earthquakes as a warning signal. When the eruption occurred, Dan and the rest of the 92nd BW cleared the runways, got the aircraft out, and then got themselves out of Dodge as fast as they could.

When things finally calmed down, Dan returned to his work in the 92nd machine shop, which supported the B-52, KC-135, T-38, T-37, UH-1N helicopters and many other aircraft, base agency, or squadron that wandered onto the base. However, Dan's primary support was for the B-52, the KC-135, and other 'cocked nuclear assets.' A typical shop day would consist of the Shop Chief assigning tasks for 'in-shop' manufacturing work like the repair and maintenance of shop equipment (machine tools), ancillary tasks like noting technical data, updates on tools, and controls records for maintenance, and so on. There was a special red phone in the shop that was known as the 'hot line'—it was a direct link to the Job Central Dispatch. Dan recalls:

> When that phone rang, the commander would tell us where we needed to go and what needed to happen … The section chief would order whoever was available to get the flight line tool book and go to the problem aircraft to assist the crew chief or other specialists in the repair. Most of the time, it was to remove damaged hardware that they couldn't get out in normal process …
>
> If the job was on an alert aircraft, only personnel verified on PRP [the Personal Reliability Program] were allowed to dispatch. One of the more critical jobs was using a ball peen hammer and a high-speed steel punch to remove a plug cover on the disarming switch on the nukes.

Hammering on a live nuclear weapon, surrounded by a dozen B-52s also loaded with nuclear weapons, often gave Freeman the 'creeps':

> Most of the hard and tedious work was done in the phase docks. The day the aircraft was brought into the shop for PHASE was the day that we de-paneled it. That usually meant hundreds of stuck screws and bolts. It was a miserable, knuckle-busting job that still bothers me on bad-weather days.

Freeman and his crew knew it was a bad day when they could hear the OMS (Organizational Maintenance Squadron) 'crews using argues to remove screws because the argues always stripped out the screw heads easily.' The weather at Fairchild was no bed of roses either:

> The weather could be -20 degrees outside and deep snow on the ground. It was extremely difficult to use your hands to manipulate tiny drill bits and trolls in that cold.

One day, it was so cold at Fairchild that Freeman's safety glasses literally shattered on his face. On the verge of frostbite, in the middle of the night, it was a tough job to deal with. However, the crews had to maintain war-readiness, and this included 'War Readiness Exercises', which happened day or night and would usually mean a twelve-hour shift—and plenty of extra duties. Freeman was out of the USAF after four years at Fairchild, but he signed back into the Air Force Reserves and was assigned to the 9540th BW at Mather AFB, California—a definite improvement over the cold weather he'd had to suffer. In 1981, President Carter started the Prior Service Program to get former Army personnel back into active duty; Freeman reenlisted that year and was assigned to Castle AFB to serve with B-52Hs. This just goes to show that once crews had the feeling for the B-52, it never left their blood.

8

Warrior Queen

The last alert status for the Air Force and the nation was canceled on 27 September 1991. SAC was standing down, and this meant changes that would eventually turn them into a new entity—Air Combat Global Command. Gone were the days of standing on twenty-four-hour alert, waiting for the terrible klaxon to sound and indicate that the world was about to end in the most profound way. Many B-52s of all variants were put out to pasture; many were just fatigued, while cutbacks claimed the rest. However, there were still some aircraft left at Minot Air Force Base in North Dakota and Barksdale Air Force Base in Louisiana, and it would emerge that these would be needed shortly—very shortly.

Operation Desert Storm

The short-term peace felt good—no wars (hot or Cold), at least for a while. There was still Russia to consider, but even here there was a type of peace (although not a restful one). Meanwhile, in the Middle East there was a major problem, and its name was Saddam Hussein—the self-appointed dictator of Iraq. Hussein was most definitely getting out of hand, trying to grab Kuwait's (Iraq's neighbour) land on the premise that he was reclaiming Iraqi land that was stolen long ago. This wasn't exactly true. On 2 August 1990, he roused his elite Republican Guard and the rest of the Iraqi troops to take Kuwait. The rest of the world, led by the United States, would not stand for it. Hussein was about to bring a mighty wrath down on himself.

Despite Hussein's belief that the United States would never have the nerve to make a move, the George H. W. Bush administration decided to act. On 7 August 1990, Operation Desert Shield began with an internal buildup of troops and armament. The US had given Hussein the chance to withdraw from Kuwait under threats, but this was not working; the Republican Guard took everything within reach, leaving many Kuwaitis dead (or worse). On 15 January 1991, it became clear that the ultimatum the United Nations had issued to Saddam would be ignored, as he refused to move his troops out of Kuwait. The United States had continued to build up its arms and also formed a coalition of other countries to support their mission; one of their main objectives was to protect Saudi Arabia from attack by the lunatic in charge of Iraq. The United States were not alone; France simultaneously enacted Operation *Daguet*, the United Kingdom enacted Operation Granby, and more troops were readied in Egypt and Syria. Eventually, thirty-two countries would be involved in some capacity. The US Navy, Air Force, Army, and the Marines were now readying for war.

The fireworks began in Iraq at 3 a.m. on 17 January 1991—just in time for the evening news broadcasts on the east coast of the USA. For many, it was a strange experience to watch a war begin while heating up their dinner, with F-117 stealth fighters lighting up the night in Baghdad.

Once again, the B-52s were called upon to do the heavy lifting of conventional bombs and missiles. The B-52 crews had to get rolling to learn the new terrain, ensuring that they were able to operate in the area at night. On 16 January 1991, a flight of B-52Gs flew from Barksdale AFB, Louisiana, to Iraq, refueling in the air *en route*. When they reached the Iraqi targets, they unloaded everything they had. Never touching the ground, the B-52s turned around and headed back home to Barksdale; the entire mission had taken some thirty-five hours, spanning 14,000 miles. This was the longest-distance combat mission ever flown, breaking the record set by a Vulcan of the RAF in 1982. This flight used 'refueling forward', which meant that B-52Gs from King Abdullah Air Base (Jeddah, Saudi Arabia), RAF Fairford (UK), and Moròn Air Base (Spain and the Island of Diego Garcia) flew bombing missions over Iraq at low altitudes. After the first three nights of raids, the B-52s moved to a high-altitude profile, which reduced the effectiveness and psychological impact on the Iraqis.

Conventional strikes were carried out by groups of three B-52 bombers. They dropped up to 150 750-lb conventional bombs over an area of 1.5 miles x 1 mile; this type of bombing created intense noise and damage. The bombings did their job of intimidating the Iraqi troops by the incessant pounding and explosions, and most of them threw down their guns and threw up their arms in surrender, surrendering to the first Allied troops they saw.

Over the course of the war, the B-52Gs flew 1,620 sorties and delivered around 40 percent of the munitions dropped by coalition forces. During the conflict, the Iraqis made several claims that they had enjoyed some air-to-air fighter success, but this was a tall tale. Just one Iraqi pilot, Knedai Hijab, successfully damaged a B-52G, firing a Vympel R-27R missile from his MiG 29 on the first night of the war. The USAF disputes this claim, stating that the bomber was actually hit by friendly fire in the form of an AGM 88 high-speed anti-radiation missile (HARM) that homed in on the fire-controlled radar operated by the B-52G's tail gun. The affected B-52G was renamed *In Harm's Way* due to the event. Immediately after the incident, General George Lee Butler announced that the gunner position on the B-52G would be eliminated, and the gun turrets were permanently turned off from 1 October 1991 onwards. The B-52s did the majority of the heavy lifting in the conflict; they pounded the Iraqis into the ground, and the crews were proud. Operation Desert Storm, the combat phase of the war, ended on 28 February 1991.

The B-52's role in Operation Desert Storm is fascinating for a bird that was already thirty years old when she went to war. She flew 1,624 missions and dropped over 72,000 weapons. She delivered 25,700 tons of munitions on the targets in the Kuwaiti theater and on the airfields, industrial targets, troop concentrations, and storage areas in Iraq. The B-52 had a mission-capability rate of over 81 percent—2 percent higher than its peacetime rate. Over the course of the fight, B-52s dropped 29 percent of all the bombs involved and 38 percent of those deployed by the USAF. Aside from the obvious destructive force, the key influence these bombers had was described by Iraqi prisoners of war—the B-52s had such a devastating effect on the enemy's morale that 20–40 percent of the Iraqi troops had deserted their units before the war ended. The coalition fighters still used precision-guided munitions to destroy pinpoint targets—real surgical strikes—but the B-52s used their power to destroy large areas. The aircraft had proved she could still carry the load, fight the battle, and win—even at thirty years old.

Strikes on Iraq in 1996

The peace didn't last long; bands of the Iraqi Army attacked Kurdish northern Iraq on 31 August 1996, enflaming the Iraqi Kurdish Civil War. As a response, the US enacted Operation Desert Strike in September, in which the Navy and USAF were tasked with handling air defense targets in southern Iraq. From 2–3 September, two B-52Hs from the 2nd Bomb Wing conducted a mission as part of this operation; they hit Baghdad power stations and communications facilities with thirteen AGM-86 conventional air-launched cruise missiles (CALCM) in a 16,000-mile round trip—a thirty-four-hour mission that spanned from Andersen AFB, Guam, and back. This again broke the record for the longest distance flown for a combat mission.

Operation Allied Force

Despite the B-52's success in Iraq, she was far from ready to rest on her laurels—on the night of 24 March 1999, she was required to attend another warzone. Operation Allied Force (also known as NATO Plan 10601) began as a response to a NATO directive issued in June 1998. General John Jumper, Commander of the USAF in Europe, started working on the plans from this date. Considered to be 'the most precise application of air power in history', the operation began with B-52 conventional bombs hitting targets in Serbia and throughout the Federal Republic of Yugoslavia. Allied Force would represent another whole year of effort; the action was led by six nations (including Russia), and its objective was to find a way to stop Serbian human-rights violations in Kosovo, one of the four areas in the Federal Republic of Yugoslavia. In 1998, the Yugoslavian army committed such violence against the Kosovo Albanians that it caused 250,000 of them to be driven from their homes and lands. With the winter months approaching, the CIA reported that thousands were in jeopardy.

By 2 May 1999, the bombings were already in their third phase. Each day in the month of May set new records for the number of NATO strikes carried out; these were now even coming from countries such as Hungary and Turkey. The attacks on Kosovo by Yugoslav forces increased as the B-52s dumped every conventional bomb they could find on the enemy. They launched ninety CALCMS (conventional air-launched missiles systems), with 70 percent of the munitions dropped within the last three weeks of the War. The US used twenty-two heavy bombers in total, of which eleven were B-52s; they carried some 12,000 weapons. Two more B-52s went to the UK on 22 February 1999 as part of the NATO buildup. By the end of the war, twenty-five B-52s belonging to the 2nd Bomb Wing and the 5th Bomb Wing (from Minot AFB, North Dakota) were still in the fight. These B-52s were bailed to the 2nd Expeditionary Force in the UK. On 10 October 1999, Secretary of Defense William Cohen ordered the deployment of six more B-52s from the 2nd Bomb Wing at Barksdale AFB, Los Angeles, to head out of RAF Fairford in the UK.

Two more B-52s came in from the 5th Bomb Wing at Minot AFB, and they traveled to Fairford on 29 April 1999. The crews would soon realize the devastation that this huge bird could cause in one single mission. The biggest B-52H missions were flown in June 1999 near Mount Pastrik, and the KLA (Kosovo Liberation Army) were nailed to the floor. More B-52 strikes followed near Gorshrub, Yugoslavia, where the B-52s continued to drop conventional weapons and carpet bomb—which is what she did best. On 10 June 1999 NATO ratified terms for an international peace plan, and the seventy-eight-day war was at an end. Once again, the venerable B-52 had made short work of the enemy.

Operation Enduring Freedom

At 8.46 a.m. on 11 September 2001, American Airlines Flight 11, a Boeing 767 with ninety-two souls on board, crashed into the North Tower of the World Trade Center in New York City, striking between the ninety-third and ninety-ninth floors. This was initially assumed to be a terrible accident, but at 9.03 a.m., United Airlines Flight 175 smashed into the South Tower, confirming that the United States was under attack. The second plane struck between the seventy-fifth and eighty-fifth floors, killing all on board and many in the towers themselves. Soon it emerged that the Pentagon had also suffered an attack; American Airlines Flight 77 crashed into the famous building, killing 125 military personnel and fifty-nine civilians.

United Airlines Flight 93 crashed on a field in Shanksville, Pennsylvania, after heroic Americans fought the hijackers on the flight and brought the plain down in a field rather than on its intended target—the Washington Capitol or the White House.

The residents of New York City and the wider United States were in shock; following the collapse of the towers, people fled across the 59th Street bridge, covered in ash and dust. All over the city, people struggled to get to a safe place or find their way home; NYC was totally shut down. When President George W. Bush arrived in the city to survey the damage, he gave a defiant message:

> I can hear you! The rest of the world hears you! And the people ... and the people who knocked these buildings down will hear all of us soon.

It did not take long for Bush to make good on his promise. On 15 September 2001, the President readied the military, and by the 19th they were starting to move. On the 17th, Bush gave a speech in which he informed the country that the US would be going after those who had destroyed the towers and killed thousands of Americans.

Operation Enduring Freedom began on 1 October 2001. The plans had begun to be formed the minute the smoke settled at Ground Zero, and the objective was to take revenge against the Taliban, Al-Qaeda, and Osama bin Laden. The operation initially took the name 'Operation Infinite Justice', but some Islamic leaders felt that only Allah could give infinite justice, and the name was therefore changed; the US wanted to show that they were at war with radical terrorists, and not Islam.

The B-52 would be called again to defend her nation, and she would do it in style. In an interview with *Stars and Stripes*, Capt. Andy McElvaine, a Weapon Officer in the 40th Air Expeditionary Groups, said: '[The] B-52 and close air support historically don't belong in the same sentence. We've been providing a lot of close air support pretty effectively.' This was yet another role for the aircraft.

The beauty of the B-52 is that the enemy never sees her and never hears her, as she can drop her weapons from 22,000 to 39,000 feet. In another interview with *Stars and Stripes*, Captain Adam (an aircraft commander who declined to give his first name) stated that most of the time crews never saw their enemies or the effect of the weapons they dropped. However, Capt. Adam mentioned one exception, which occurred during a night mission; in this instance, a 2,000-lb GBU-31 bomb 'lit up the entire night sky when it hit the target.'

The hunt for Osama bin Laden was a main aspect of this battle. Four aircraft carrier groups were already in the region and setting up their targets; the former Soviet Republic of Uzbekistan, which is situated off the northern border of Afghanistan, allowed the US to use one of its air bases, which would put the US closer to the center of battle. The US also had bases in Pakistan, on the western border of Afghanistan. In Guam, Diego Garcia was going to handle the heavy bombers like the B-52s and the B-1Bs.

The B-52 did what she does best—carpet bombing with conventional munitions or 'dumb bombs.' Putting it mildly, the B-52s slammed the Taliban, with the B-2 Stealth making a 7,200-mile trip to start hitting them with precision-guided munitions. The B-52s continued carpet bombing the Taliban troops with dumb bombs, cluster bombs (a particularly nasty type explosives), and the 15,000-lb BLU-82 Daisy Cutter, which is the most powerful non-nuclear weapon in the United States' arsenal. It can cremate anything within 600 yards.

As always, the continuous pounding of the B-52s demoralized the enemy. The Taliban couldn't stand up against the explosions, especially when they couldn't see or hear where the bombs were coming from; all they could do was hide in their trench holes. Much like the others who had previously faced the B-52, it did not take long before the enemy was running and hiding from this huge bird, decimating anything she aimed at.

After the completion of Operation Enduring Freedom, the US had to contend with the Tora Bora mountain range; military intelligence indicated that Osama bin Laden was hiding in a maze of caves around this area. In the last week of December 2001, B-52s with BLU-82 Daisy Cutters and AC-130 Spectre gunships blew the living hell out of those mountains. Many of the Taliban and al Qaeda fighters were killed by US Special Forces, who went from cave to cave and took them out. Many more ran to the southern border with Pakistan to hide.

By December 2001, most of al Qaeda in Afghanistan had either died, surrendered, or fled. By January 2002, the US-led war was winding up—but it wasn't over by any means. US troops were still going after insurgents, rogues, and the remaining Taliban and al Qaeda fighters. An interim government was established in Afghanistan, with Hamid Karzai as its leader, but while the war was slowing down, the battles refused to end.

Operation Anaconda—Enduring Freedom

Operation Anaconda began with a focus on a collection of caves in mountains in the eastern region of Afghanistan. As in Tora Bora, it was known that some al Qaeda fighters were hiding up there with refugee Taliban fighters. However, even with the early start to Operation Anaconda's planning stage, the outcome was not looking good; there were many issues in arrangement of command that were not solved, and these led to bigger problems later on.

All the US forces—air, land, and sea—needed to come together to pull this mission off. Air operations were particularly muddled; the required level of air integration was proving difficult to reach, and by 5 February 2002, the officer in charge at the air liaison office knew that ground troops were already pushing into the region. Central Air Force Command (CENTAF) was said to have been routinely provided with information and copies of various messages from the Combined Joint Task Force (CJTF) about the operation from its inception, but no formal move was made by anyone in command of the land operation to involve the air component commander. US Air Force Lieutenant General Michael T. Moseley and his staff were planning other things—even looking ahead to after Operation Anaconda would change from a low-level operation to a major one. The planned operation date for the major stage was 28 February.

The major bombing for Operation Enduring Freedom had finished nearly two months beforehand. Lieutenant General Moseley was looking far into the future—perhaps to a possible invasion of Iraq in 2003. He was even touring the Gulf region in the build-up to Operation Anaconda, indicating that his eye was firmly off the ball. This meant that the Central Command (CENTCOM) of the Air Department were unaware of the latest developments with the operation. While Moseley was in the Gulf, General John Corley of the Combined Air Operations Command (CAOC) instructed his staff to create an inventory of the required assets that would be needed for Anaconda; upon discovering Moseley's absence, it dawned on the Air Support machine exactly how unprepared they were. By 24 February, Moseley and the CAOC staff were desperately trying to put together the required air assets for the operation—at this stage, no one had even figured out how much jet fuel would be required. It took until 26 February—two days before the start of the operation—to get their ducks in a row.

Anaconda went ahead on schedule, but not in style. The Enlisted Tactical Air Controller (ETAC), the officer who was in command of the Tactical Air Control Party that controlled the air group (and all Air Force) aircraft, stated, 'We jumped off the [helicopters] right into the middle of a hornet's nest.' Machine-gun fire blew up everything in sight, with mortar fire thrown in for good measure; they were stuck. The ETAC was pinned down for fifteen hours within 546 yards of his original position, where the helicopters had dropped them. In the last few minutes, when it looked like his position was about to be overrun, he called for a JDAM hit on the hillside.

In another battle, the same ETAC reported that he was taking mortar fire at his position, and he yelled for a laser-guided bomb drop (LGB) from an F-16 that was overhead. The ETAC directed the F-16 to the spot the where LGB would do the most good, and it was deployed perfectly. In this battle, the 10th Mountain Division had been pinned down for some six hours in the Shah-I-Kot valley, being pounded by merciless mortar fire. A B-52 that was part of the group called out of Diego Garcia (and had no pre-assigned targets) destroyed an al Qaeda position. The story goes like this:

> An ETAC called out on the radio: 'B-52, I want you to put every fucking bomb you have on the fucking ridgeline, right fucking now!' When the ETAC's commander reminded him that someone was most likely taping this radio conversation, he replied: 'Sir, if I survive this, they can court-marshal me for poor radio exchange!
> 'Roger that.'
> His commander responded: 'B-52, you heard the man, bomb the fucking ridgeline with everything you've got right fucking now!'

As Anaconda continued, things improved. On the evening of 4 March, air support was called on again to retrieve some survivors from Roberts Ridge. The B-52s, B-1s, F-14s, F-15Es, F-16s, and F/A18s were ready, along with the ever-popular A-10 Warthog. One of the biggest problems with Anaconda's communication issues was the coordination of air strikes and extraction of the aircraft without an accident. The problem here was not running out of aircraft, but running out of airspace. Some of the B-52s were stacked as badly as aircraft over a commercial airport in bad weather.

As always, the B-52s were dropping JDAMS from an altitude of 39,000 feet, through the flight paths of B-1s and fighter formations that were staged at 22,500–25,000 feet; this was a recipe for disaster if there ever was one. However, Anaconda ended successfully, with the B-52s once again the heavy hitters in the ninth inning, with two out, a man on third, and the count 3–2. There were no second chances, and the B-52 just didn't seem to need one.

Operation Iraqi Freedom

Operation Enduring Freedom had overthrown the Taliban and routed al Qaeda out of Afghanistan. The next objective for the US was to get rid of Saddam Hussein. The US and the UK led a coalition to take Hussein out of Iraq, once and for all. This was the result of a highly contested declaration that Iraq possessed weapons of mass destruction, and the countries were hard-pressed to prove the existence of these weapons to their citizens. The United Nations remained unconvinced, but the operation went ahead.

Two of the component operations of this Iraq War were called 'Northern Watch' and 'Southern Watch'; they had the USAF flying from Turkey to Northern Iraq and from Kuwait and Saudi Arabia to Southern Iraq. The Combined Force Air Component Commander (CFACC) controlled the moves in Operation Iraqi Freedom, the main operation of the war; General Michael T. Moseley was in command, despite his controversial role in Afghanistan. According to General Moseley, the primary objective was to create and maintain 'a stable Iraq with its territorial integrity intact and a broad based government that renounces WMD development and use and no longer supports terrorism or threatens its neighbors.' The top three objectives of the combined force commanders were to defeat the Iraqi forces or compel their capitulation; to neutralize the regime's leadership; and to ensure the Iraqi theater was free of ballistic missiles and WMD delivery systems.

Northern Watch and Southern Watch brought down the Iraqi Air Force defense system. The Iraqi Air Force was essentially out of business, but the combined forces were still concerned about them; during the initial invasion of Iraq, the USAF saw more than 1,000 AAA firings and more than 1,600 SAMs sent their way. Despite this, the USAF lost only one A-10 Warthog aircraft to enemy fire and two mobility aircraft (AMC) to SAM damage, out of 236 attempts to bring them down.

The first operation in Iraqi Freedom was the leaflet campaign, an example of psychological warfare that attempted to set the Iraqi citizens up for the coming operations. On 9 March 2003, leaflets were dropped from the skies over the country; they preached non-interference and support for the coalition, and sought to win over the people Iraqi citizens themselves.

On the evening of 19 March 2003, one day prior to the start of combat operations, USAF F-117 stealth fighters hit the Dora Farms complex in south-west Baghdad, based on intelligence that Saddam was hiding in the area; however, this intelligence was faulty.

Combat operations began on 20 March, and the USAF started it off by hitting target areas around Baghdad proper, with more than 1,700 sorties flown. Similarly to in Operation Enduring Freedom, 68 percent of the weapons used in the first six weeks of the operation were all precision-guided weapons. Turkey had refused to allow the US to access its air bases to get troops and supplies into Northern Iraq, so the US did the next best thing—they took an air base in Northern Iraq itself.

On 21 March, B-52Hs launched 100 conventional air-launched cruise missiles (CALCMs) during a night mission. In April, a B-52H was fitted with the Northrop Grumman Litening II Laser Targeting pod, which was used to hit targets in the north of the country. This new laser was a multi-sensor targeting and surveillance system, which allowed the crews to detect, acquire, auto-track, and identify targets at a very long range, for weapons delivery or non-traditional intelligence, or surveillance and reconnaissance missions. The Litening's 1K forward-looking infrared radar (FLIR), charged-coupled device (CCD), laser-imaging sensors, advanced image processing, and digital video output provide superior imagery, permitting crews to identify and lock on to targets in many different combat roles.

On 13 December Saddam Hussein was captured, hiding in a hole in the ground, near his home in Tikrit, by American forces. On 5 November 2006, he was tried and hanged for his crimes, including the murder of 148 Iraqis.

North Korea and Simulated Military Exercises

The United States consistently works to keep their military forces sharp, and this is done with various military exercises that run constantly; an example would be Red Flag, one of the USAF's military games. The Navy also has its own exercises, testing submarines, destroyers, and aircraft carriers. In February 2013, the US conducted simulated nuclear bombing raids on North Korea as part of its continuing military exercises in South Korea.

It is widely recognized that North Korea has a history of provoking other countries (especially the United States, South Korea, and Japan) by carrying out its nuclear tests. The country conducted its third underground nuclear test on 12 February 2013, prompting a response from the US—during a visit to South Korea, Deputy Defense Secretary Ashton Carter stated that the B-52 would be making flights over North Korea as an 'extended deterrence.' Carter said:

> I should note the presence of strategic bombers taking place in flight training in the Korean peninsula area in particular, for example, but this is routine. There will be a B-52 flight tomorrow.

George Little, the Pentagon press secretary, told the press that B-52 bombers from Andersen AFB, Guam, would also run a training mission over South Korea on 8 March 2013, during a war game called 'Exercise Foal Eagle.' Little added:

> It's not any secret that we are in the midst of sending a very strong signal that we have a firm commitment to the alliance with our South Korean allies.

These flights showed the US resolve in protecting South Korea, and the bomber flights were part of the increased training endeavors. They were part of the US Pacific Command program called 'Continuous Bomber Presence', and the Guam base had been in use since 2004 for the rotational deployment of strategic bombers. George Little pointed out:

> The B-52 Stratofortress can perform a variety of missions, including carrying precision-guided conventional or nuclear ordnance ... We will continue to fly these training missions as part of our ongoing actions to enhance our strategic posture in the Asia-Pacific region.

It was unusual for the Pentagon to make such an open statement about the use of strategic nuclear forces in the region. The Foal Eagle maneuvers highlighted both the nuclear and conventional abilities of the B-52, but it was noted that the flight would be routine. George Little remarked:

> Despite that challenges with fiscal constraints, training opportunities remain important to ensure US and [South Korean] forces are battle ready and trained to employ airpower to deter aggression, defend South Korea, and defeat any attack against the alliance.

The US had stored nuclear bombs and missiles at the Guam base until the early 1990s, but they were then moved back to the continental United States. Recently, two Russian TU-95 Bears (of the same age range as the B-52) were recently intercepted as they were prowling around Guam; CIA analysts claim that this was a show of force by the Russians.

With the combination of conventional-forces exercises that started in early March (as part of the maneuvers called 'Key Resolve'), this exercise included some 13,000 US and South Korean troops. A second group of exercises ran through the end of April. North Korea was once again angered by new UN resolutions that condemned their underground nuclear testing, and announced that it was pulling out of the 1953 armistice agreement that had ended the Korean War. This meant that the US had to keep the lid on the North Koreans with these military exercises, and there was no stronger deterrent than a fleet of B-52Hs, fully loaded, flying just overhead.

As the B-52 was updated and missions rolled in, she continued to serve on the front lines, demoralizing and demolishing the enemy. It is good to know that she is still in the inventory, ready to destroy and dishearten wherever her crews are told to go, in defense of the United States and to support those who depend on them.

9

Still Defending the Skies

The B-52 had begun her life on 23 November 1945, after a request from the Air Force for a long-range bomber. Since 1955, the B-52 has flown continually, meaning that she has spent sixty years in Air Force service; she is still the backbone of manned strategic bombing in the US Air Force. The B-52 is the strongest beast in the USAF's fleet and represents the most formidable conventional weapon in its inventory, carrying the heaviest and most deadly conventional, non-nuclear weapons. She has often flown from the US air bases to her target and back, non-stop, utilizing air refueling. Her crews are some of the most highly trained officers and enlisted men and women in the USAF, and they regard flying with the B-52 as an honor. While she may not be as sexy as one of the USAF fighters or the B-2 bomber, she remains the biggest hammer in the toolbox—the full realization of her genius design.

There have been many updates to the B-52's airframe, which remains solid for some 19,000 hours. The bomber is capable of subsonic speeds and altitudes of up to 50,000 feet, and two B-52s can monitor over 140,000 square miles of ocean surface over two hours. Technological advances have meant that today the B-52 can be outfitted with two electro-optical viewing sensors, along with forward-looking radar (FLIR) and advanced targeting pods that can upgrade her arsenal and improve her flight safety.

Pilots now wear night-vision goggles, which enable them to enhance their performance during night missions. They allow a greater safety ratio due to increased visibility for the pilots, allowing them to see clear terrain, to avoid enemy radar, and to see other aircraft in the area with their lights out. The B-52H was upgraded from the Litening Advanced Targeting pods to the Sniper Advanced Targeting pod, providing improved long-range target identification and continuous stabilized surveillance for all missions—including close air support for the ground forces. The Sniper pod's advanced targeting and image-processing technology significantly increase the combat effectiveness of the B-52 during the day and at night—and ever under poor weather conditions—while attacking ground targets with a variety of standoff weapons, including laser-guided bombs, conventional bombs, and GPS-guided weapons. While SAC is no longer extant, it has been reborn as Air Force Global Strike Command—a name that even Gen. LeMay would approve of.

The use of aerial refueling gave the B-52 a range that is limited only by crew endurance. Even without this, she has an unrefueled combat range in excess of 8,800 miles. When she reaches her target, the B-52 is capable of dropping or launching the widest array of munitions in the US inventory, including gravity bombs, cluster bombs, precision-guided missiles, and joint direct attack munitions. Updated with the twenty-first century technology described above, she is more than capable of continuing as the heart of the nation's manned strategic defense. The aircraft's flexibility was evident in the nation's most recent wars—in Vietnam, Desert Storm, Allied Force, and Iraqi Freedom, for example. The B-52 struck at troop concentrations over a wide area, fixed installations, and bunkers, decimating the morale of all who found themselves in her sights.

As of February 2015, the pilots and crews of the B-52 are convening at Barksdale Air Force Base, Louisiana—the home of the aircraft—for the 'Air Force Global Strike Command Bomber Force Improvement Program.' The program sent five teams to visit the bomber units, where they will advise those working on bomber duties and work with the airmen to resolve the issues they face. The bomber's force improvement program operation recognizes the necessity of reorganizing the B-52's mission set, enabling her to continue to operate until 2040. The team have recommended to Lieutenant General Stephen Wilson, Deputy Commander of US Strategic Command, that this reevaluation of the B-52's priorities and the changes to its training programs will bring its capability up to that required by future warfare. The main goal of these changes is to improve the quality of combat pilots who graduate from flight training, increasing the instructor-to-student ratio, increasing the speed of training, and concentrating on the aircraft and weapons.

Major Michael Green, the Air Force Global Strike Command Bomber Operations Division Realistic Training Manager, remarked:

> A training tiger team was created from the findings of the Bomber FIP. We had a good mix of personnel, including maintenance, bomber, aircrew, and aircrew from other combat platforms. Areas of evaluation included training, capabilities, battle rhythm, and morale.

According to Captain Derek Williams, Chief of Bomber Operations and the programs of the AFGSC Applied Capabilities office:

> The tiger team knew the B-52 community needed to adapt training to the new security environment. FIP gave us the opportunity to address training gaps and provide solutions to leadership.

This restructure of the training priorities and methods would still not completely set a crewmember up for the challenges that a B-52 crew could face in twenty-first century warfare. The best way to fix this problem is to increase the scope of the initial B-52 qualification training, ensuring that instructors build a supply of the most combat-ready airmen possible.

The findings of the Bomber FIP gave the tiger team the chance to develop a thirteen-person High Performance Team to totally rebuild the B-52 training program. Within four months, these High Performance Team trainers came up with three new training courses, with the support of the 93rd and 11th Bomb Squadron Formal Training Unit. The team will continue to build on this new platform by overhauling mission-qualification training over the rest of the year. Lieutenant Colonel Erik Johnson, Chief of Safety for the 2nd Bomb Wing, remarked:

> We had a good lead-in from the tiger team. It gave us our vector, set boundaries for us, and framed the problem. This new program will assign a one-to-one student-to-instructor ratio, which would improve the quality of instruction for each student, and moving training objectives, which would enhance the learning experience and increase the trainee proficiency.... This will reduce the number of training sorties required, while also providing more effective B-52 combat aviators in the end.

The changes made to initial qualification training (IQT) included de-emphasizing mission qualification duties, giving operation squadrons MQT responsibility. Derek Williams stated:

> The tiger team wanted IQT to focus on building a strong foundation. Through interviews and personnel experience, we witnessed compartmentalization and gaps in core skills throughout the crew force that hindered the B-52's ability to increase combat effectiveness.

Lt Col. Erik Johnson added:

> This product will greatly differ from what IQT previously created. We're expecting aviators to be more proficient in their fundamental operation of the

aircraft, a greater capacity for students to learn on their own after graduation and more effectively use the time given at the field training unit.

Johnson went on to say that the successful overhauling of training was due to a 'total force effort. He remarked: 'This wasn't just the effort of a handful of us, the whole field training unit pitched in. It wouldn't happen without their buy in and support. Major Michael Green concluded:

> We wanted to affect the B-52 culture. We wanted a lasting, holistic approach to training. We want aircrew progressing to a higher level faster by not just shortening the time it takes to qualify, but increasing their quality and capabilities.

With all this restructuring of training for the B-52 crews, the next step is the upkeep and restructuring of the B-52 herself.

New Engines for a Warrior Queen

The head of the USAF Global Strike Command, Lt Gen. Stephen Wilson, wanted the service to consider the installation of new engines in the B-52. She has been flying with the current Pratt and Whitney TF-33, the low-bypass ratio that was built around the successful J-57 engine many years ago; the commercial JT-3 flew for the first time on 22 June 1960, on the Boeing 707. The TF-33 powered its first B-52H on 6 March 1961, and has remained there ever since. Of course, there have been upgrades to the engine itself, but the USAF is now at a stage where it feels it is time to totally re-engine the B-52H; the problem has been working out how do this and with whom. Lt. Gen. Mike Holmes, Deputy Chief of Staff for Strategic Plans and Requirements, said that the service 'is looking to get creative on potential powerplant replacements' for the aircraft. The last upgrade to the TF-33 was in the 1980s, and the current incarnations are now inefficient. Lt Gen. Holmes stated:

> To go out and buy new engines for the B-52, you'd have a really hard time fitting that into our programme … But that's why we're interested in a public-private partnership, which would be a different way to amortize those engines over time and pay for them in the savings that they actually generate, instead of paying for them out of savings that you hope for.

While this idea would allow the USAF to get new engines without breaking the bank, the non-budgetary problems have to be figured out before any agreement can be reached. Lt Gen. Holmes continued:

> There are contractor proposals to do some public-private partnerships in kind of creative ways … We have to work through policy and legal and legislative hurdles to be able to do that. The idea is [that] in a public-private partnership, somebody funds the engine and then we pay them back over time out of the fuel savings … Our government has a way to do that with [military construction] facilities. We don't have a way to do that with airplanes and we are exploring whether there are alternative ways that would let us do that.

Back in October 2014, Lt Gen. Stephen Wilson told the press that he had people 'looking at' installing new engines on the bomber fleet, which is expected to keep operating until 2040:

> Look at what the airline industry is doing—they are all re-engining. Why? Because it saves you a lot of money. If there is a commercially available engine which can give a 25–30 percent increase in either ranger or loiter, you have my attention.

Later, analysts finally came up with a choice for a replacement—this was the Pratt and Whitney PW2000 engine, also known as the F117 on military aircraft. That engine was closed for production about ten years ago, but it is used by the C-17 heavy-airlift aircraft. Bennett Croswell, the head of Pratt's military engines department, told the press that his 'company has made some very attractive offerings' to the USAF. Croswell also said that while the F117 was a logical choice, in the past there have been problems with control of the aircraft that might require a re-wing to mount the more-powerful engines. The problem was solved, Croswell claimed, and he argued that the company has offerings that can help keep the current B-52 '8-8' configuration. Croswell continued:

> I think that it's just going to be affordability … There would be some significant savings in terms of the fuel economy of the engines … we have some attractive options for the Air Force to consider.

Should the B-52 engine program go in for bids, there are two other candidates who are likely to put their hats in the ring—General Electric and Rolls Royce. In 1996, Rolls Royce bought into the Allison engine company, and finally got a foot in the door to business with the USAF. The company proposed a lease program for the RB211-535 to the Pentagon, which would eliminate the cost of buying 400-plus new engines; however, there were many legal problems with the lease deal, and the proposal dropped like a lead balloon. In Washington, DC in 2004, the Office of the Under Secretary of Defense (Acquisition and

Logistics) revised and updated the 'Defense Science Board Task Force on B-52 Re-Engining.' The study yielded some interesting results:

1. The B-52 is the most flexible and cost-effective weapon system in the USAF bomber inventory, and re-engining would create an even more favorable position.
2. The B-52H has the uppermost mission-capable percentage of any of the three bombers (B-1, B-52, and B-2), and remains the only competent conventional air-launched cruise-missile system (CALCMS) in the stock of the USAF.
3. Any further significant lessening of the B-52H task force is considered unlikely in the near future because the entire assigned inventory (TAI) bomber fleet is being abridged from 130 to ninety-six
4. The B-52H is exceedingly competent when accomplishing its allotted missions.
5. The B-52H is adaptable and able to be modified for future missions.
6. The USAF chose to retire more than twice as many B-1 airframes as the B-52H airframe.
7. There is no bomber aircraft currently in development (however, the LRS-B is almost at the point of choosing a contractor—although no-one knows how long that will take).
8. The B-52 re-engining represents a small technical risk to the aircraft.
9. The B-52H re-engining would allow for a greater operational flexibility and range, which would reduce the amount of fuel burn and tanker on-site demand, producing noteworthy reductions in fuel-maintenance costs and manpower reserves.
10. B-52H re-engining is an excellent lead program for increasing the use of energy-saving presentation in contracts that are beyond fixed facilities, allowing them to develop into a mobile system.
11. The task force concludes that both economic and operational reimbursements outweigh the total cost of the re-engining program.

Despite this all being investigated in 2004, in 2015 the re-engining program has still not been completed. In the above list, we see a thorough recommendation for the initiative—it is cost-efficient, suitable for the aircraft and airframe, and it will save money on maintenance, among other benefits. It is surprising that the Air Force has not yet come to a conclusion on the future of the aircraft. However, they did make an error in calculating the period over which the cost of the adjustment would be paid back using the fuel pricing on the ground; they failed to see that the fuel being carried by a KC-135 was something approaching fifteen times more expensive. The Defense Science Board told the USAF to immediately proceed with the new engine based on these incorrect figures, and the proposal quickly vanished. This was not the first mistake the USAF had made when calculating costs—in 2009, the same thing had happened with the E-3 Sentry and the B-1B Lancer bomber.

Pratt and Whitney offered an engine that it made for its commercial Airbus A32Neo, while General Electric offered eight of its CF34-10s, which were more efficient than the last engine they offered. While the economics for re-engining the B-52 should have worsened since the 2004 Defense Science Board Report, they have not; if anything, they look better, because new engines burn more efficiently and will stay on the wing so long that they would last for the rest of the B-52's lifetime.

In the USAF's 2016 fiscal year budget request, they asked for $149 million for B-52 modifications; this is a decrease from the $179 million they received in the 2015 fiscal year. According to the USAF inventory, it holds seventy-six B-52Hs with a certified life of 27,701 flight hours, of which there are an average of 9,169 hours left as of January 2015. In addition to the effort to re-engine these aircraft, the USAF is also tracking many other B-52 modifications, including: an enhanced data link (EDL); a multi-mode receiver-2020 instrument-landing system; anti-skid replacement; advanced-weapon integration; and Air Education and Training Command trainers (AETC).

Another Upgrade

In 2013, the USAF started a fleet-wide technology upgrade for the B-52Hs. This new program was called 'Combat Network Communication Technology' (CONECT), and it was intended to modernize the electronic communications systems, computing, and avionics in the cockpit. CONECT upgrades included hardware and software such as new servers, modems, radios, data links, receivers, and digital workstations for the crew.

One new piece of in the suite was called the 'ARC-210 Warrior', which is a beyond-the-line-of-sight software featuring a programmable radio capable of transmitting voices, data, and information in-flight between the B-52, ground command, and control centers. This allows for the transmission and receipt of data with updated intelligence mapping or targeting information. This has been useful in long-endurance missions since it allows in-flight updating of targets that may have moved while the B-52 was in the air. The upgrades cost $1.1 billion overall, and will take several years to compete; however, funding has been secured for thirty B-52s, and the USAF hopes to complete ten CONECT upgrades per year.

The B-52 weapons upgrade included the 1760 Internal Weapons Bay Upgrade (IWBU), which gave a 66 percent increase in carriage ability, using a digital interface and rotary launcher to increase the weapon payload. This will also allow the B-52 to carry the AGM-158B JASSM and the ADM-160C MALD-J. The IWBU effort is expected to cost roughly $313 million, and all 1760 IWBUs should be online by October 2017. When completed, two B-52s will be able to carry forty weapons, as opposed to beforehand, when three B-52s could only carry thirty-six weapons; this gives the USAF the option of deploying more weapons to targets from the same number of aircraft. The 1760 IWBU also allows for precision-guided weapons to be deployed from inside the weapons bay, increasing the number of guided weapons a B-52 can carry and reducing the need for guided bombs to be carried externally on wing hardpoints. The first phase will allow a B-52H to carry twenty four 500-lb JDAMS or twenty 2,000-lb JDAMS, with later phases accommodating the JASSM (long-range, semi-autonomously guided, conventional, air-to-ground, precision standoff missile) and MALD (ADM-160 Miniature Air-Launched Decoy) family of missiles. Alongside the obvious benefit of carrying more smart-bombs, moving them internally from the wings results in a 15 percent full saving on range by reducing drag on the aircraft.

Will There be a Replacement for the Warrior Queen?

There will come a time when the B-52 will need to be replaced, but this is not as easy as it sounds. The aircraft has been the backbone of the United States Military inventory for the past sixty years, which is remarkable when one considers her combat history—flying in wars in the 1960s, '90s, and the early 2000s. After each of these conflicts, she came home and retained the stability that the USAF needed to maintain its bomber force. She outlived the B-58 and the B-70, and still flies side-by-side with the B-1B and the B-2.

The B-52H proved to be a multi-talented strategic and tactical operator, and she could still deliver a nuclear warhead if needed. This is in addition to her proficiency in deploying ACLMs, CALCMs, conventional bombs, laser-guided bombs, small-diameter bombs (SDBs), joint air-to-surface standoff missiles (JASSM), joint standoff weapons (JSOW), and wind-corrected munitions (WCM). Anything that is thrown at a B-52H can be thrown right back.

Part of the B-52H's longevity has been due to her many upgrades and variations since entering service; there have been airframe reinforcements, Sniper and Litening pods, new networks and datalinks, and improved ECM suites. Many commanders still rely on her abilities and her cost-effectiveness compared to the B-2. For the wing of B-52Hs (of which there are eighty-five-plus), running costs per aircraft are $53–90 million, compared to $283 million per aircraft for the B-1B and $737 million per aircraft for the B-2.

When it comes to replacing the B-52, one of the biggest problems for the USAF and the aviation industry is research and development. Developing a new, 'state-of-the-art' aircraft takes time and money, and the United States aviation industry is not what it once was; it has lost its productive edge when it comes to R&D. One of the reasons for this is that the military no longer has the wherewithal to spend money on this department when every dime has to go to keeping its fleet intact. Meanwhile, the private aviation industry is fighting against taxes, lack of interest from new Engineering graduates, and the cost of doing business in general. This is all within the context of increasing focus on research and development in countries like Japan, China, and Russia.

Where will the next generation of bomber come from? The designers and engineers that birthed the B-52 are a rare breed, like Ed Wells, Art Carlson, Maynard Pennell, H. W. Withington, Vaughn Blumenthal, and George Schairer. Besides, the B-52 has a big hangar to fill; as the consummate military aircraft, whatever follows must have a higher level of stamina, cost-efficiency, technology, and prospective longevity. The talent is out there somewhere, and hopefully in the United States. Plans for a long-range strike-bomber (LRS-B) were still being kept under wraps by the USAF in late 2015, while they were trying to decide who the contract would go to. The competitors were paired off in teams, with Northrop Grumman on one side and Boeing and Lockheed-Martin on the other. On 28 October 2015, it emerged that Northrop Grumman had won the contract, but the Boeing/Lockheed team were unsatisfied with the results of the contest. This means any work is delayed while the GAO looks into the complaints. Northrop's first aircraft was slated to come off the production line by the late 2030s, in time for the B-52's retirement in 2040; it might be a long wait, but hopefully it will be a fruitful one.

Epilogue: The *Ghost Rider* Soars Again

The B-52 Resurrected and Reclaimed

The story of the B-52 is not over by any means; she will remain a part of the USAF and an American legend for many years to come. There are some B-52Hs that have been stranded at Davis Monthan, retired many years ago, and that would be hard to upgrade or refurbish after their long slumber. Despite this, the 307th Bomb Wing would come calling for one of these old birds after one of their B-52s suffered a cockpit fire that decimated the bomber beyond repair. The 307th Bomb Wing travelled from Barksdale AFB, Los Angeles, to Arizona and the boneyards of Davis Monthan AFB to replace her.

Out in the many acres of the Air Maintenance and Regeneration Group (AMARG) at Davis Monthan, part of the 309th Aerospace Maintenance and Regeneration Group, there was a field of B-52Hs that were put out to pasture many years ago due to mission cutbacks and funding issues. In February 2015, for the very first time, the USAF pulled out one of these retired B-52Hs and returned it to duty. Out of all the birds across the boneyard, this one B-52 was found sitting in the desert, waiting, hoping for a return to service.

The B-52H named *Ghost Rider* was the lucky one chosen from the AMARG inventory, having been decommissioned since 2008. Due to Davis Monthan's dry, desert climate, the many Navy and USAF aircraft held there are often in a good state of preservation, with little erosion and rusting. However, the arid weather can play havoc with the aircrafts' interior, and being in the hot Arizona sun for so long did cause some sections of *Ghost Rider*'s exposed aluminum skin to bleach out until it was almost white. Dry rot also affected the fuel lines and tires, but none of the damage was so bad that the aircraft could not be refitted. 'Our first engine start was a sight to see,' said Staff Sgt Matthew Cocran, Crew Chief of the 2nd Aircraft Maintenance Squadron. 'Out of the exhaust came a black cloud of smoke, then a huge flame as it roared to life.' Her eight engines were checked out in late January, and they started up without hesitation; she passed her tests perfectly. Next, she taxied down the runway to test the steering on the landing gear.

On the day that *Ghost Rider* was due to leave Davis Monthan, an old friend came to see her off. One of the AMARG tour guides, a gentleman in his eighties, served as her crew chief when she first arrived at Homestead AFB, Florida, way back in 1962. Right after coming off the production line, *Ghost Rider* took off for Florida and to this new, very young crew chief by the name of Jerry Fugere. He took the new aircraft in hand to 'show her the ropes.' Fugere said, 'Every time I came on the base [Davis Monthan] I would see her sitting out on the field and she would bring back a swell of fond memories.' On 13 February, Jerry got to see his old friend take off again to return to service, all eight engines roaring away as she lifted off into the desert runway, heading to Barksdale AFB in Shreveport, Louisiana. 'Aircraft 61-007' is airborne.' It was an emotional moment as the two warriors bade each other farewell; Jerry's old buddy was on the way to a new life, just like when she had left Homestead AFB for her first assignment.

Ghost Rider was piloted by Col. Keith Schultz, who reported: 'I've been flying B-52s since the '80s and it surprised me that after seven years ... she cranked up just fine and we had no issues with flight control systems.' Col. Schultz is the 307th Operations Group Commander, with over 6,500 hours of flight time to his name; he is the most experienced B-52 pilot to fly in the USAF today. He reported that *Ghost Rider*'s trip from Davis Monthan to Barksdale took three hours, and they were fortunate to enjoy good weather since the 'inertial and navigational equipment was not yet installed.' The Air Force regeneration team thought it would take some ninety days to complete the restoration, but they actually got it done in seventy days. Air Force Global Strike Command had never attempted anything like this before, and they weren't sure how quickly they could complete the assignment; it turned out that they had little to worry about.

When *Ghost Rider* arrived at Barksdale, she was greeted by some very excited airmen—her new family at the base. Col. Schultz remarked:

> This aircraft has made it through Jerry Fugere's career, through the twilight of my career, and it could very well perform through those young maintainers' careers who once again brought her back to life.

This is an amazing statement, and serves to underline the magic and durability of the B-52.

Ghost Rider was later transferred to Tinker AFB in Oklahoma and treated to a complete refit and overhaul, bringing her up to date and flight-ready; she is now part of the Barksdale family of B-52Hs. Her story proves that anything is possible, even for a B-52 that was drying out in a boneyard in Arizona.

This would be a fitting conclusion to the B-52's tale, but this is not an ending; the aircraft strives on, a monument to the folks who conceived her at Boeing, the Generals who believed in her and fought for her (like Gen. LeMay), and to the many, many crews who have flown her. She an 'old friend' who many of the Vietnam crews remember—some fondly and some with regret, but always with respect. Her age is nothing to be ashamed of, and her longevity emphasizes the potential of such an aircraft when treated with love, intelligence, and consideration. As the powerhouse of democracy, the new upgrades that are coming her way will ensure that the B-52 will remain the towering strength of the USAF until 2040. The Warrior Queen will continue to serve her crew, the USAF, and the United States as a whole for many years to come.

Bibliography

Books

Adams, S., *First Hand Report: The Story of the Eisenhower Administration*, (Library of Congress, 1961)

Atkinson, R., *Crusade: The Untold Story of the Persian Gulf War*, (Houghton Mifflin, 1993)

Bacevich, A. J., and Cohen, E. A., *War over Kosovo: Politics and Strategy in a Global Age*, (Columbia University Press, 2001)

Bamford, J., *Book of Secrets: Anatomy of the Ultra Secret National Security Agency from the Cold War through to the Dawn of a New Century*, (Doubleday, 2001)

Betts, R. K. (ed.), *Cruise Missiles: Technology Strategy Politics*, (Brookings Institution, 1981)

Chinnery, P. D., *50 Years in the Desert Boneyard: Davis Monthan AF Arizona*, (MBI Intl, 1995)

Coffrey, T. M., *Iron Eagle: The Turbulent Life of General Curtis LeMay*, (Crown Publishers, 1986)

Door, R. F., and Peacock, L., *Boeing's Cold War Warrior: B-52 Stratofortress*, (Osprey Aviation, 1995)

Ethell, J., and Christy, J., *B-52 Stratofortress*, (Charles Scribner's Sons, 1981)

Friendman, N., *Desert Victory—The War for Kuwait*, (Naval Institute Press, 1991)

Gavin, Lt Gen. J., *War and Peace in the Space Age*, (Harper Press, 1958)

Harder, R. O., *Flying the Black Hole: The B-52 Navigator Bombardiers of Vietnam*, (Naval Institute Press, 2013)

Lambeth, B. S., *Air Power Against Terror: America's Conduct of Operation Enduring Freedom*, (National Defense Research Institute, 2006)

McMaster, H. R., *Dereliction of Duty: Lyndon Johnson, Robert McNamara and the Joint Chiefs of Staff and the Lies That Led to Vietnam*, (HarperCollins, 1997)

Morris, C., *Iron Destinies/Lost Opportunities: The Arms Race between the USAF and USSR 1945-1987*, (Harper Row, 1960)

Nalty, B. C., *The Vietnam War*, (Barnes and Noble, 1988)

Office of Technology Assessment, *Strategic Defenses: Ballistic Missile Defense Technology: Anti-Satellite Weapons, Countermeasures and Arms Control*, (Princeton Press, 1986)

Pollack, K., *The Threatening Storm: The Case for Invading Iraq*, (Random House, 2002)

Power, Gen. Thomas, with Arkym, A. A., *Design for Survival*, (Coward McCann, 1964)

Rumsfeld, D., *Known and Unknown: A Memoir*, (Sentinel Press, Penguin, 2011)

Sheehan, N., *A Bright Shining Lie: John Paul Vann and America in Vietnam*, (Random House, 1988)

Sheehan, N., *A Fiery Peace in a Cold War: Bernard Schriever and the Ultimate Weapon*, (Random House, 2009)

Tapper, J., *The Outpost: An Untold Story of American Valor*, (Little, Brown and Co., 2012)

Weiner, T., *Legacy of Ashes: History of the CIA*, (Doubleday, 2007)

Yenne, B., Boeing Company, (MBI, Zenith Press, 2005)

USAF Documents

'Defense Science Board Task Force on B-52 Re-engining (Revised and Updated 2004)', Office of Undersecretary of Defense for Technology Engineering and Logistics, (June 2004)

Lamy, USAF Col. P. L., *Barrel Roll 1968-73: An Air Campaign in Support of National Policy*, (Air War College, Air University, Maxwell AFB, 10 May 1995)

Nalty, B. N., *The Air Force Role in Five Crises 1958-1965*, (USAF Historical Division, Liaison Office, June 1968)

Rayfield, Col. R. E., and McCarthy, Brig. Gen. J. R., 'Linebacker II: A View from the Rock', *USAF Southeast Asia Monograph Series*, Vol. 8, Monograph 8, (Office of Air Force History, 1985)

The B-52-E Standard Characteristics, (1 October 1958)

Articles

'B-36 Last Production Model Rolls Off', *Aviation Week and Space Technology*, (23 August 1954)

'B-52 Follow On Funds may be Sought in 1966', *Aviation Week and Space Technology*, (21 October 1963)

'B-52 Targeted-Washington Roundup', *Aviation Week and Space Technology*, (22 April 1968)

'B-52 Toll Spurs ECM Antenna Changes', *Aviation Week and Space Technology*, (8 January 1973)

'B-52 Wing Requested', *Aviation Week and Space Technology*, (15 May 1961)

'B-52 X-15 Sets Record', *Aviation Week and Space Technology*, (18 September 1961)

'B-52G Test Turbo Fans', *Aviation Week and Space Technology*, (1 August 1960)

'Boeing Frontiers', *Combat Ready*, (September 2007)

'DOD Seeks Single SAC Polaris Command', *Aviation Week and Space Technology*, 16 October 1961

'Electronic Countermeasures for B-52H', *Aviation Week and Space Technology*, (5 October 1959)

'Initial Hound Dog Production for B-52 G-H', *Aviation Week and Space Technology*, (7 September 1959)

'Internal Conventional Bomb Loads for B-52', *Aviation Week and Space Technology*, (4 October 1965)

'JFK Stands Firm on Bomber Funds', *Aviation Week and Space Technology*, (6 November 1961)

Donald, D. (ed.), *US Air Force Air Power Directory*, (Airport Publishing Inc, Wesport, CT, 1992)

Garamone, J., 'Interagency Team Checking for H-Bomb Lost in 1958', *American Forces Press Service*, (Washington, 4 October 2004)

Tavares, E., 'Night Flight to Iraq', *Aviation Week and Space Technology*, (19 January 1991)

Index

A-12 59
AGM 69 missile 116, 126, 132
AGM 86 missile 116 -117, 128, 181
Air Materiel Command 59, 65
AN/ASQ 151 electro-optical viewing system 131
ANACONDA 185, 186
Andersen AFB, Guam 121, 140, 141, 143, 145, 146, 151,153, 158, 161-162, 164, 168, 181
Arc Light 140, 141-142, 144-147, 149, 151, 154, 162, 185

B-1B Bomber 123, 184, 196, 198
Barksdale AFB 144, 180, 182, 199, 200
Barrel Roll Operation 148
Big Belly 74, 141, 169, 170

CALCM (Conventional air-launched cruise missiles) 181-182, 187, 195, 197
Captain Hook 134
Castle AFB, California 104, 109, 118
CFACC (Combined Force Air Component Commander) 185, 187
Chrome Dome 125, 126, 172, 185
CIA 189, 203
Cold War 1, 13, 15, 17, 19-21, 23, 25-26, 54, 61, 76, 94, 96, 117, 123, 129, 171, 174, 176
Combat Skyspot 142
CONECT 196
Consolidated Vultee 12, 17
Convair 12, 17-18, 22-24, 27-28 , 30, 32, 63
Cuban Missile Crisis 122, 130

Davis Monthan AFB 109, 112, 126, 199
Desert Shield 179
Desert Storm 123, 136, 174, 179, 181, 191
Diego Garcia 180, 184, 186

ECP-1050 130
Edwards AFB, California 106
Eisenhower, Dwight D. 56-57, 137, 138
Engines:
Pratt and Whitney 14-15, 18, 20, 22, 63, 65-66, 75, 98, 103-104, 115, 142, 193-194, 196
Wright 14, 19, 33, 35, 48, 61, 99

F-111 TFX 54, 58, 64, 85, 98, 101, 152
FCS (Fire Control System) 103, 105, 108, 114
Flying Wing YB-49 46, 63
Fowler flap 39, 75

GAM 72 ADM 20 decoy 115
Ghost Rider 199-200, 201
Guam AFB 41, 68, 121, 133, 140-144, 149, 151–152, 154, 160-161, 164, 167, 181, 184, 188-189

Homestead AFB 119–200

ICBM 60, 77, 80, 97, 117, 123
IRAN (Inspect, Repair if Necessary) 114, 129-130

JASSM 197
JATO (jet-assisted take-off) 49-50
Johnson, Lyndon B. 139
Jolly Well 112, 131
JT 3 Pratt and Whitney engine 193

Kadena AFB 115, 140, 143-146, 151, 154, 164
KC-135 tanker 89, 99-102, 121, 125, 127, 143, 152,
154, 164, 166
KC-97 tanker 39, 46, 50, 86, 120
Kennedy, John F. 138-139, 171
Khrushchev, Nikita 138
Kuwait 179-181, 187

Lam Son 151
LeMay, Gen. Curtis 27, 50, 56, 61, 85-86, 88, 90, 92, 94, 101, 105-106, 122, 191
Liberators B-24 13-14
Linebacker I 151
Linebacker II 152-169
Loring AFB, Maine 82, 107, 109, 119, 130, 156, 159

MACV (Military Assistance Command Vietnam) 142, 144, 146
MAD (Mutually Assured Destruction) 174
MADREC 132
MAJCOM 119
Mather AFB 118, 144-145, 178
McNamara, R 123, 135-136, 141, 145, 171, 174
Minot AFB, Nevada 115, 117, 131, 182
MITO 43, 121

NASA 58, 106, 175
NB-52 106, 175
Nixon, Richard M. 134, 150, 151
North Korea 26, 28, 38, 88, 144, 150, 188, 189
Northrop Litening II Laser POD 187
Northrop, Jack 13, 63

OAS modification 132
Oppenheimer, Robert 24

Pacer Plank, Operation 79, 132, 175
Parrot's Beak 147, 150
Pennell, M. 65-67, 198
Persian Rug 115
Power, Gen. Thomas 87, 122, 125
Pueblo, USS 144, 150, 151

Quick Clip 129
Quick Kick 100
Quick Start 77, 133

RB-47 43-45, 47-48, 52-54, 75
RB-50 75, 90
RB-52 81-82, 104-107
Reflex Action 87, 121, 172
Rivet Ace 133
Rivet Rambler 133

SAC 172-174, 176, 179, 191
Salt II Treaty 97, 128, 135, 176
Schairer, G. 66-67
SIOP (Single-integrated operation plan) 123, 172, 174
Spaatz, Carl 'Tooey' 60, 92
SRAM (Short-range attack missile) 77-78, 97-98, 116, 126, 130, 132
Stratojet B-47 28, 36, 39, 61, 64, 66
Stratotanker KC 135 48, 86, 89, 99-100, 121, 127, 140, 143, 151-152, 154, 164-165, 176, 295
Symington, S. 61, 63

Tagboard 134
Thermal reflecting paint 82, 107
Thule AFB, Greenland 125
Tinker AFB, Oklahoma 201

United Kingdom 120, 180
USSR 26-28, 32, 43-44, 51, 57, 94, 97, 110, 125, 136, 138, 171, 174
U-Tapao (Thailand) 144-146, 157, 160-163, 167, 201

Van Cleve Hotel, Dayton, Ohio 65, 67
Vietnam War 95, 113, 123, 137, 141-142, 150-151, 169-172

Wells, Edward 35, 63, 66-67, 198
Wright Patterson AFB 65

XB-47 35-40, 45-46, 48
XB-52 63-69, 71, 103
XB-70 Valkyrie Bomber 43, 85

YB-52 48, 69, 71, 85, 95, 103
YB-60 30-31